THE
THEOLOGICAL
IMAGINATION

THE
THEOLOGICAL
IMAGINATION

Constructing the Concept of God

BY

GORDON D. KAUFMAN

THE WESTMINSTER PRESS
Philadelphia

BOOK DESIGN BY DOROTHY ALDEN SMITH

First edition

Published by The Westminster Press ®
Philadelphia, Pennsylvania

PRINTED IN THE UNITED STATES OF AMERICA
9 8 7 6 5 4 3 2 1

Library of Congress Cataloging in Publication Data

Kaufman, Gordon D.

   The theological imagination.

   Includes bibliographical references and index.
   1. God—Addresses, essays, lectures.
2. Theology, Doctrinal—Addresses, essays, lectures.
I. Title.
BT102.K35   231'.044   81–12960
ISBN 0–664–24393–2   AACR2

In remembrance
of
H. RICHARD NIEBUHR

Contents

Continued

Though it does indeed sound dangerous, it is in no way reprehensible to say that every man creates a God for himself, nay, must make himself such a God . . . in order to honor in Him the One who created him.

Immanuel Kant

. . . none is absolute save God and . . . the absolutizing of anything finite is ruinous to the finite itself.

H. Richard Niebuhr

Preface

The present volume may be regarded as a sequel to my earlier collection of essays, *God the Problem* (Harvard University Press, 1972). In that work I was attempting to reflect on and respond (in a tentative way) to the highly problematical status of concern with God in modern intellectual culture. Some essays proposed ways of interpreting Christian talk about God, and certain problems with that talk, that seemed to me reasonable and worth further exploration; other essays probed into the meaning and uses of the word "God" itself and its foundations in human experience and life. All were tentative and exploratory. The present volume goes beyond that earlier one in hewing to a specific proposal for understanding the meaning and significance of the symbol "God" today, and, accordingly, for understanding what theology is and how it is to be done.

I have become persuaded that theology is (and always has been) essentially a constructive work of the human imagination, an expression of the imagination's activity helping to provide orientation for human life through developing a symbolical "picture" of the world roundabout and of the human place within that world. In the course of history the fertile human imagination has generated, in the great religious and cultural traditions of humankind, a number of very diverse views of the world and of the human. Among these are those monotheistic perspectives

11

—largely descendant from ancient Israel—in which the symbol "God" provides the ultimate point of reference and orientation for human life, indeed for understanding all of reality. This symbol has provided meaningful and effective orientation for human existence through a very long past, partly because, from the eighth-century prophets to the present, it has been continuously reexamined and reconstructed, as new historical situations placed new demands upon it. Thus, a diverse and sophisticated theological tradition has developed over the centuries, analyzing and exploring the meanings, uses, and functions of the symbol "God"; and along with it has gradually emerged what I call "the theological imagination." The theological imagination devotes itself to the continuing critical reconstruction of the symbol "God," so that it can with greater effectiveness orient contemporary and future human life.

Between the unsureness and tentativity of approach in the earlier volume, and my present commitment to a definite way of doing theology, occurred the reflection which culminated in the publication of my *Essay on Theological Method* (Scholars Press, 1975; rev. ed., 1979). In that little book I was able to work through to what seemed to me a coherent and compelling position—foreshadowed to some extent in the essay on "God as Symbol" in *God the Problem*—on the meaning and function of the symbol "God," and the way in which and reasons why that symbol is constructed by the human imagination; and hence I was able to make specific and definite proposals about how theology, as self-conscious and critical imaginative construction, should proceed in its work.

The present volume brings together a number of recent essays in which I attempt to work with methodological self-consciousness and clarity at the central theological task, which I would now formulate as *constructing toward God*. Nearly all these essays were written since the publication of my proposals on theological method, a few while that work was being composed. They represent deliberate attempts to employ, with varying degrees of explicitness, and with respect to a variety of theological problems, the method outlined there. Collectively, therefore—even though the occasions for which they were originally prepared were quite diverse—they adumbrate a systematic position, and they should give the reader a clear view of both the promise and the limitations of this understanding of theology. Half of these essays have been previously published, but these have all been revised, some of them substantially.

Even though the essays resist any neat classification, I have divided them into three groups according to certain dominating themes. The three chapters brought together in Part One serve to introduce the volume by sketching the principal features of the image/concept of God, as it has taken shape in those traditions heir to ancient Israel, and by setting out something of the understanding of theology with which I am working. Although there is frequent reference to "Christian" views and perspectives in these pages, most of what is said in Part One, I think, unless it is identified as peculiarly Christian, applies to the concept of God as such, as that concept has developed in Western history. The essays in Part Two, then, attempt to make clear the special qualifications and transformations which are worked in the conception of God (and also the conceptions of the world and the human) by specifically Christian faith and reflection; and they also make some suggestions about the significance and the proper interpretation of these Christian claims in the face of the religious and cultural pluralism of which today we are so conscious. Finally, Part Three further explains the conception of theology with which I am working by exploring the importance as well as the metaphysical difficulties for theology of the concept of "nature"—so prominent in much contemporary understanding of humanity and the world, especially in the light of the complex of ecological issues now forcing themselves upon us—and by examining the relations of theology and metaphysics to each other; and it brings the book to a conclusion with a summary exposition of Christian theology conceived as imaginative construction. Although this volume is concerned throughout with issues important in Christian reflection, these are all considered within the context of an understanding of theology as not primarily a parochial or churchly activity but a public discipline dealing with the inescapable human problem of orientation in life and in the world.

In these essays I have referred sometimes to the "concept," sometimes to the "symbol" of God, sometimes to the "image" and sometimes to the "idea" or "notion" of God. In some of the earlier essays I probably regarded these as significantly and appropriately distinguishable from each other, and I was particularly interested in the "concept" or "idea" of God. Later I became convinced that the complexity of meaning which the word "God" bears cannot be adequately understood as simply "conceptual," and in some of the more recent essays published here I have used the term "image/concept" to make this point. In the present collection of essays, then, my use of a variety of terms should not be taken to suggest important technical distinctions which I am committed to following. Rather, by intermixing such terms I hope to keep myself and my readers aware that the infinite complexity of meaning which the word "God" bears cannot be subsumed under any single rubric. Conceptual, symbolic, and imagistic elements are each involved in all serious uses of "God-talk," and failing to recognize this will impoverish and falsify our understanding. It is only this many-layered complexity that enables this "symbol" to function in the prayers of the humblest peasant as well as in the reflection and speculation of the most sophisticated philosopher. I do not believe that two such diverse uses are equivocal; the possibility of each—indeed, perhaps the inevitability of each—is grounded directly in the multiple dimensions of meaning which the word "God" bears and which is the key to both its religious and its philosophical power, and thus to its real human significance.

Probably I should also clarify my use of the word "theism" in the following pages. I do not use that term to refer to particular philosophical conceptions of God, or particular philosophical or theological positions, or a particular way of speaking about or conceiving of God (as some writers do). I use it as a convenient way to refer to any and all religious and philosophical positions in which "God" is a significant or central symbol. This volume is concerned with "theistic" issues throughout, therefore, though it is not intending to expound a particular philosophy of religion called "theism."

When *God the Problem* was published (not quite ten years ago), I had little or no awareness that the almost exclusive use of male gender terminology in virtually all Western discussion of God and of humanity has destructive and oppressive consequences for women (and also for men, in another way). Since then, the work of a number of "women's liberation" theologians has made that point absolutely undeniable, and the necessity to change our theological language has therefore become imperative. The changes that are required here are of the most fundamental sort, both in the material content of theology—for which such symbols as "father" and "lord" have been central—and in the masculine linguistic forms and conventions, including pronouns, which have long been taken for granted in our talk about God as well as in our talk about the generically human (about "man"). Indeed, I suspect it was in part the realization of how radical must be the theological reconstruction that is now required—a reconstruction for which there is no clear precedent or legitimation in the Bible (or elsewhere in the tradition), since the Bible itself perpetrates and is a major source of the problem—that helped me to see that theology could no longer be properly understood as contemporary retranslation and re-presentation of traditional themes (supposedly authorized by "divine revelation") but must be viewed as imaginative construction through and through. In any case I am completely convinced both for theological and for humanitarian reasons—that is, for the sake of what we understand "God" to be, and because of the oppressive effects the traditional language has on humans—that we must eliminate sexist thinking and sexist grammatical forms and linguistic expressions from theology. I have attempted to follow this principle in editing the present essays (many of which were first written in what I would now regard as sexist language). This has resulted upon occasion in some infelicities of style (and in the regular use of the neologism "Godself" instead of "himself," when referring to God); but significant innovations in language are bound to seem awkward and difficult until we get used to them.

Most of the ideas elaborated in this volume had their initial public exposure in classes and seminars at Harvard Divinity School; a few, at the United Theological College in Bangalore, India. I am indebted to students and friends at both of these institutions, first, for listening carefully to what I had to say; second, for giving me significant and helpful criticism. These persons must for the most part remain anonymous, but there are several whom I wish to acknowledge here by name. Dr. John McDargh made some significant critical suggestions regarding the previously published version of Chapter 2, which have been of help in revising it; Dr. Sheila Davaney's critical observations on early drafts of several chapters, particularly Chapter 1, helped me to sharpen and tighten, as well as broaden the significance of, my arguments; Professor Helmut Koester gave me helpful criticism of Chapter 5; Dean George Rupp's comments on preliminary drafts of a number of these essays aided me in formulating certain issues more clearly. Finally, Evelyn Rosenthal faithfully typed and retyped the many versions through which these essays had to go before they could be opened to public view. I am grateful to all these, named and unnamed, without whom I could not have written this book.

I have dedicated this collection of essays to the memory of my teacher, H. Richard Niebuhr. It is not, I think, a book that he would have written, for, despite his emphasis on the importance of the imagination for faith and for theology, more is made here, I suspect, of the imaginative character of what we take to be God than he, with his powerful conviction of God's rock-firm reality, would have found acceptable. And yet, the central theological emphasis of this book, well expressed in his words in one of its opening mottos, I learned from him: everything in this world—including especially our own convictions, ideas, faith—is relative, limited, transitory; only to God, therefore, may our ultimate loyalty properly be given. The fundamental theological task, as well as our most profound and difficult human task, is to distinguish between God and the idols.

As one seeking to discern what this distinction between God and the idols might mean in contemporary life, it is my deepest desire that this collection of essays might prove helpful, in some small way, to others similarly searching.

G.D.K.

Cambridge, Massachusetts

PART ONE

THE CONCEPT
OF GOD

God is a highest conception, not to be explained in terms of other things, but ex-
plainable only by exploring more and
more profoundly the conception itself.

Søren Kierkegaard

1 / Constructing
the Concept of God

Whether in prayer or sermon, biblical exposition or theological analysis, use of the word "God" involves important imaginative and constructive activity that is often not recognized. God is not a reality immediately available in our experience for observation, inspection, and description, and speech about or to God therefore is never directly referential. Thus, we are unable to check our concepts and images of God for accuracy and adequacy through direct confrontation with the reality *God,* as we can with most ordinary objects of perception and experience; instead, our awareness and understanding here is gained entirely in and through the images and concepts themselves, constructed into and focused by the mind into a center for the self's devotion and service. God is said to be father of us all, creator of all things both visible and invisible, lord of history, judge of all the earth. These images, each drawn from ordinary political, social, or cultural experience, and suitably qualified to enable them to suggest (a) being transcending everything finite and particular in glory, majesty, and power, then become the constituent elements out of which the image of God is put together by the mind. Again, God is said to be eternal and transcendent and absolute, one who alone has aseity and on whom all other beings depend for their existence. Concepts such as these are taken to characterize in religiously and metaphysically distinctive ways who or what God is, and thus they also become constitutive of this focus for devotion, life, and meaning. The mind's ability to create images and characterizations, and imaginatively to weld them together into a unified focus[1] for attention, contemplation, devotion, or address, is at work in the humblest believer's prayers as well as in the most sophisticated philosopher's speculations. In this respect all speech to and about God, and all "experience of God," is made possible by and is a function of the constructive powers of the imagination.

It is not difficult to see why this must be the case. From Kant onward it has been understood that even the simplest experiences of objects are possible for us only because of the elaborate synthesizing powers of the mind: these enable us to bring together and hold together in enduring conceptual unities what is given to us only piecemeal and in separate moments of experience. How much more must pictures or conceptions of that "ultimate reality" which is taken to ground and unify and comprehend all experience and being be a work of our constructive and synthesizing powers. The idea of God gains its own distinctive and unique meaning for us through contrast with all the particulars of experience, and also contrast with that structured whole within which all experience falls and which we call the world—even while being built up and put together out of images and analogies drawn from this very experience. This idea is in many ways the mind's supreme imaginative construct, related to all other dimensions, realities, and qualities of experience and the world and yet seen as distinct from and grounding them all. Little wonder that, as the tradition has always recognized, God is not an object of ordinary perception, directly accessible to us, but is believed to be transcendent and mysterious, hidden from our sight, even unknowable.

> Lo, he passes by me, and I see him not;
>   he moves on, but I do not perceive him. . . .

Behold, I go forward, but he is not there;
   and backward, but I cannot perceive him;
on the left hand I seek him, but I cannot behold him;
   I turn to the right hand, but I cannot see him.
                                        (Job 9:11; 23:8–9)

Of course no individual human mind constructs the idea of God from scratch. All thinking about God and all devotion to God take place within a cultural and linguistic context in which the notion of God has already been highly developed through the imaginative work of many preceding generations. So the idea of God with which any particular individual works is always a qualification and development of notions inherited from earlier worshipers and prophets, poets and thinkers. For much of Western history the Bible has been the principal resource collection of earlier stages of reflection on and construction of the concept of God, and biblical attitudes toward God have been built in at deep levels of Western consciousness of life, humanness, and reality.

But the Bible's significance for Western thinking about God has gone far beyond mere informal influence of this sort. The Bible was long regarded as the locus of God's revelation to humanity (the "word of God"); it therefore carried an authority powerful enough to override ordinary human experience and rational argument. Although the "creator of the heavens and the earth" was not an object available for direct confrontation and observation, and knowledge about God could not be gained in any ordinary way, this lack had been, in God's graciousness and mercy, divinely supplied in and through the Bible. The presence of this authoritative resource for normative images and concepts of God meant that God's being and activity could be regarded as completely objective and "real"—indeed, even more real than the objects and qualities of ordinary experience. For the Bible presented the story or history of all the world and of humanity, a story of which we humans also are a significant and living part. And in that story God is the supreme active character: the creator of the world, the lord and principal mover of history, the one in relation to whom human life finds fulfillment and meaning, and in turning from whom it withers away and dies. For those who lived out their lives with this story as the fundamental context within which events and experiences were understood, every occurrence had a divine significance. It was God with whom one was actually dealing in every moment and relationship in life, and there was little question of God's reality, power, or significance.

The authority of the Bible, and the reality and power of God within the biblical story, assured that questions about the mode of God's presence to the mind—through the mind's own activity of imaginative construction—would not quickly arise. This was so even though God's reality in the Bible was that of a character in a story, and though this reality was apprehended by believers in much the same way that they grasped other story-characters—through powerful acts of imaginative reconstruction carried out in and by their own minds as they read or heard the text.[2] However, after two centuries of modern historical scholarship, it is possible to see both that the image/concept of God in the Bible is a product of imaginative construction and also something of the various historical stages through which that construction developed. Thus, we can gain some understanding of why and how the notion of God came to have the particular shape and content which has been so authoritative in the West. This in turn puts us into a position from which to ask whether and to what extent we should continue to use biblical motifs and images in our own contemporary attempts to construct an adequate concept of God.

I

According to modern critical historical scholarship, the fundamental biblical picture of human life is rooted in very ancient Near Eastern mythological traditions. Out of these remote mists Yahweh appears as a distinct character in the Mosaic period. He[3] rescues a group of slaves from Egypt, makes a covenant with them in the desert, and goes before them to destroy their enemies and to give them the land of Israel. At first Yahweh seems to be essentially a "mighty warrior" who fights—and wins—his people's battles for them, so long as they remain faithful to him. Before long, however, that simple picture proves insufficient. With the settling of the land, the rude desert nomads who were Yahweh's devotees become farmers and city dwellers, and Yahweh must expand his capacities to deal with the new problems arising in these new situations. So in prophets like Hosea and Jeremiah, we can see Yahweh increasingly envisioned as one who gives the rainfall and fertility to the crops, who heals diseases, and who performs other activities which had earlier been ascribed to other gods and to goddesses. Moreover, with the rise of civilization among the Hebrews and with increasing economic stratification and centralized political power, new social problems appear in the cities; and so Yahweh, through the mouths of prophets like Elijah and Amos, becomes a strong advocate of social justice. Above all, with the crisis of political defeat and renewed enslavement, first by Assyria and then by Babylon, it becomes necessary thoroughly to reconceive Yahweh, from one whose being and activities are essentially an extension of the wishes and needs of his people to one who is totally independent of them and their desires: Yahweh becomes understood as the creator and lord of all the world who directs the movements and activities of all nations and peoples according to his own inscrutable purposes and who is free and able to allow Israel simply to die or be destroyed, if the people do not keep the (now somewhat expanded) covenant made with him. The eighth-century prophets (with the help of the preceding "Yahwist" historical writer[s]), and above all Second Isaiah, are the first to come to this exalted vision of the one God, "high and lifted up" above all things earthly and human, the creator of all the world and its sole lord.

All this, of course, could be sketched in much greater detail, and this historical development of the conception of Yahweh could be followed further into the Christian era and into the subsequent mixing of Hebraic and Hellenic cultural and religious traditions. But it is not necessary to do so here. The point I wish to emphasize is that this Hebraic world-view focused in its lordly creator-god, like other great religious frameworks, gradually developed as the seers, poets, and prophets of the community found it necessary to come to terms with new situations and new experiences. The mythic imagination was able to shape and reshape the early Near Eastern stories of a hierarchy of warring gods into what became ultimately a picture of a unified world ruled over by the one God, Yahweh, its creator and lord, who was working in that world to accomplish his own purposes. The whole of human history was thus caught up in a movement toward the goal which Yahweh had posited for it from the beginning, and to which he would ultimately bring it. Within the overall sweep of this cosmic historical movement the Christian acclamation of Jesus as Yahweh's Messiah came as a climax and principal turning point.

It is important for us to observe here that the notion of God which was gradually emerging in the biblical history, and the interpretation of human life as God's gift and human existence as "under God," are parts of, and essentially functions of, an overall world-picture that was gradually developing. Political and personal metaphors were utilized as the fundamental building blocks in these conceptions. The world which God had created is like a "kingdom." It is ordered by God's sovereign will, ruling through earthly intermediaries (kings and/or prophets and priests) who know what God wants done and seek to carry it out. This High King, however, was not to remain simply an arbitrary imperial potentate or a rigid legalistic judge and protector of law and order; in course of time he became understood as a heavenly "father," one who loves and cares for his children, one who continuously seeks to extricate them from difficulties into which they have fallen. Within this picture human life was to be lived out in response to, and under the love and care of, this just, merciful, and almighty God, who is the fundamental Reality behind all other reality, and relationship to whom gives life its only proper orientation and meaning.

Every feature of experience and life is interpretable within this framework. Even events of suffering and apparent meaninglessness or absurdity are given significance here, because they also come (though we cannot understand how) from the hand of the absolutely trustworthy God: "Though he slay me, yet will I trust in him" (Job 13:15, KJV). Since God is the ultimate point of reference in terms of which all else is understood, and apart from which nothing can be rightly grasped or known, God's own reality or existence is absolutely certain. In later formulations, this was put very strongly: God is the ultimate reality, the only being with absolute aseity, the one whose very essence is to exist, that than which nothing greater can be conceived.

An overall framework of interpretation of this sort, which gives meaning to existence, is indispensable to humans. We cannot gain orientation in life and cannot act without some conception or vision of the context within which we are living and moving, and without some understanding of our own place and role within that context. Such a framework of interpretation, however, is like the air we breathe: it does not easily or quickly become an object directly perceived or noticed. In consequence, it is seldom realized that the terms or foci, which structure the framework and give it its peculiar pattern of meaning, in fact function only within and as a part of the framework itself. This can be seen most readily, perhaps, when we consider world-views to which we are not closely attached. Terms like "Brahman," "karma," "nirvana," "yin/yang," "mana," all gain their meaning, not through particular beings or experiences which they name, but rather as essential constituent elements within the frameworks of interpretation of the whole of life to which they belong. The same can be said for such (contemporary) terms as "evolution," "class struggle," "creativity," and "universe." When these notions are used in setting out or explicating an overall view of life and reality, they articulate the human imagination's attempt to grasp and understand and interpret the *whole* within which human life falls; their creation and use is thus a function of the imagination's power to unify and organize and synthesize into one grand vision what comes to us only episodically and in fragments. It should not surprise us to discover that in the various separated geographical settings in which humans gradually created great civilizations, quite diverse conceptions of the world, and of the human place within the world, developed, as the imagination generated and followed increasingly different perspectives in the several great cultural and religious traditions. Since the terms and images which articulate these world-conceptions or world-pictures are never simply representations gained in direct perception, they should not be understood as directly descriptive of objects (of experience). As products of and constitutive of a poetic or imaginative vision, they are properly understood as essentially elements within and functions of that overarching vision or conception.

In a radically unified world-view such as a monotheism, the central focus of meaning, "God," easily becomes reified into an independently existing being. But the constituting elements of frameworks of interpretation are not distinctly locatable objects of this sort at all (and it is significant in this respect that the tradition was well aware that God could not be directly "seen"). It is a mistake, therefore, to regard qualities attributed to God (e.g., aseity, holiness, omnipotence, omniscience, providence, love, self-revelation) as though they were features or activities of such a particular being. Rather, in the mind's construction of the image/concept of God the ordinary relation of subject and predicate is reversed. Instead of the subject (God) being a *given* to which the various predicate adjectives are then assigned, here the descriptive terms themselves are the building blocks which the imagination uses in putting together its conception. As the principal character in a great dramatic story God is conceived as absolute, all-powerful, all-knowing, holy, and the like—or, in the more mythic and wholistic mode in which the imagination first did its work: as a "mighty warrior," a "stern judge," "king of kings and lord of lords," "maker of heaven and earth," "heavenly father." This character, then, often lifted out of the original story-context which gave it life and meaning, becomes the core of the notion of God; and all of life and the world are grasped as ultimately grounded upon and centered in this God.

God, thus, is the ultimate point of reference in terms of which all else is understood, and the ultimate focus of life and of human devotion. The technical theological vocabulary—including concepts like aseity, sin, creation, salvation, trinity, providence, miracle, revelation, incarnation, and the like—was developed over the centuries as an articulated schema for expressing and interpreting this claim, and it remains a principal resource and tool for theological work today. However, contemporary theological construction needs to recognize that these terms and concepts do not refer directly to "objects" or "realities" or their qualities and relations, but function rather as the building blocks or reference points which articulate the theistic world-picture or vision of life. For this reason it is a mistake to take over traditional vocabulary and methods uncritically, since these were worked out largely on the assumption that God-language was directly objectivist or referential, and thus they are usually cast in a reifying mode.

Theology has always been constructive in character. In its original mythopoeic form theological images and concepts were utilized to create a world-picture in which all of life was seen to be derived from and ordered to God; and this vision was gradually developed and shaped—constructed and reconstructed—under the impact of centuries of prophetic criticism and insight. When Greek culture was encountered, theology became philosophically self-conscious and critical, and thus attended more directly to problems of conceptual analysis and systematic conceptual construction, but it remained wedded to the reifying referential mode in which its mythic origins had cast it, and it understood itself to be attempting to express in human words and concepts what was objectively and authoritatively given in divine revelation; the thoroughly constructive character of theology was not clearly recognized. With the contemporary theory of world-views and conceptual frameworks, however, more adequate understanding of the human function and the logical standing of religious and theological language is made possible, and this deficiency is overcome. Theological work, therefore, can now be carried on as a fully critical and self-conscious constructive activity, in a way that has never before been possible.[4]

II

If we can no longer presume that theology is working directly from an authoritative divine revelation, how are we to proceed? What are we to construct here, and in what way? It is clear that we cannot fabricate a concept of God simply out of whole cloth. Of what elements is it to be composed and how should they be put together? Is it really possible to set out a meaningful concept of God once the radically constructive character of theology is acknowledged?

A framework of interpretation for life and experience cannot be artificially built up from scratch, and then simply "adopted" by persons who find it attractive and plausible. Since all experiencing, thinking, and acting presuppose a world-view or perspective which shapes the questions being formulated and provides the categories by means of which life will be grasped and interpreted, we are never able to get to a presuppositionless point from which we can freely and without bias choose our framework of interpretation. We are always already living in and operating out of one (or more) world-picture(s). The most we can hope, therefore, is to become sufficiently conscious of the stance within which we are living and acting so as to become critical of it to some degree, and thus in a position significantly to reconstruct it.

It is in response to meaning already abroad in the culture and language, meaning given in and through the symbol "God," that theological criticism and construction arises. (In this sense theology always begins in "faith" and in response to "revelation," and is always in the service of faith.) When a theologian becomes conscious that the images and forms mediating this meaning are not adequate to convey it precisely or effectively, so that the meaning comes through stunted or distorted and subject to misunderstanding, criticism and reconstruction are undertaken in the attempt to enable the symbol to become a more valid and effective center of orientation for modern life. In the earlier pages of this chapter we have already begun this task of theological reconstruction. I have been arguing that God is to be understood not primarily as a "freestanding" separate or distinct "object" or being (a mistake into which we are often led by our imagery), but as an important constituent of, and simultaneously a function of, an overarching world-view. We must now attempt to work out what God can mean positively and significantly when the logical standing of God-talk is reconceived this way.

To begin let us ask, What sort of function does the symbol "God" have for those to whom it is significant? We may give a summary answer to this question by saying that the image/concept of God serves as a focus or center for devotion and orientation.[5] Value-claims of many sorts attract our commitment and loyalty: family, nation, truth, pleasure, power, work, political causes, beauty, health, charismatic leaders, sex, sports, ideologies, physical discipline or indulgence, and many more. Particular moments—or major segments—of life may be oriented in terms of one or more of this immense variety of fascinating objects which come to our attention. The attraction in diverse directions of incompatible values may threaten on occasion to pull us to pieces; intemperate subservience to particular values may enslave and ultimately destroy us. In contrast with all such "idolatrous" attachments, however, the symbol of God claims to represent to us a focus for orientation which will bring true fulfillment and meaning to human life. It sums up, unifies, and represents in a personification what are taken to be the highest and most indispensable human ideals and values, making them a visible standard for measuring human realization, and simultaneously enabling them to be attractive of loyalty and devotion which can order and continuously transform individuals and societies toward fulfillment (i.e., bring "salvation").[6]

As modern biblical scholarship has discovered, Yahweh became known first and primarily as the savior and protector of his people; only later was he identified as the creator of the heavens and the earth, the source and ground of all that is. It was to reinforce the propriety and significance of the belief that Yahweh is *our* God, *our* savior, the one on whom we can and should depend and to whom we can rightly devote ourselves, that the more metaphysical claims about Yahweh's being the first and the last besides whom there is no other God (Isa. 44:6), the very creator of all that is (Isa. 45), developed. Thus, the metaphysical claim that God is "ultimate reality" or "being-itself" or "the source and ground of all that is," is made to undergird and make plausible the religious claim that God is the single appropriate object for ultimate human devotion and service. But it is the performance of this latter religious function that identifies God as *God.* An abstract metaphysical conception of the "ultimately real" in and of itself does not warrant, and can hardly attract, full human devotion; that high place is given only to those metaphysical conceptions which explicate and secure the significance and standing of meaning that already is providing an important focus for affection and orientation.

Every conceptual frame or world-picture can demonstrate some grounding for what it holds ultimately significant. But since it is never possible to step entirely "outside" the frame of orientation being examined onto "neutral" ground, to see whether and how well it "corresponds" with "what is really the case," the metaphysical "truth" of an all-inclusive conceptual framework can never be directly and easily ascertained. (The notions of "correspondence" and "what is really the case," it should be noted, are themselves concepts of ours, given meaning by their place in the frame of orientation which Western philosophically trained minds have come to take for granted.) The best way to assess the appropriateness or adequacy of a particular frame of orientation is through comparison with alternatives. One can attempt to observe and evaluate the different styles and modes of human existence and community, and the forms of human realization, made possible by the various world-pictures and conceptual frames which the several great human civilizations have employed. This is an exceedingly difficult task, one for which we are barely beginning to acquire the necessary tools, and which, in any case, cannot be undertaken here. It looms as important work for future theologies and philosophies of religion. The most that can be attempted here is to sketch the outlines of a critical modern theistic position, including some suggestions about its metaphysical grounding. At some later time, perhaps, this could be laid alongside other critical modern world-views—for example, Buddhist, Marxist, secular evolutionary-humanist—for comparative evaluation and for the metaphysical assessment which such comparison would make possible.

I want to turn now to an analysis of those characteristics in the monotheistic notion of God received from the tradition which make God a suitable and appropriate object of human service and devotion. If we can see something of how and why it might justifiably be claimed that love of this God does promote (or is even indispensable for) what might plausibly be regarded as human fulfillment and meaning,[7] we will have gained some understanding of how the concept of God has functioned in the past and we will be in a position to consider what sort of claims might be made for its continuing importance. Then in the concluding sections of this chapter we can briefly explore the sense in which it might be said that this God "exists."

III

The word "God" has been used in many different ways in Western literature, and I shall make no attempt to explore them all. I will confine my attention here to certain features of what I take to be the central monotheistic strand of the Christian tradition, but this should not be taken to imply disparagement of or lack of interest in other conceptions and formulations.

The concept of God as the sole proper object of unqualified human devotion and service appears to be structured by a unique and powerful internal dialectic. On the one hand (as we have already noted), God is conceived as a humanizing center of orientation, one who brings about human salvation and who is (usually) conceived in quasi-human or anthropomorphic images. On the other hand, however, God is envisioned as mysterious and beyond all human knowing, the all-powerful creator of the heavens and the earth and the determiner of destiny, one who "builds" and "plants" but who also "plucks up" and "breaks down," "destroys" and "overthrows" (Jer. 1:10), the relativizer of everything human and finite. God is thus conceived to be radically independent of all human striving and desiring—certainly no product of our fantasies and wishes—while at the same time it is only in relation to God that genuine human fulfillment is to be found. God transcends all things human, indeed all things finite, even while being that which creates, sustains, and nourishes the entire finite order. I want to argue that either of these dimensions taken without the other would undermine and ultimately destroy the function and significance of God as the proper object of human devotion and service; but they need very careful formulation if we are to avoid the reification so characteristic of the tradition.

Let us consider first the motif of God's radical transcendence and otherness. This theme is particularly developed in the image of God as the creator of the heavens and the earth, the lord of history and judge of the world. It is also expressed in the notions of God's eternity, transcendence, aseity, and absoluteness. In all these conceptions God's otherness from and radical independence of the human and all else finite is underlined. God is not to be understood as our tool or device, to be used for our advantage or as we please. We are God's servants, not God ours. We must subject ourselves to the order which God imposes; God is not subject to our arranging and ordering.

What seems to be at stake here is a claim that human individuals and communities need a center of orientation and devotion outside themselves and their perceived

desires and needs if they are to find genuine fulfillment.
As finite beings seeking security and satisfaction, we all too
easily make ourselves the center of life, rearranging all
else so that it simply conforms with our wishes. Our relations within the finite order are all characterized by reci-
procity and mutual interdependence, and this makes it
possible for us to employ them in ways directed toward
the fulfillment of our own desires, to utilize the finite realities to whom we are related as "means only" rather than
treating them as "ends in themselves" (Kant). Our narcissism as individuals seems inevitably to lead to corruption
of these relationships, and our similar ethnocentrism as
communities and anthropocentrism as a species lead to
warfare among peoples and to the exploitation of the resources in our environment. What is needed to break
through this curved-in character of human existence is a
center and focus of meaning which can evoke from us
devotion and service that draws us out of our preoccupa-
tion with ourselves and our own wishes. The image/con-
cept of a God radically objective to us, entirely independent of all our desires and not susceptible to any remaking
or reshaping in accord with our wishes, that which we can
in no way control, has traditionally performed this function. God has been a center of devotion and service which
could draw selves and communities out of themselves,
thus overcoming the warfare of a thousand centers each
attempting to order everything in its own terms, and
opening up human life to structures of order and meaning
otherwise outside its reach.

It was the employment of objectivistic images like creator, lord, and judge, which emphasized God's radical transcendence and over-againstness while simultaneously suggesting God's absolute authority and power over human
existence, that gave the symbol of God its great power to
evoke this kind of human self-transcendence. These same
images, of course, have been the basis for the understanding of God as (an) existent being, as the ultimate reality on

which all other reality depends; and it may seem that belief in God's existing over against us is essential to God's functioning as a center of orientation and devotion which can draw us out of ourselves. I do not, however, think that is necessarily the case. For it was not so much God's objectivity and existence in the present that gave the traditional images their great power of evocation, as it was memories of what God had done in the past and hopes for what God would do in the future.[8] To live "under God" was to live remembering God's "mighty deeds" already performed and expecting that future which God was about to bring. This would be a "kingdom" in which all evil, unrighteousness, and falsehood were overthrown, and truth, peace, and love were ushered in—whether this was understood in terms of individual guilt and sin and the hoped for release of forgiveness and salvation, or in terms of the transformation of the whole sociocultural order in a great consummation of history. "God" and the "kingdom of God" signified, thus, a movement through history from a past of sin and bondage to a future of judgment and salvation, and it was in terms of that great historical movement that the image/concept of God actually exercised its power, both through the terror it evoked and the love it inspired. The fulfillment of human life (both individual and social)—or its absolute destruction—was in God's hands: it was this awareness that was the real ground of God's power to draw human existence outside itself.[9]

These observations reinforce a point made earlier in this chapter: in actual practice the image/concept of God does not function simply as referring to some being which is grasped and understood just in terms of itself; on the contrary, it functions as the principal focal point of an overall world-picture, and it is in terms of that interpretive frame that it must be understood. The world-picture within which the biblical God functions is historicist in character. All of life and reality are seen as a vast historical movement, from creation to eschaton, and God is the principal

actor in that movement. It is within this context that
human life is to be understood and is to find its proper
place and fulfillment. So it is as true to say that the meaning of human life is found within the ongoing movement
of (God's) history as to say that it is found in relation to God
—for the two expressions come down to the same thing.
Living within the world-view which has God as its focus
is no different from living in significant relation to that
God who is the focal center for this world-view. In either
mode of expression human existence is understood in
terms of its relation to and dependence on a reality other
than itself, a reality which calls it into being, sustains it in
existence, and gives it a ground for hope of fulfillment
(salvation). In the one case this Other is seen as a particular
being, God, who is working in and through history; in the
other case it is seen as the cosmic historical movement
ordered by God's purposes.

Since (as we have seen) it is an error to reify God into
an independent being, the two forms of expression are
really equivalent. But from the point of view of contemporary theological reconstruction, the understanding in
terms of world-historical movement is distinctly prefera-
ble. For it provides a way to speak of an independence and
otherness and even aseity over against the human—the
requisite condition for breaking our narcissism and anthropocentrism and drawing us out of ourselves—without
positing a particular existing being (named "God") as that
in which this otherness is lodged. The historical movement as a whole, and in particular its moving forward
toward future possibilities which we cannot now envision
but for which we must become open, can now be seen as
that independent Reality in relation to which our existence and activity must be oriented. Since the characteristically modern interpretations of the overall context of
human existence and experience—of the "world" within
which our lives fall—are evolutionary-historical in pattern,
the shift in emphasis which I am advocating here enables

God to be seen not
as a par-
ticular being
but as
cosmic
historical
movement

our theological reconstruction to establish effective contact with major presuppositions and perspectives of modern intellectual and cultural life.

For the moment I do not wish to elaborate further the way in which the motif of God's otherness or transcendence—that dimension of the concept of God which relativizes and calls into question all human wishes and concerns, ideas and ideals—would be developed in the theological reconstruction being proposed here. Let us turn, rather, to the other equally important motif in the concept of God, what I would like to call God's "humaneness," God's concern for and active promotion of human well-being and fulfillment. In some traditions the gods have been believed to be indifferent to human needs and suffering, or even malevolent; in the traditions growing out of Hebraic culture, however, God came increasingly to be depicted as representing the epitome of humane virtues and as being thoroughly devoted to the welfare of humans and other creatures. Thus God was thought of as *good*, not only powerful, as just, merciful, caring, loving, and forgiving. In the Christian version of the divine activity God is represented as sacrificing self without reservation—sending "his only son"—in order to rescue fallen humanity from the mass of sin and perdition into which it had fallen. The use of such anthropomorphic imagery in depicting God contributed to the overall impression that God was thoroughly "trustworthy"; so one could give oneself without reservation in service and devotion to God. God was like a thoroughly humane, just, and loving father, and we are the children for whom God has unlimited care, for whom God's only desire is that we reach maturity and fulfillment. But this is no mere "wish" of God's: God is also pictured as a powerful will, the very King of the Universe, who is working effectively to accomplish the humane objectives set from creation. In the "end" a humane communal order of justice, mercy, and love—the "kingdom of God"—will be fully established and we human children and loyal subjects of God will reach our destined salvation. However much it is necessary to curb our superficial wishes and desires in order to worship and serve God, ultimately our own deepest interests and needs will be realized, for God's will and work for us is unqualifiedly humane.

This emphasis on God's humaneness in the traditional theistic world-view meant that the events and processes of the natural order within which human life fell were not to be understood in wholly impersonal terms: they were themselves in some sense the expression of (the humane) God's purposive activity, and in and through them God was working to create and sustain human life and bring it to its proper fulfillment. We can put this point in more contemporary terms. There have been tendencies and forces working in and through the evolution of life which have eventuated in the appearance of human beings; and in the history of that humanity which subsequently unfolded, interest in, attraction toward, and commitment to what we call "humane" values, attitudes, ideologies, and institutions appeared, and in some historical strands began effectively to transform and shape personal and social life. One can speak, thus, of a movement of cosmic history which has eventuated in the production of the human and the humane, and one might hope for a further development of this historical tendency toward a more genuinely humane society—what in the traditional mythology was expected as the "kingdom of God."

Within such an evolutionary-historical understanding of the world, and of the appearance of humanity within the world, the image/concept of God continues to have a significant place and function. As finite but self-conscious beings within the ongoing evolutionary-historical process —beings capable of shaping and directing our own development in certain respects—it is important that we be able to focus our attention on those features of the over-arching cosmic process which create and sustain and fulfill us as specifically *human.* That is, we need to be able to focus our devotion, our reflection, and our activity on that which grounds and fulfills our humanity, that which can enable it to come to its highest and most mature expression, that which, therefore, can open us to that fuller realization of humanity toward which (we may dare to hope) history is moving. *God* is the symbol which holds all this together in a unified personifying image/concept suitable for devotion, meditation, and the orientation of life. As such, God symbolizes that in the ongoing evolutionary-historical process which grounds our being as distinctively human and which draws (or drives) us on toward authentic human fulfillment (salvation). In this interpretation, God continues to symbolize that which is outside and other than the human, that which effectively relativizes present human existence and consciousness, that which draws the human out of itself, opening it to new possibilities in the future.[10] And ritualized devotion to God in religious cult as well as in the private disciplines of prayer and meditation still has an important function to play in life.

IV

There has always been considerable tension between the two central motifs in the symbol of God—humaneness, with its tendencies toward anthropomorphism and its emphasis on human fulfillment; and transcendence or absoluteness, with its emphasis on God's radical otherness, God's mystery, God's utter inaccessibility. This tension gave the symbol much of its power and effectiveness as a focus for devotion and orientation in human life, but it was also a source of instability in the symbol's meaning. When a proper balance was not maintained between these two motifs, God either lost attractiveness and power as a center of devotion, or the devotees of the now lopsided God themselves became twisted and warped, possibly dangerous.

[handwritten margin note: Unbalances / If focus on / humaneness / of God / over / stressed ↓]

Consider first the consequence of overemphasis on
God's absoluteness at the expense of God's humaneness.
This tended, in the first place, toward reification of the
solitary, absolute, and independent being, *God,* as alone
worthy of any interest or attention, and thus to disregard
of or lack of attention to the significance of the conceptual
frame or world-picture within which "God" had meaning,
significance, and value. This in turn sometimes led, in the
second place, to a complete destruction of God's attractiveness as a center of devotion. In the West this happened
in two ways.

On the one hand, overemphasis on God's tyrannical omnipotence so offended many sensitive and thoughtful humanists (J. S. Mill, Bertrand Russell, Albert Camus) that
they found it impossible to worship or believe. The hor-
rendous evils in human society, especially as these have
come clearly into view in the twentieth century, suggest
that only a terrible monster-God could have been responsible for our world. If God is indeed omnipotent, the one
whose will is being realized in our history, God is not one
whom we should serve but rather one whom we should
loathe and despise and against whom we should struggle
with all our strength. Worship of such a being could, in
fact, evoke from devotees harsh and authoritarian attitudes and actions similar to those attributed to God. Of
course devotion to a God of this sort—often inspired more
by fear or terror than by love, as Calvinism, for example,
shows—may also be a source of great power in human
affairs, as men and women seek above all else to carry out
the will of the Almighty. As some historians have argued,
much of the dynamic of Western culture may be traced to
the worship of this all-powerful and terrifying oriental
potentate. But a dynamic not qualified and restricted by
humane concerns is always dangerous and destructive,
and in recent years we have begun to awaken to the rape
of other peoples and of the environment, which Western
society, too much devoted to this God, has consummated.

On the other hand, the motif of God's absoluteness and transcendence may be developed so as to emphasize God's wholly-otherness, God's transcendent mysteriousness and unknowability. This also has occurred in modern times, with the consequence that for many God has become simply an unknown "X," the ultimate Mystery which is the horizon bounding all our experience and knowledge but which we can never penetrate or comprehend. Such a God has become empty of content and meaning and thus ultimately irrelevant to the day-to-day concerns of human life, one who can safely be ignored or neglected. Much modern agnosticism and religious indifference is an expression of this loss of meaning and significance in the symbol of God. "God" has become something of which we no longer need take serious account.

Overemphasizing the motif of God's humaneness, however, at the expense of God's absoluteness, has had equally deleterious effects. A God without transcendence and otherness is a God without independence of the human, a God who is simply our creature, the extension of our own wishes and desires. Such a God may in many ways be attractive to us, as the personification of all that we want, and we may be quite happy to serve such a God devotedly. But in the end worship of this sort proves self-stultifying. Not only can this God easily be exposed as simple projection and wish-fulfillment (Xenophanes, Feuerbach, Nietzsche, Freud), a product of self-deceit and of cowardly unwillingness to face the hard facts of human life; but this God also proves to be as fickle and changing as its devotees, and is capable, finally, of maintaining only sentimental interest. A God who gives easy divine approval to our projects, and is the means for legitimating and even sanctifying what we already are and believe, places too little tension on us to draw us out of ourselves, out of our fixed habits and attitudes and ideas. A symbol of this sort —all too often imaged as white and male—has often functioned ideologically, helping to shore up the class and sex distinctions, and the unjust institutional structures, of society. Instead of providing a critical principle which enabled persons and communities to come to some awareness of their shortcomings, failures, and perversions (the "judgment" of God), it has helped to reinforce and maintain unjust and inhuman social practices and structures, blinding and corrupting the consciences of worshipers. Since every society, and every group within society, tends to divinize its own desires and needs, a multitude of these henotheistic gods always appears, each at war with all the others and each promising salvation to its devotees; and the divisions and separations already so destructive to human life and well-being become further magnified. Instead of providing a center of devotion which could draw humanity, with its petty distinctions and divisions, into a wider community, God breaks down into a plethora of little gods, each reflecting but sanctifying the interests of its worshipers and thus each contributing further to the warfare and chaos of human affairs. Such gods are constructed too much in the image of our own humanity.

There are, of course, wide differences in understanding of the human among individuals and among societies. The anthropomorphic elements in the image/concept of God, especially those elements which define what I have called God's humaneness, naturally reflect these differing views of human nature and human fulfillment—and this accounts in part for the diversity of conceptions of God. A fully argued reconstruction of the concept of God would require a thorough consideration of these matters, but that cannot be undertaken here. However, I would like to suggest that it is at this point that specifically *Christian* theology becomes interesting and important, because of the special constraints laid upon it.

For Christian faith Jesus Christ has had a double normative significance (Chalcedon): he provided a basis for understanding what the human truly is and how it is to comport itself, and also for understanding who God is and how

God acts to and for humans. Thus, for Christian theology the humaneness of God was not to be understood simply or primarily in terms of our own ideas and experience of the human: *Jesus* provides the model on the basis of which our notions of humaneness (whether God's or ours) are to be developed. There are of course wide differences in view among Christian theologians about who Jesus was and what he did, and about the way in which Jesus' character, actions, and fate help to define and determine how God is to be conceived. I cannot here address these matters in detail,[11] but I would like to point out certain radical implications which can follow from taking Jesus as the paradigm for understanding humaneness. When one proceeds in this way, such qualities as love, mercy, and forgiveness—even "nonresistance" (Matt. 5:39) or "weakness" (1 Cor. 1:25) in the face of aggression—will be given prominence in the conception of the truly human and in the understanding of God.[12] Since these qualities all tend toward a universalistic and humane ethic rather than toward ethnocentric or politically and socially chauvinistic positions, emphasis on their importance presses the anthropomorphic or "humane" side of the conception of God to break through from its henotheistic tendencies to the full universalism of "radical monotheism."[13]

When developed in this way, the motifs of humaneness and of absoluteness in the concept of God, though remaining in a certain tension, reinforce each other instead of undercutting and threatening to destroy each other. It now becomes clear that God's (and history's) absoluteness cannot be identified with that tyrannical power which destroys its enemies mercilessly, nor is it to be understood as some inscrutable mystery that ultimately fades into the complete emptiness of an unknowable "X"; it is, rather, that which creates, sustains, and continues to nurture humans even in the face of hostility and rejection, so as to effect their transformation and ultimate fulfillment. And God's (and history's) humaneness is not some simple real-

*These
are
the
antropological
values
underlying
K's
construction.*

ization of our wishes or desires but rather the insistence, which we in our self-centeredness always resist, that we become transformed into beings who love and serve each other, that we become a "new humanity" characterized preeminently by such virtues as love, freedom, reconciling forgiveness and openness, and creativity.

The import and meaning for human life supplied by an image/concept of God constructed in this way should be obvious. Though such a focus for devotion and service would not solve all, or even any, of our immensely difficult concrete problems, it would help to mobilize our energies and intelligence to attack those problems by combating the ego- and ethno- and anthropo-centric tendencies in our lives, opening us up for that universalistic "benevolence toward being in general" (Edwards), without which a truly orderly, and at the same time genuinely humane, world can scarcely be conceived.

V

I have attempted here to sketch desiderata for the image/concept of God which are rooted in the Christian tradition. In the present argument, however, the significance of these desiderata is not grounded on the supposed authority of "revelation," but instead on the claim that it is both appropriate and humanly desirable for our devotion and service to be focused on a symbol defined in this way. It is clear that much fuller discussion would be required to show that a center of orientation of this sort would indeed promote genuine human fulfillment, but I think perhaps enough has been said to suggest the lines along which such further elaboration might be undertaken. I want to turn now to a summary assessment of this whole approach to theology by considering briefly the question of God's "existence."

We must not be misled here into repeating the common error of searching for some particular being or reality to which the name "God" can be applied. As we have seen, "God" is the focal term of an overarching conceptual framework (in terms of which all experience is grasped, understood, and interpreted), and is not the name of an object perceived or experienced apart from that frame. The question, therefore, to which we must attend—often improperly posed as asking about the "existence of God" —is really concerned with the viability and appropriateness of this whole frame of orientation. To what extent and in what respects does this conceptual scheme provide a "true" or "valid" understanding of human existence in the world? I have already indicated that proper and full treatment of this question would require comparative studies of a sort I cannot here undertake, but it is possible to say something further about it.

Human ideals and values, foci for devotion and loyalty and the standards in terms of which humans judge themselves, do not and could not exist independently of and without regard to "how things are." If they had no significant connection with or relationship to "the real world," it is inconceivable that they would provide useful guidance and orientation for beings living and acting within that world. In this respect every mythology or world-view which the human imagination has conceived—even those which seem grotesque, supersititious, and completely unbelievable to us today—must in its own way bear some significant relation to the reality in which its devotees live. What, now, can be said about a frame of orientation centered on and symbolized by God—more specifically, by a God constructed according to Christian criteria? Does or can devotion to this God in fact provide us with significant and valid orientation in the "real world"? If it does, then this frame of orientation must in some significant sense "correspond" to "how things are," and talk about God, the symbolical focus of this perspective, must represent something "real." I have argued above that the terms articulating a frame of orientation cannot be expected to corre-

spond directly to "existent realities." But it would be hard
to conceive how the ruling focus of a highly centered
frame of orientation could be completely out of touch with
that which is metaphysically real. I am not here preparing
to develop an "argument for the existence of God": I am
claiming that the symbol of God must in some way correspond to or represent something metaphysically real, if it
is in fact true that devotion to that symbol provides proper
orientation for human life. What in "reality," then, might
one contend this symbol stands for?

The Christian image/concept of God, as I have presented it here, is an imaginative construct which orients
selves and communities so as to facilitate development
toward loving and caring selfhood, and toward communities of openness, love, and freedom. Other ways of understanding God or other foci of devotion—other value
schemes or frames of orientation—would, presumably,
lead human development and realization in other directions. Clearly there are many different ways in which individuals and communities can grow; there are many different ways of being human. And the models and images
which humans accept as their own have much to do with
the style of life which will ultimately become theirs. The
question we must ask here is: Are there some styles of life
in which human possibilities come to fuller realization
than others? Though it is exceedingly difficult to define
criteria which will enable ranking different forms of existence according to the degree in which human potential
is realized, few, I suppose, would hold that every form
human life has taken historically is equivalent with every
other. Some are exceedingly frustrating and ultimately
prove abortive; others open up human life to a wide range
of values and meanings.

The question about the validity or truth of a theistic
frame of orientation is the question about the degree to
which it reflects the actual situation of human existence
and thus opens up the possibility for persons and com-

munities to come to full(er) realization (i.e., to "salvation").
To speak of God's "reality" or "existence"—i.e., to speak
of the validity or truth of the theistic perspective—is to
maintain that the modes of life made possible, when existence is oriented according to this perspective, are a full
and genuine realization of the actual potentialities of
human nature, are in accord, that is to say, with "how
things are." That is, it is to say that life which comes to
expression in love for and concern for other persons, and
in the creation of communities of justice and freedom, is
grounded in *actuality,* not merely fantasy. Doubtless it is
difficult, or even impossible, to establish scientifically the
existence of vital cosmic forces undergirding and even in
some sense "working toward" the establishment of human
existence conceived in this way. Nonetheless, in the long
course of the evolution of life on this planet, human forms
eventually emerged; and in the course of human history,
full self-consciousness, love, and freedom gradually came
into view as possibilities for human life. To see these possibilities as ultimately normative for human existence is to
hold them to be grounded in and expressive of "reality"
in a way not true of significantly different modes of life.
Speech about the Christian God as "real" or "existent"
expresses symbolically this conviction that free and loving
persons-in-community have a substantial metaphysical
foundation, that there are cosmic forces working toward
this sort of humanization. To the extent that there has
been in fact a genuine evolutionary movement through
cosmic history toward the production of our humanity, the
ancient mythic notions of the will and purposes of God
working through time toward the realization of humane
ends begin to become intelligible in modern terms.

We are here at one of the great divides which separates
theistic faith from unbelief. Faith lives from a belief in, a
confidence that, there is indeed a cosmic and vital movement—grounded in what is ultimately real—toward humaneness, that our being conscious and purposive and

thirsting for love and freedom is no mere accident but is undergirded somehow in the very nature of things. This is a momentous claim. For those subscribing to it, our efforts toward building a more humane world are not simply our own, but are themselves the expression of deeper hidden forces working in nature and in life. In striving for such a world we are supported and sustained and inspired by a dynamism in the foundations of the universe. Such a faith can give a grounding and confidence in struggles for a more just and humane world which may be the only antidote, in our desperate times, to an ultimate and enervating despair.

This attention to and reliance on the ultimate cosmic grounding of our humanity is what is focused and concentrated by belief in God. "God" is the personifying symbol of that cosmic activity which has created our humanity and continues to press for its full realization. Such a personification has a considerable advantage for some purposes over abstract concepts such as "cosmic forces" or "foundation for our humanity in the ultimate nature of things": the symbol "God" is concrete and definite, a sharply defined image, and as such it can readily become the central focus for devotion and service. Sympathy and love and care and trust and loyalty are evoked from us by other personal selves; it is to other persons, with whom we are in active interrelation, that we can most fully and unreservedly give ourselves. The image, then, of a divine Person who has created us, who sustains us, who loves and cares for us, and who is seeking our full realization (our salvation), presents vividly and meaningfully to human consciousness that to which we should be devoted, if the further realization of our human potential is to be achieved. "God" is a symbol that gathers up into itself and focuses for us all those cosmic forces working toward the fully humane existence for which we long.

Human existence conceived as defined essentially by love, freedom, and creativity would hardly have gained as important a foothold in consciousness and history as it has, apart from the mode of life, and the confidence and insight, engendered by devotion to the God who loves and cares, who is free and creative. This humanizing image has disciplined and shaped the consciousness of those who held it before themselves in devotion and adoration, helping to generate norms for authentic human selfhood and community. The concept of God—properly demythologized and rightly constructed and defined—still has much to contribute in the proper focusing of our energies and affections toward realization of a more humane society. Some may find sustenance and support for living and acting humanely in the abstract concept of a "cosmic movement" toward our fuller humanization; but for the larger part of humanity the symbol of a loving God will surely remain the principal focus of devotion and affection and service which has truly humanizing effects. For this symbol represents with great vividness and power the fact that we are created, sustained, and fulfilled as human and humane, not by our efforts alone, but from beyond ourselves, from resources in the ultimate nature of things.

VI

The concept of God which I have been sketching here requires and enables us to employ varying sorts of representations falling on a continuum running from highly mythical and symbolical images—God as a personal being who loves and cares—to the more abstract notion of the cosmic ground of our humanity. Its strength resides precisely in the contention that images and concepts along this entire continuum must be used in constructing an adequate contemporary concept of God; to concentrate on one extremity at the expense of the other can only result in misunderstanding and failure. If one emphasizes only the mythic and anthropomorphic characterizations that make God religiously attractive, one increasingly moves away from plausible metaphysical talk about God, as suggested by the actual cosmic and evolutionary foundations of our humanity, and the concept becomes empty; but conversely, if one emphasizes abstract metaphysical concepts about a "cosmic movement" toward, or "cosmic ground" of, our humanity, to the exclusion of more anthropomorphic and personalistic imagery, the concept loses its religious power and attractiveness as a focus for devotion and orientation. However difficult it may be to do so, the mythic and the metaphysical dimensions of the image/concept of God must be held together for that notion to function properly.

Contemporary efforts to construct an adequate conception of God have met with great difficulties at this point partly, perhaps, because it has seemed important to interpret the meaning of "God" in purely (or largely) immanent or intramundane terms. This move brings the referent for our God-talk in very "close" to our experience and observation, so to speak, thus exposing clearly the tension —almost the incoherence—generated in the idea by the juxtaposition of the mythic and the metaphysical. This tension was not felt so strongly in more traditional constructions of the concept of God, because God, as "creator" or "ground" of the world, was posited as utterly "transcendent" of it. God's "essence" or "nature" was thus in principle inaccessible to human experience and reflection, and the incoherence or lack of "fit" between the more anthropomorphic language and the abstract characterizations could be regarded as somehow resolved in the ultimate mystery of God's being. As long as it was believed that divine "revelation" certified God to be both truly absolute and truly humane—simultaneously metaphysically ultimate and our savior—this traditional solution did not raise unmanageable problems. God could function both as the focus for worship and the orientation of human life, and also as the ultimate point of reference in terms of which all else was understood and which relativizes all.

Constructing the idea of God with this emphasis on God's transcendence of and distinctness from the world has the undeniable strength of highlighting the respects in which human existence is ensconced in impenetrable Mystery; it thus underlines in a valuable way the relativity and incompleteness and potential error of all our experience and knowledge. But it gains these advantages at the expense of positing an ultimate dualism between the world and God, between the context of our lives and (a) "being" which "exists" somehow "beyond" or "outside" that context.[14] Once it is recognized that all speech and ideas about such (a) being are grounded in our own imaginative powers and in the necessity for us to construct world-views—and that even claims about "God's revelation" from this "beyond" are thus our own construction— this way of interpreting the meaning of God-talk tends to lose plausibility. I have attempted in earlier sections of this chapter to show why this is the case.

If one gives up the cosmological dualism which underlies and is implied by the notion of God's existence as (a) transcendent being, several alternative ways of dealing with the tension between the mythic and the metaphysical dimensions in the concept of God seem to be open. The first and simplest is, of course, to give up one or the other side of the concept. One may, for example, develop a largely mythic notion and make no real attempt to explain how this relates to the rest of our experience and knowledge; that sort of move was characteristic of much neo-orthodox theology. Or one may confine oneself to conceptions that are metaphysically plausible but that have little or no religious power.

A second move appears to acknowledge that it is necessary to attend to both the mythic and the metaphysical dimensions of the concept of God but does not work through their interrelations and interdependence conceptually. Thus, one may hold "God" to be the religious name simply for "what is," for "the structure in things," for "being-itself."[15] When one goes this route, there is no question about God's metaphysical absoluteness and reality, but there are many questions about whether God can or should be worshiped, whether God is "good," whether God can in any sense be said to "love" humankind or to be "working toward our salvation." Despite all the evil in human affairs and in the world, despite the evidently impersonal and uncaring character of the cosmic process, this view declares that "whatever is, is good," the foundation of the world is loving and caring, it is steadily gifting its salvation to us. Here an overwhelming tension develops between the motifs of humaneness and absoluteness in the concept of God. Moreover, there seems to be no way to relieve this tension; it must be simply ignored—or it may be obliterated in a rhetorical *tour de force.*

In this chapter I have attempted to hold together the mythic and the metaphysical dimensions in the concept of God and to show how they are related to each other. By identifying God with the mundane cosmic, vital, and historical powers which have given rise to our humanity and which undergird all our efforts to achieve a fully humane society, I have attempted to provide a metaphysically plausible referent for a religiously significant symbol. With this move the tension between the mythic and the metaphysical is somewhat reduced by qualifying both God's "absoluteness" and God's "humaneness." God's absoluteness is qualified by identifying the referent of "God" with those specific cosmic forces that undergird our distinctively human forms of being; God's humaneness is qualified by interpreting God as a symbol for humanizing and vital powers instead of as "a personal being." By compromising each of these two motifs a bit, they are pulled together into a symbol/concept which can claim both metaphysical plausibility and some religious power.

It may be objected that this conception results in a "finite God," and that it thus gives up any credibility as a monotheistic position. That is certainly one possible interpretation, though not the only one. With an evolutionary-historical cosmology it is possible (though certainly not necessary) to hold that the temporal movement from a material order, through the various stages of life, to the appearance of humanity and historical forms of order, expresses the basic character of Reality, and is not simply one among many cosmic developments. On this view, speaking of God would signify not only the fact that our humanity is cosmically grounded and sustained: God would symbolize a fundamental telos in the universe toward the humane. The creation, sustenance, and enhancement of our humanity, then, would be in some significant sense an expression of the whole cosmic order, not simply of one complex of cosmic powers among many. Choice between such a monotheistic interpretation and a finitistic one would depend, on the one hand, on the relative plausibility of this conception of cosmic teleology and, on the other, on the relative weight given to the religious need for a single unified ultimate center of orientation and devotion for human life.

It is, of course, not necessary in every situation in which theological language is used to attempt to resolve the question of the relationship between the mythic and the metaphysical dimensions in the concept of God. In liturgical or homiletical situations, or in performance of pastoral activities intended, for example, to strengthen the church as a cultic community devoted to Christ, it would hardly be appropriate to raise such issues; and theological writing directed to such uses could well skirt them also. Instead, using the mythic mode which makes both God's humaneness and absoluteness so vivid and appealing, one might speak simply of "God's self-revelation," "God's 'mighty acts' in history," "God's direct responses to personal prayers," "God's sending forth 'his only begotten Son.'" Such language, however, should be used with great care and discrimination, and one must be prepared to back it up with a fuller theological interpretation if it is to retain its meaning. Sophisticated lay persons increasingly find such mythic modes of expression unintelligible or incredible, and they have become a stumbling block for many who otherwise desire to be serious and committed believers.

Mythic language is so commonplace in the life of the church, and in the work of leading theologians, that it is often regarded as the only appropriate language for theology; and it is sometimes assumed that piety, if it is to be genuine, must take this language in a literalistic reifying way. For any who hold this position, the carefully qualified interpretation of the concept of God which I have given in this chapter may seem unacceptable. To them it will seem that God's reality must be much "harder" and "firmer" than is allowed by talk about a "focus" for orientation and devotion provided by a world-view or conceptual frame. I do not believe, however, that careful examination of the work of leading theologians of the twentieth century will uncover any who in fact take such a "stronger" position. It is true that one may discover many loud and confident *assertions* in the rhetoric of piety about God's existence, nature, and activity, but when one examines the grounds on which these are made, they inevitably turn out to be subjective feelings of confidence and conviction ("faith") in combination with biblical and other traditional authorities—i.e., the appeal is to precisely what I have described here as the Christian or theistic world-view or conceptual frame. (Some might wish to take exception to this claim in behalf of certain Whiteheadian theologians who do not seem so fully bound to traditional theistic conceptual schemes, but I do not think this exception really holds: in this case the authoritative conceptual framework is simply drawn largely from Whitehead instead.) What this chapter represents is an attempt to analyze more fully—and perhaps more candidly—just what this grounding of theological work in a world-picture or conceptual frame actually means, and to propose that theology now be done with direct and full consciousness of this.

Making the moves advocated in this chapter should strengthen theology and its credibility as an intellectual discipline. The understanding that all thought and experience are decisively shaped by the overall world-picture or conceptual frame within which they occur is strongly confirmed on many sides today. Epistemological studies, psychological studies of perception and belief, studies in comparative religion and comparative linguistics, in the sociology of knowledge and the sociology of religion, in the history of science—all bear witness to this newer understanding, and theologians must take its implications for their work seriously, if theology is to remain a significant intellectual enterprise.

2/Attachment to God

I

Much psychological study has been devoted in recent years to the phenomenon of attachment of human beings to each other in love and trust and loyalty.[1] It is now becoming clear that such attachment—far from being an optional or merely morally desirable characteristic, or a socially induced attitude necessary in complex highly differentiated societies—has biological roots going far back in the evolutionary process, and is an indispensable and ineradicable characteristic of our human nature. We are social beings to the deepest recesses of our nature. The attachment of infant to mother and of mother to child, of members of families and other intimate groups to each other, and later the wider loyalties to community, guild, and nation, are expressive of our fundamental inter-dependence as human beings. The atomic, individual human being—Robinson Crusoe on his lonely island or each of us in our imagined self-subsistence—is literally an abstraction: the real human being exists only in community, in a network of relationships which sustain her or him

This is a revised version of an address originally prepared as a contribution to a symposium on psychotherapy and religion (1974), and first published in the *Andover Newton Quarterly* (1977), 17:258–270. Used by permission.

biologically, psychologically, and culturally and without which he or she could not exist. Particular attachments among human beings, therefore, are not merely expressions of our conscious interests or even our unconscious desires: they constitute the very structure of our existence to the deepest levels of our being. Our selfhood is incorrigibly social.[2]

Healthy productive human existence, even in strictly biological respects, develops only where the individual is sustained and supported by a network of social relationships and connections. At the level of consciousness this social interdependence expresses itself in the need to know there are others who care for us sufficiently that they will be there to help us, to comfort and support us, in our hour of need, and to rejoice with us in our achievements and triumphs. As John Bowlby puts it, summarizing his analysis of many relevant empirical studies:

> Human beings of all ages are found to be at their happiest and to be able to deploy their talents to best advantage when they are confident that, standing behind them, there are one or more trusted persons who will come to their aid should difficulties arise. The person trusted provides a secure base from which his (or her) companion can operate. And the more trustworthy the base the more it is taken for granted.[3]

The strong undercurrent of anxiety which most of us experience much of the time appears to be directly correlated with the absence, or potential absence, of such supporting figures. Again quoting Bowlby:

> In the presence of a trusted companion fear of situations of every kind diminishes; when, by contrast, one is alone, fear of situations of every kind is magnified. Since in the lives of all of us our most trusted companions are our attachment figures, it follows that the degree to which each of us is susceptible to fear turns

in great part on whether our attachment figures are
present or absent.[4]

If the principal thrust of these claims about our structural interdependence as selves, down to the deepest levels of our being, is correct, it will be clear that there are
certain inevitable but insoluble problems which all human
beings must face. We depend for our very lifeblood as
selves on the presence and availability of certain trusted
attachment-figures; but at the same time, as we mature to
adulthood, we become aware that no human beings can be
absolutely relied upon, that all are susceptible to incapaci-
tation by accident or illness, to failure in meeting their
responsibilities because of ignorance and moral lapse, to
total and final removal from our lives by death. Every
human being—even the most trustworthy and reliable—
is finite and limited, fallible and weak, and may not be
available to us in our moment of most desperate need. The
child's mother may die; the close associate may be away
on other business and out of reach; the most trusted friend
may betray or prove disloyal precisely when one's situation has become most difficult and need of him or her has
become most urgent. I do not say that these things have
to happen, or even that they do happen most of the time.
But we all know well that the conditions of human life are
such that the failure of our trusted companions to be available when needed is always in principle possible. Even
though in actuality we may seldom have to deal with crises
of this sort, they are contingencies for which we must
always be prepared.

Unlike other animals, human beings have the power of
imagination, the ability to envision possibilities which do
not actually exist. This power to entertain the merely *possible,* the not-now-actual, and then to work to make these
possibilities into actualities has enabled creation of the
whole distinctively human world of culture and history; it
has freed humanity from being bound to the actual, the

given, in the way all other animals are bound. But this
same power of imagination opens us to the awareness of
unhappy and destructive possibilities. And our knowledge
of human finitude and failure, of sin and death, makes it
impossible for us to rest absolutely secure in any of our
human attachments. To do so would be folly: it would be
to set ourselves up for greater disaster that would befall
when those on whom we had depended absolutely were
not there to support and sustain us. So we attempt to
withdraw to a certain degree and to maintain a certain
independence from all human attachments, however
needed or alluring. And we are wise so to do. For no
human being or community of human beings, after all, is
able—physically or psychologically—to be absolutely dependable.

Thus, if the modern analysis of human selfhood as social
to its deepest roots is correct, every human being is confronted with a difficult dilemma. On the one hand, we
depend on our close attachments to other human beings
for the creation and sustenance of our selfhood; and if such
highly dependable attachment relationships fail to develop in childhood, or if they rupture at critical moments
then or later in life, the result seems inevitably to be a
crippled personality. So it would seem that human health
and well-being are best served if we give ourselves to each
other in strong unconditional attachments. But on the
other hand, we all know that no human being can or
should be relied on absolutely, that each of us is fallible and
weak and subject to all sorts of failure, and that therefore
it is indispensable that we keep ourselves free enough
from each other to be able to survive potential ruptures or
failures in our relationships, able to move forward into
unexpected situations and new conditions without breaking down completely. Doubtless it is true, as Bowlby
argues, that the level of anxiety or fear increases in inverse
proportion to the presence of trusted and loyal companions, but we must beware lest we draw from that claim the

false conclusion that there are certain optimum conditions of attachment in which anxiety would be virtually eliminated. This can never happen, for however ideal the particular human relationship may be, it always remains finite and weak in various respects and subject to destruction; and he or she who was not aware of this and did not have some consequent anxiety would be foolish indeed.

Anxiety at this level and in this respect is a function of our situation as finite human beings and is not to be eliminated; it is an inevitable concomitant of our awareness of the fragility of the network of relations and attachments in which we humans stand, and its absence would testify not to our healthiness or wholeness but to our lack of sensitivity to what it is to be human, to be finite. In this respect, as Paul Tillich has argued,[5] human anxiety is "ontological"; it belongs to our human existence as such, as beings who are both conscious and finite, and we should not expect it to be overcome by better methods of child-rearing or more adequate psychotherapy. Doubtless this fundamental anxiety can be much exacerbated by failures of human attachment, and can be made more tolerable and productive by healthy and sustaining human relationships, but it cannot be overcome or dissolved by any combination or mode of human attachments.

Although it may well be true, as Bowlby and others argue, that attachment between human beings is biologically rooted in the need for survival and has its proper analogies in lower forms of life, the tendency to withdraw from absolutely firm attachments to other humans, to sit a bit loose in our relations to others, is not to be accounted for solely in terms of experienced failures of attachment in childhood or later. Doubtless experiences of disloyalty and betrayal have their sorry effect, but there is another fundamental root of the tendency to seek independence from overly binding relationships to other human beings: such withdrawal is an inevitable consequence simply of growing consciousness. It quite naturally occurs as one becomes aware of what it means to be finite, and it should not, therefore, be understood as strictly correlative to attachment behavior. Because we are able to think, to use concepts, and with the aid of those concepts to come to self-awareness and self-understanding, our problems of attachment and withdrawal become exceedingly complex.

II

We will be able to understand this complexity better if we examine a bit more closely the phenomenon that we call self-awareness or self-understanding. In self-awareness the self is related essentially to itself, not to something else with which, for example, it is being compared. There are not two objects here, A and B, of which we can say A is to the right of B, or B is larger than A, or A is round and B is square, or A is aware of B. There is only one very complex reality, the self, turning back on itself and relating itself to itself. To be self-conscious is not to be conscious of something other (though that is also always involved) but rather to be conscious of the very self that is conscious.

Self-awareness is made possible for us above all by the word "I," a very complex word and one that we learn to use only slowly and painfully; under certain extreme conditions—for example, of autism or of mental breakdown—humans may not learn to use this word at all, or they may cease being able to use it. Unlike other nouns and names which can be used indifferently by any speaker to refer to the various objects experienced or observed by one or more persons, the word "I"—and other related first-person words—can be used by a speaker only to refer to herself or himself. When I utter or think the word "I," I am simultaneously involved in acting and in responding to that very action—acting, in that it is I who speak the word; responding, in that I take this word to be referring to myself as speaker and not to anything external to myself, and to be demanding my continuing acknowledgment. The word "I" thus both requires and enables attention to myself; it is a self-reflexive word. I am never directly aware of myself as I am of an object of perception; I become aware of myself *as* myself only indirectly or mediately through the mediation of this very complex little word "I." Learning to say "I," therefore, is not merely one more step in the child's acquisition of language; it is made possible by, and itself helps to make possible, the creation of self-consciousness, and thus the very discovery of one's self. It is a very considerable achievement indeed.

Although the word "I" refers to this present speaking self, it has built into it a reference beyond anything and everything present and observable, namely, to both past and future. On the one hand, to say "I" is to identify this present existing reality with that whole complex of memories of past experience through which I have gone and which has shaped me into what I now am; on the other hand to say "I" is to identify this present reality with that somewhat dim and unstructured future into which I am moving, sketched as it is in my plans and projects, my hopes and fears. Neither past nor future is present or actual here and now: both are present only symbolically in the form of memory and imagination. Yet both are constitutive of this "I," of my sense of who I am and what I am doing. The word "I," thus, is not simply a label for some directly present or visible sort of reality: it is a complex symbol which binds together the conceptual and imagistic realities of past and future with this presently existing physical organism and all its needs, binds them into the psychophysical unity we call a self.

Our knowledge of objects (including other persons) is made possible by our direct observation and experience of them over against us; but our knowledge of ourselves, our self-awareness or self-consciousness, is mediated to us in a much more complex way through the use of this word "I," and the images and ideas it carries with it.[6] In the case of external objects—my house or my wife or the town I live in—my original or basic consciousness and knowledge is formed by directly experiencing or observing the objects; I am then able on other occasions to (as we say) "call them to mind" by means of words—for example, by thinking now of "my house" or "my wife," I am able to attend to those realities even in their absence. Words thus function as a substitute way of attending to objects. But in the case of myself there is no original experience of an object which I then later "call to mind" with the help of the word "I," for the self is never in this way a perceivable object. The original experience here is of myself as "I." It is as I learn to say "I," and only as I learn to say "I," that I become conscious of myself not merely as an object but as an active agent, a subject, an experiencer, a doer. The idea or image of "I," thus, is not simply a symbolic substitute for an absent object; it is an indispensable element of the original consciousness of self. Thus conceptual and imagistic elements—at least the concept or image of "I"—are constitutive of our very selfhood; selfhood, involving as it does self-awareness, could not exist without the self's idea or image of itself.

Since symbolical materials are thus constitutive of our very beings as selves, we should not be surprised to find that certain sorts of human problems—for example, what we have called "ontological anxiety"—are grounded directly in our consciousness, and that developments in our consciousness will affect those problems. Consciousness of human frailty and limits, for example, becomes a dimension of my awareness of myself as this particular "I." Whenever I say "I," I am implicitly aware of myself as finite, limited, weak, and struggling and threatened in a variety of ways. This consciousness of my own finitude is not, of course, something directly given in infancy nor even with the original learning of the use of the word "I" in the early years of life; it comes only with growing experience and increasing reflection on oneself and one's experience. But it becomes an integral and indispensable moment of every mature person's self-consciousness.

I am contending, thus, that symbolic elements—images, concepts—are constitutive for every instance of human self-consciousness, and that in this sense conceptual and imaginative activity is in at the ground floor of selfhood. Getting our consciousness or our ideas straight is thus an indispensable part of becoming a healthy well-functioning self, and should not be derogated as somehow less important than, say, "getting in touch with our feelings." As a matter of fact our feelings about ourselves are often generated by the underlying ideas and images with which we constitute ourselves. Thus, if I think of myself as evil or ugly, I may feel deep self-revulsion or self-hatred; if I take myself to be creative or good, I am better able to affirm and accept myself.

Among the ideas constitutive of our selfhood, when we have become mature human beings, is the idea of our finitude or limitedness, and of the fragility of all the relationships in which we stand. And among the feelings that accompany or are generated with this idea is the profound and pervasive underlying sense of insecurity that we call anxiety. "Ontological" anxiety belongs to our very selfhood; but it belongs to our selfhood on the conceptual or symbolic side, not the physical or bodily side, however inseparable these may be. That is, it is because we are conscious or thinking beings that we suffer from ontological anxiety, not simply because we are animals who have unfortunately not attained a proper attachment-relationship to our mothers or to other humans. And for this reason it will be only through developments in the sphere of consciousness, the sphere of ideas and images, that this problem can be properly addressed. No amount of attention to the attachment of mother and infant can resolve this problem—however important such attention may be for certain purposes, including the control of certain forms of anxiety and the creation of free and creative selves—for this problem does not arise fundamentally out of attachment between humans but rather out of the emerging consciousness of the inevitable inadequacy of all such human attachments for dealing with the deepest insecurities and helplessness of the self, i.e., its finitude. It is rooted in our sense of the fragility of those connections and relationships which constitute our very being as selves.

III

It is at this point, now, that we can begin to see something of the significance and meaning of the idea or image of God. The idea of God is the idea of an absolutely adequate attachment-figure. This is made clear by the images in and through which the notion of God has traditionally been spelled out.

In the Christian tradition God has been described preeminently as a father—not just any sort of father but a loving father who cares for his children. We need not debate here whether mother-imagery or father-imagery would be more to the purpose: the point is that God is thought of as a protective and caring parent who is always reliable and always available to its children when they are in need. (In the context of the patriarchal Hebrew society where this idea grew up, father-imagery could certainly express this more powerfully since the father was the head of the family and its protector against all dangers.) But parental imagery by itself would not be sufficient to develop the notion of an ideal attachment-figure: as we have seen, all human beings, including parents, are weak and failing in important respects and cannot be relied upon absolutely. So God was thought of under other images as well, particularly that of lord and warrior, one mighty in battle who can and does defeat all the enemies of the faithful.

> Lift up your heads, O gates!
>> and be lifted up, O ancient doors!
>> that the King of glory may come in.
> Who is the King of glory?
>> The LORD, strong and mighty,
>> the LORD, mighty in battle! . . .
>> he is the King of glory!
>>> (Ps. 24:7–8, 10)

It was this image of the "mighty warrior" which was apparently dominant in the early Mosaic period of Israel's history, when the idea of God was just beginning to gain sharp and clear outlines.[7] God was the one who had overthrown the host of Pharaoh and had brought the people of Israel out of bondage in Egypt, and God was the one who led them into the promised land of Canaan, destroying their foes before them.

But the warrior-imagery, however powerful and dramatic, also has its limitations. Not only is it the case that every warlord is ultimately overthrown and replaced by another. Even in his successful days the warrior is constantly engaged in struggle against foes with power comparable in at least some respects to his: his power is far from absolute, and for just this reason there is always considerable risk involved in depending absolutely upon him. So a further image emerged, overcoming these defects: the conception of God as creator, creator of humankind and all the inhabitants of the earth, and of the heavens and the earth as well, the origin and source of all power everywhere.

> . . . the LORD is a great God,
>> and a great King above all gods.
> In his hand are the depths of the earth;
>> the heights of the mountains are his also.
> The sea is his, for he made it;
>> for his hands formed the dry land.
> O come, let us worship and bow down,

> let us kneel before the LORD, our Maker!
> For he is our God,
>> and we are the people of his pasture,
>> and the sheep of his hand.
>
>> (Ps. 95:3–7)

When conceived as creator of all that is, source and foundation of all power, God has the strength to be absolutely dependable. God can be relied upon in a way that no human being can, whether powerful warrior or faithful father. For the creator is the eternal one who is always there, always available.

> Put not your trust in princes,
>> in a son of man, in whom there is no help.
> When his breath departs he returns to his earth;
>> on that very day his plans perish.
> Happy is he whose help is the God of Jacob,
>> whose hope is in the LORD his God,
> who made heaven and earth,
>> the sea, and all that is in them . . .
>
>> (Ps. 146:3–6)

But the picture is still not complete. God must have absolute power in order to be one who can be relied upon absolutely in all contingencies, but power by itself is not enough: raw power can be destructive, demonic, terrifying. God must also be conceived in terms of the moral attributes of faithfulness and justice, compassion and mercy. So the psalmist goes on after the passage just quoted and rejoices that the Lord "who made heaven and earth" is one

> who keeps faith for ever;
>> who executes justice for the oppressed;
>> who gives food to the hungry.
> The LORD sets the prisoners free;
>> the LORD opens the eyes of the blind.
> The LORD lifts up those who are bowed down;

the LORD loves the righteous.
The LORD watches over the sojourners,
  he upholds the widow and the fatherless;
  but the way of the wicked he brings to ruin.
(Ps. 146:6–9)

The conception of God is now fully drawn: God is creator, lord, father, one characterized by absolute and eternal power and also absolute justice and mercy. God is thus one who can be depended upon absolutely, in every contingency and crisis as well as in the day-to-day routines of ordinary life. God is the perfect attachment-figure to whom one's absolute loyalty and devotion can and should be given, in a way not possible or appropriate even with loving parent or faithful friend.

IV

There is, however, a problem. Although the idea of God, the symbol which is built up through the variety of images we have been examining, is of one who can be relied upon absolutely, the idea of God remains just that: an idea, a symbol. "No one has ever seen God," as the Gospel of John puts it (John 1:18); God is not present to us as are the ordinary objects of experience, to be pointed out or touched, felt or experienced. Indeed, it is difficult to imagine what "experience of God," except in a highly metaphorical sense, could possibly be like. What would it be to encounter the creator of this vast universe? How would one recognize such a being? With what faculties could one possibly take God in or comprehend who God was? We can barely think the idea of the universe: certainly we cannot imagine what it would be like to *meet* the universe. How much more confusing is it to try to imagine meeting God or experiencing God. The very characteristics that give the symbol of God its power and attractiveness— God's being all-powerful creator and all-loving parent—

distinguish God absolutely from everything known and available to us in our ordinary experience. Though the piety of every age has wanted to say, "He walks with me and he talks with me, and he tells me I am his own," it is obvious that this walking and talking are of a very different kind from that ordinarily meant by these terms. The ordinary meanings are radically qualified by the prior knowledge and acceptance of a distinctive *idea,* namely, the idea of God as a unique and incomparable reality.

In this sense, God is present to us and known by us primarily and fundamentally *in idea,* in symbol, rather than in person or in fact—if we mean by the latter the presence of a directly and empirically perceivable object. Doubtless in its most popular versions the symbol of God includes the idea of God's presence here and everywhere and the idea of God's ready availability to our cries and prayers; and it also includes the idea of God's responding to our needs and answering our petitions. But we should not confuse the fact that these are all features of the symbol of God with the supposition that the mode of God's presence and the character of God's responsiveness are of the same sort as another person's in the same room with us. Often believers, in their enthusiasm for their faith, have spoken as though God were in our midst in this way, and have even supposed that they directly felt the divine presence. Such claims have given rise to many controversies among religious people and to much misunderstanding between believers and unbelievers. But God does not answer prayer with the direct and unambiguous speech with which my friend responds to my comment; God is not present to be touched and seen and heard as is the person to whom I am speaking, and we only confuse ourselves and others by thinking this, however important to us may be our faith, or the experiences in which we feel our faith has been confirmed. God is a very different sort of attachment-figure from any human being, and the transfer of attachment from parent, for example, to God will involve a move not from one concrete present person to another, but from a concretely present finite person to the image or idea of the absolutely dependable eternal Person. Attachment here is to a symbol, not to a directly given or perceptible object.

However deeply moving and profoundly convincing religious experiences may be, their actual content and their explicit meaning is always framed in terms of conceptions and symbols derived from the culture and beliefs of the individual involved. It is notorious, for example, that though a Roman Catholic may encounter the Virgin Mary, a Protestant almost never does; though a Christian may have communion with Christ, a Buddhist or a Jew does not. Relationship to God is established and maintained preeminently through the idea or image of God that has been given in language and tradition, however much particular experiences may deepen, intensify, vivify—or undercut and weaken—this relationship.

This does not mean that attachment to God will not be as firm or significant as that between human beings. Indeed, because of the way in which God is conceived, it can often involve a more profound loyalty, trust, and hope than attachment to any human; for every human, as we have noted, is finite and limited and simply cannot be depended upon absolutely as God—when God is believed in—can. But the attachment in this case is, nonetheless, to a symbol—a symbol that takes up into itself all of the positive meaning of the most profound human attachments while omitting the characteristic limitations and negative accompaniments of all such relationships to finite objects; the attachment is not to a directly experienced being. It is only in idea, in symbol, that the magnitude and comprehensiveness and meaning of what is intended by the word "God" can be grasped by humans. Even such realities as cosmos or universe, to say nothing of perfect justice or perfect love or all-powerfulness, can be grasped by us only in idea or concept, never directly in experience;

how much more, then, is this the case with God, who is
supposed to comprehend and include them all.

This contention, that God is present to us fundamentally
in symbol or image or idea, not in person, may seem at first
somewhat shocking to believers and nonbelievers alike.
For does it not suggest that God is somehow less than real?
We have been taught in our culture to regard ideas and
symbols—particularly those that cannot be confirmed by
reference to directly experienceable objects—with suspi-
cion as misleading or unreal. But this is unwarranted. I
have already shown that there is an imaginative or conceptual element built into our very selfhood. My awareness of myself, for example—of the "I" that I am—is
awareness of an idea or image, not the perception or experience of an object. It is fundamentally by means of such
images and ideas that we grasp our experience and the
world, and that we orient ourselves in life. Through the
system of ideas which we come to hold—about the world,
about persons, about what is important in life, about what
is real and what is illusory, about how to comport ourselves, about what is worth doing—we organize or build
up a symbolic map or model of the context within which
we live and of our place within it. With the help of this
map we understand who we are and what we can do, and
we project and plan how we are going to live and what we
shall try to achieve. The system of ideas and images by
means of which we apprehend ourselves and our place
within the world is among the most important of our
possessions; we simply could not function without it as
living, acting human beings. Doubtless there are forms of
life that do not need such structures of symbols in order
to function, but they are indispensable to us humans because we are fundamentally agents or actors, beings who
are capable of anticipating—in idea, in imagination—the
future, seeing alternative possibilities before us (in image
or idea), and then choosing from among those alternatives
and acting to realize those chosen. For beings such as we

it is essential to have a system of symbols by means of which to grasp the reality in which we exist, and through which to project possibilities for action as we move into an open future.

Almost none of our ideas or symbols, of course, do we create from scratch. Rather, we inherit them from our culture and acquire them through the educational processes in which we are immersed all our lives. Above all, it is in learning to speak that we gain the basic symbolic structure with which we operate through most of life, for in the acquiring of language we gain an elaborate and detailed structure of ideas and images which sorts out, orders, and organizes all that we ever can or do experience.

The most important and profound symbol which we in the West have inherited, and in terms of which, therefore, we can understand ourselves and our world, is *God*. We have already seen something of the meaning and significance of that symbol: the idea of God is the idea of the supremely adequate attachment-figure, the idea of one to whom we can give ourselves in absolute loyalty and devotion without fear of ever being betrayed or let down. God thus provides the anchor for a relationship which can overcome that ontological anxiety which naturally and inevitably emerges in the course of our growing into full self-consciousness.

A danger inherent in all our finite attachments is that they become idolatrous objects of devotion and thus destructive of the self. On the one hand, if our finite objects of loyalty are many and diverse, they will pull us in inconsistent and contradictory directions, thus undermining our integrity and threatening to destroy the self. On the other hand, if our attachment to a finite object is single and unrivaled, we may become enslaved in a fanatical devotion which twists and cripples the self. If the self is to gain its own unique integrity and become truly free, all finite attachments must be restricted and delimited by the self's loyalty and devotion to that highest reality which is above and behind and under them all. Attachment to God, through relativizing all other attachments, can free the self from idolatrous bondage to them. God, thus, is finally the only appropriate counterpart to the self-conscious self. "I" and "God," both known to us only in image or idea, are polar realities which establish and sustain and reinforce each other: a strong "I," a strong and self-confident sense of self not overcome by ontological anxiety and not bound in idolatrous enslavement, is made possible by and sustained by a firm confidence in and reliance upon God.

For the self in a godless world, human existence, and the most characteristic and cherished human values—loyalty, love, truth, justice, beauty, meaning—have no secure grounding or foundation in the ultimate scheme of things. Without God those things which are most important to us appear to be but cosmic accidents which we can treasure for a while if we choose, but which surely will soon fade away or be destroyed in some uncaring cosmic catastrophe. In contrast, to believe in God is to believe that trust and loyalty, truth and love—relationships indispensable to the creation and sustenance of free and healthy selves— are not simply accidental developments in that evolutionary stream that produced hominids but are grounded ultimately beyond the human realm in the original source of all that is.

V

This discussion of attachment to God has involved vast oversimplification. I have written, for instance, as though there were a single idea of God, and I have tried to suggest something of what attachment to that God could and does mean. But there are many ideas and images of God abroad in our culture, and they overlap and interrelate in complex ways which I have not been able to discuss. Clearly some of these images and ideas are highly destructive of

human well-being and human moral existence—as when
God is viewed essentially as an arbitrary tyrant whose
wrath must be appeased at all costs and who, at a mere
arbitrary whim, is able and willing to destroy or torment
in hell. And there are some downright silly ideas of God,
as the kindly old man who gives us pretty much anything
we want, a kind of cosmic cornucopia—ideas thoroughly
destructive of self-reliant and free selfhood. These ideas
are related to, but corruptions of, the basic conception
that I have been trying to sketch here. Obviously I am not
interested in defending such views as these, nor is there
space here to show how they have developed or why they
have gone astray. But it should be evident that some images and ideas of God are exceedingly dangerous, destructive of human life and of the possibility of developing
creative and productive selves and communities. Just
what one means when one uses the word "God," thus, is
far from a matter of indifference. The meaning of devotion to God and of peace with God will depend very much
on the idea or image one has of God and what it is believed
God requires of us; likewise, the question whether one's
feelings of alienation, self-hatred, and guilt will separate
one from God, or whether the relation to God will prove
the basis for dealing creatively with these destructive feelings and attitudes, will depend very much on the conception of God one holds. It is therefore of the greatest importance to formulate and use the symbol of God critically
and with care. The task of theology, as I understand it, is
to think through and make explicit the criteria for an
adequate understanding of God and then to reconstruct
traditional images and ideas on the basis of these criteria,
so that God will be grasped in faith and life as in significant
creative relationship to our actual experience.[8] The theological task, however difficult and problematical, is absolutely indispensable so long as the idea of God plays any
significant role in our culture.

Let me try to draw together the main lines of this chapter in this way. Picking up on the contemporary psychological interest in the inevitability and significance of attachments of one person to another, I have attempted to show both the limitations of such attachments for dealing with what we have called ontological anxiety and the importance, in just this connection, of attachment to God. However, unlike persons who are present to us bodily as objects of perception, God is present to us fundamentally in image or idea. This means that attachment to God, though it can be very strong, should not be understood as directed toward a particular concrete object of experience, as in the case of attachment to other human beings; but it also means that attachment to God can be relevant to the problem of ontological anxiety, grounded as it is fundamentally in consciousness and reflection (i.e., in ideas and symbols), in a way that attachment to finite persons can never be. Of course these different modes of attachment are never entirely separable from each other in any particular instance; and even though they can and should be distinguished analytically, they are always interconnected and always affect each other. Moreover, their respective sorts of aberration or disorder, though distinct, are also interconnected. The failure of inadequate attachment between persons in childhood can usually best be remedied by the development of adequate therapeutic attachments with actual human beings in later periods of life; however, a new understanding of God, together with a transformed attachment to God, may have its significant effects in such a case. Again, even though attachment to God is attachment to a symbol, difficulties and failures here may be affected by transformation and healing of one's relationships to other human beings, as well as by new and deeper understandings of who God is (i.e., by changes in one's ideas and images).

As we have seen, the image or idea of God, like my

image or idea of myself, has very deep roots in the self—in its primordial interpersonal experiences and attachments, and in the system of symbols by means of which the self gives fundamental order and orientation to its life. The way in which I view God, and whether I think of myself and the human community generally as living within God's purposes, affects everything I think and feel and experience. To change this symbol, then—to give it up if one has once believed in God, or to come to believe when once one had thought of the fundamental context of human life as a cold, impersonal, material order—is to change one's deepest attachments as well as one's whole understanding of life and of one's self, and thus to be changed in every dimension and at every level of one's existence.

Thus, though they are analytically distinct from each other, it is clear that attachment to God can never really be separated from our attachments to other persons. It is in and through our attachments to other human beings that our selfhood emerges and we become self-conscious beings; it is with our growing self-understanding that we come to realize both what it is to be a self and how frail and weak all of our finite human relationships ultimately are; it is in correlation with this awareness of human finitude and its meaning that we come to understand who God is and come to have whatever attachment to God will be ours; it is with attachment to God that we are given strength to live and act, even in our imperfect human communities, with loyalty and trust and love. Attachment to God and attachment in loyalty and trust and love to fellow humans thus belong together and mutually reinforce each other; weakness or absence of either mode of attachment threatens the vitality and strength of the other.

This of course is no new discovery of mine. Long ago Jesus was making just this point when he declared that the first and great commandment is, "You shall love the Lord your God with all your heart, and with all your soul, and with all your mind," and the second is like it, "You shall love your neighbor as yourself. On these two command-ments depend all the law and the prophets" (Matt. 22:37–40).

3/The Idea of Relativity and the Idea of God

There is no relativity which does not reflect a vanished absolute which can never be wholly obliterated, since it is this absolute which makes relativity relative.

Karl Barth[1]

In certain important ways the concept of relativity or relativism is correlative with the concept of God, and this correlation bears on the way in which we conceive all finite being, especially all human reality. We will be able, then, to understand better both what we mean by "relativism" and what we mean by "God," if we see these two concepts in relation to each other.

I

In Western usage the word "God" has come to have a very special meaning: it designates the ultimate point of reference for all action, consciousness, and reflection. No regressive reflection seeking to push back to an ultimate starting point, no creative action moving toward an unstructured future, no appreciative feeling of worship or devotion expressing the orientation of the whole life of a self or community, can intend some reality "beyond" God.

This paper was originally prepared in 1975 as a contribution to a collection of philosophical essays on the problem of relativism, but the book for which it was intended was never published.

This is what is meant by calling God the "First Cause" or "Creator": God is the ground and foundation of everything that is, and therefore there can be nothing behind or beyond God which in any way founds or grounds anything in us or in our world. This is expressed also by the claim that God alone is holy, the only one worthy of the full devotion and worship of every self. Again, it is expressed in the acclamation of God as the Alpha and the Omega, the first and the last, the one "from [whom] and through [whom] and to [whom] are all things" (Rom. 11:36). I am not arguing that *empirically* God is the beginning and end of everything that is, as though this were something that could be observed. Rather, this is a conceptual matter: the *idea* of "God" is the idea of that absolute beginning and ending point beyond which it is never possible to move. Many different titles have been used to express this in the tradition: God is said to be "absolute," "unconditioned," "infinite," "necessary being," "perfect being," and so forth. Perhaps the best succinct characterization that makes this point is that of Anselm: God is that "than which nothing greater can be conceived."[2]

As Anselm already saw, this means that the idea of God is unique; "God" does not (cannot) function like any other noun or name. As ultimate point of reference, God cannot be conceived as simply one more of the many items of ordinary experience or knowledge, in some way side by side with the others: God must be thought of as "beyond" all the others, not restricted or limited by any of them but relativizing them all. Without such unique logical status, God would be conceived as of the same order as the many things which need to be grounded beyond themselves, rather than as the ground or source of them all. The notions of God's absoluteness or unconditionedness or aseity attempt particularly to make this logical point. God is able to meet the fundamental religious need for an ultimate ground of security in the face of such human crises as death, natural catastrophe, or military conquest precisely

because of the special logical standing which these conceptions suggest.[3]

It is only in a monotheistic scheme that God functions
in this unique way, rather than simply as one more of the
many powers to which we are subjected. And precisely
this unique logical standing makes it possible and necessary to distinguish radically between God and all the idols
—all merely finite realities mistaken for God: God
becomes the One who unmasks all idols, showing them to
be unreliable shams. That is, it is with reference to and in
contrast with the concept of God—i.e., because of the
cultural availability of the concept of God—that the deficiency of ultimate power and reliability in everything else
can be discerned, that the whole of our world and everything in it can be seen as *finite.* Our modern Western
notions of human finitude or limitedness did not develop
simply on their own: they are direct descendants of the
theological notion that we and all our world are creatures;
it is thus in correlation and contrast with the idea of God
the creator that the full significance of the meaning of
finitude is brought out.

God is not to be conceived, therefore (as so often in
popular religion), as one more object like all others, as like
one of those many things of which we can ask rather simply, Does it exist? and then devise straightforward procedures for finding the answer. In contrast with our concept
of ordinary objects of experience, which can be readily
observed and can be examined in various ways, the concept of God functions as a *limiting idea,* as the idea of
something which can only be approached but never actually reached, certainly not surpassed. This makes "the existence of God" very problematical and controversial (and
often misunderstood). Moreover, in the case of God we are
not just speaking of some ordinary limit of experience: we
are speaking of the *absolute limit,* the limit of all limits,
"limit" raised to a second power. We are attempting to
speak of that in terms of which all else is to be understood,

which therefore so transcends everything else that it cannot gain its meaning or being by reference to anything else. This does not mean that God is *experienced* as somehow isolated from everything else or that God is known without reference to knowledge of anything else. Rather, once again, this is a *conceptual* matter: the *idea* of God is the idea of that on which all else depends but which itself depends on nothing else, the idea of absolute aseity.

The term "God," then (in Western cultures), has stood for or named the ultimate point of reference or orientation for all life, action, devotion, reflection. I have been expressing this matter abstractly here, trying to bring out the peculiar logical character of the idea. In actual religious life and experience all this is usually expressed much more concretely in images which speak directly to the existential needs of persons: God is spoken of as "our Father in heaven"; as our "Lord" or "King" to whom all devotion is due; as the "Creator of the heavens and the earth," "the Maker of all things visible and invisible"; as the "Judge of all the earth" who will effect a final separation of the good from the bad, the righteous from the wicked, the wheat from the chaff; as our "Savior," the "good Shepherd," who leads us "through the valley of the shadow of death" to our ultimate destination where "goodness and mercy" shall be our portion "for ever." Ordinary human speech about God is not abstract logical talk about an "ultimate limit" but rather talk about life and the world, about our deepest human problems, about catastrophe and triumph, about human misery and human glory. It is about what is really important in life, how we are to live, how comport ourselves, which styles of life are truly humane and which dehumanizing. But it is this, and it can deal significantly in this way with all features and dimensions of human life, only because it claims to be about that ultimate point of orientation from which all else gains its meaning and to which it all must finally be referred. It is the peculiar logical standing of the idea of God

which enables it to raise the concrete (finite) images in
which that idea is ordinarily expressed to a level where
they can bear such profound religious meaning.

II

One can understand the concept of God as essentially a
product of and tool for growing human critical self-understanding.[4] I do not mean by this to suggest that those Old
Testament writers (and their successors) who are largely
responsible for developing our idea of God did so with a
view to expanding human critical powers; their interests
were much more directly religious and moral. But this
concept which they gradually and painfully created and
refined did in fact function as a powerful instrument of
criticism for them; and from the vantage point of centuries of cultural development, culminating in a period
when human critical powers are valued very highly and
are cultivated for their own sake, we may see this as one
of its most significant features.

For these writers God was understood as the source of
all reality and as the lord over all. The entire world and all
its contents, including especially human persons and communities, existed only because God had willed and acted
to bring them into existence; and God was continuously
working with creation to shape it in new ways and bring
it to the ultimate realization of the divine purposes. The
finite order, particularly humanity, was far from what God
intended it to be—in fact, it was in a kind of rebellion
against the divine sovereignty—so it was necessary for
God to work toward its transformation into a "kingdom"
where the divine will would be perfectly realized; the
biblical account traces the history of God's working with
humankind to accomplish this end. Not only humanity was
being transformed through God's work: the whole finite
order was gradually being brought to its consummation.

However difficult it may be for moderns simply to take over a mythic framework of this sort, it has certain features which are well worth noting. Most important is the claim that finite reality cannot be understood simply in terms of itself. The various orders of finite being will not be grasped aright if they are not seen in relation to the purposes of the God who has created them; one cannot understand what is really going on in the world apart from some awareness of that Reality beyond the finite order who is moving it all toward the realization of transcendent ends. Thus, the idea of God (and of the purposes and work of God) functions as a kind of Archimedean point beyond the world in terms of which all that is in the world—and the world itself—can be understood and evaluated. Everything within the world, including especially human institutions and practices, is to be assessed and criticized, not simply by reference to its own intentions and desires, or to its present nisus, mode of being or structure, but by reference to the transcendent God for whom it exists and who has specific purposes for it. The great prophets, particularly, found it possible to bring the most devastating social and moral criticism to their society because of their conviction that it did not measure up to God's transcendent requirements. They were not criticizing the social order simply in terms of what they took to be *human* standards of justice or mercy: human conceptions as well as human practices needed to be transformed. And they found the insight and the personal courage to make this critique—even to the face of thoroughly autocratic kings —only because of their conviction that they were mouthpieces of that transcendent reality beyond everything human, that by reference to which everything human was to be judged and assessed. Thus, the idea of God and of God's will functioned as a transcendent point of reference in terms of which everything human and finite could be evaluated. A major strand of the biblical story is this continuous struggle to assess and transform the human social and cultural order with reference to the demands of transcendent reality.

Moreover, the idea of this transcendent reality was itself continuously undergoing criticism and purification. At first, perhaps, Yahweh was thought of simply as one god among many, the one to whom the Israelites had bound themselves in a special way; and it is not really too surprising that apostasy to the gods of other societies was a frequent problem for an Israel in interaction with them. But with the thorough destruction of the Hebrew states and the exile of many of the people, the great prophets came to see God as utterly unique, not to be confused with or likened to anything that was finite or this-worldly:

> To whom will you liken me and make me equal,
>   and compare me, that we may be alike? . . .
> I am the first and I am the last;
>   besides me there is no god.
>
> (Isa. 46:5; 44:6)

God's utter uniqueness as creator of all meant that God transcended all human images and ideas, and that these also, along with everything else in the world, must stand under judgment. To confuse humanly constructed images or concepts with God was the most serious sin of all—idolatry—and much of the Old Testament is given over to the struggle to distinguish God from all idols, including previous or received notions of God. The idea of God thus gradually developed into a highly dynamic conception, always reaching beyond itself toward more appropriate understanding and formulation, never adequately realized or expressed. Not only was God the point of reference in terms of which all else could be assessed and criticized; the idea of God gradually developed into a highly dialectical principle of self-criticism, a principle with a sensitivity to the inadequacy of its own every formulation.[5]

I certainly would not claim that every believer in God

has been aware of the critical implications of that idea for self and society, as well as for itself. The idea of God has been used as a bulwark of highly oppressive social orders, and appeal to the will of God has been used as a justification for virtually every sort of crime. Marxist and other humanist critics are correct in maintaining that the legitimation of institutions and customs by reference to God has been one of the most powerful constraints against necessary social change. This has been made possible, of course, because of precisely that unique feature in the idea of God which I have been attempting to elucidate: if God is the final point of reference in terms of which all else is to be understood and judged, a kind of ultimate and unsurpassable legitimacy will be given to any institution or custom or act which is believed to conform with God's will. Thus the idea of God—precisely because of God's transcendence, precisely because God is the ultimate court of appeal—can be, and often has been, put into the service of human corruption and of the most vicious sorts of inhumanity; it is a very dangerous idea[6] indeed, when improperly understood or when put to cynical uses. But the idea of God can function in this way as a bulwark of conservatism or tyranny only when its highly dialectical character is overlooked and its demand for continuous self-criticism, in the light of that which is ultimately transcendent and cannot be domesticated, is forgotten or ignored. If God is not converted into an idol sustaining and supporting our own projects, but is apprehended as truly *God,* the judge of all the earth, the self is forced into a posture of humbleness in its claims, and a principle of revolutionary criticism of all the structures and orders of the human becomes effectual.[7]

The idea of God, thus, by calling into question everything finite—including every formulation or expression of the idea of God itself—can be a powerful instrument of criticism. In contrast with God every finite being, value, and claim is seen to be incomplete, insubstantial, inadequate in important respects. In short, they are grasped as *finite:* as limited, questionable, relative, requiring continuous criticism and reassessment. The idea of the finite and the idea of God are correlative and interdependent parts of a conceptual whole which for many centuries in the West provided the context within which all experience and reality were grasped, and it is questionable, therefore, whether the full significance of either of these ideas can be grasped apart from the other.

III

We are now in a position to turn to the notion of relativism. I suggest that the modern much-debated idea of the relativity of all truth and value is an offspring of the (theological) conception of the finite, which we have just been examining, and that some of the logical and other problems connected with that idea are illuminated, and possibly dissolved, when this parentage is understood. The claim that every human judgment of truth or value is relative to the social or historical context in which it appears—or to the psychological makeup of the individual who makes it—and therefore cannot be regarded as absolutely or universally true or valid, is a direct implication of the theological understanding that every human individual and community is finite. As finite, each has a particular locus, within the orders of nature and history, from which the world is viewed and from which judgments are made, and what is seen or understood from that position will be relative to it in certain crucial respects. It will be different from what would or could be grasped from any other locus, and it therefore cannot claim to be universally true or valid.

This idea of universal or absolute truth, with which the notion of relative truth is always (implicitly or explicitly) being contrasted, is nothing other than a secularized version of the old theological idea of "God's truth." For God is the one with an all-seeing eye, the one who is never deceived, the one "unto whom all hearts are open, all desires known, and from whom no secrets are hid." God alone is omniscient; only God's truth is absolute, perfect, eternal. It is this idealized notion of what truth "really is" that lies behind both the relativists' contention that all human judgments of truth and value are relative and limited and that only modest claims dare be made for them, as well as the insistence of the critics of relativism that such limited or relative truth is really not *truth* at all, for truth must be absolute and universal.

However, once the theological foundations of this distinction between relative and absolute truth or value—between our truth and God's—have been forgotten, confusing and interminable arguments develop. On the one hand, there are those (the "relativists") who are persuaded that every truth-claim, every value-judgment, however insightful or significant it may be for those persuaded of it, must inevitably be bound to its social and linguistic context in such a way as to make it less than universally true or valid; indeed, it may be so infected with racial, gender, and class bias or prejudice as to be largely ideological. On the other hand, there are those who claim that no proposition or judgment which is situationally bound in this way can properly claim to be true or valid; it is at most the expression of mere opinion. Moreover, insofar as relativistic theory itself claims to be "true," it implicitly invokes a universal and absolute standard which it dare not acknowledge, lest it systematically undercut its own claims to credibility. Existentially and factually the relativists seem to be stating something hardly controvertible, yet they find it difficult to deal with their critics' charge of inconsistency and incoherence. Conversely, the logically airtight case of the critics seems to ignore, and even to blind them to, patent historical and psychological facts.

This disagreement is difficult to resolve so long as its theological roots remain unrecognized. For, without real-

izing it, the opponents are passing each other in the dark.
Each has seized one side of the creature/creator polarity
and has (rightly) defended its importance; but since, with
the secularization of modern philosophical thought, the
polarity itself has dropped out of view, neither side recog-
nizes its actual interdependence with the other.

The relativists, with the help of much historical, ethno-
graphic, and linguistic data, are articulating in secular
terms a doctrine of human finitude (and even sinfulness!)
—showing limitations that obtain for our knowledge (including science) and values, as well as for our more obviously transient customs and institutions. For this they are
certainly to be commended, and they should be encouraged to explore as far as possible the lines which have been
opened up by Marx and Freud, by the sociology of knowledge, and by comparative linguistics. Such studies have
made possible profound insights into our human nature,
its possibilities and its limitations. Thus, they help to enhance growing human control over our historical destiny;
but simultaneously they throw into sharp relief the limitations of and constraints on all human knowledge and
power, thus, as we may dare to hope, helping to keep us
more humble about our projects and claims and open to
other quite different insights and perspectives.

The contemplation of human finitude and sinfulness has
always had this double potential of helping to make actual
a greater human freedom as well as true humility. The
symbol of "God" (and of "God's truth"), standing over
against the human and in judgment upon it, made it possible to see with a kind of sharpness and clarity both the
possibilities in finite human existence and the constraints
upon that existence. And the contemporary concept of the
relativity of all human truth and value preserves that insight into our finitude, even though the polar concept of
God's absoluteness, which completes and makes fully intelligible this notion of finitude, remains largely implicit
and unarticulated.

I say "largely" (rather than "entirely") implicit, because the critique of relativism—that it does not really do justice to the dimensions of absoluteness and universality in the idea of truth, and thus cannot adequately account for its own claims—seems to be a veiled expression of the awareness that a radical and genuine doctrine of finitude can be made fully intelligible only in partnership with a correlative concept of an "absolute" which sustains the finite. Most of the critics of relativism, of course, are far from understanding their position in this (theological) way. Seeing that doctrines, which hold all truth and value relative, are inherently unstable and incoherent, that they seem to presuppose some absolute about which they nevertheless remain silent, it often seems necessary to those critics to argue that absolute and universal truth must in some sense or some respect be accessible to human minds, and that the relativistic claims about radical human finitude (and sinfulness) are thus misconceived. What other alternative is open once the concept of God, as thoroughly relativizing the human, has dropped from view? Truth absolute and universal, which in the theological tradition could properly belong only to God, is now claimed for us.

If the implicit hubris and idolatry of such claims does not come clearly into view, it is because the concept of God —which is the basis for such insight—itself is no longer part of the conceptual frame within which the analysis and interpretation are proceeding. In consequence, exaggerated claims for human insight into and judgments about truth and value may be made, and critical leverage against these claims may be difficult to achieve. Complacency about the possibilities of human knowledge, and about the methods for pursuing knowledge, is the result, and this in turn tends to reinforce in a conservative way present cognitive and axiological methods, viewpoints, and conclusions. When the concept of God is eliminated from our conceptual framework, there is no Archimedean point in terms of which critical leverage against every human insight and claim can be maintained, so humans easily fall into self-destructive hubris and idolatry.[8]

Thus, the relativists are right in emphasizing the import of the existentially bound character of all human thought and valuation, and their critics are right in seeing that such an understanding of the human situation has absolutistic presuppositions which it ought to acknowledge. But the relativists are wrong if they suppose their position can be coherently formulated without some point of reference in terms of which all else is seen to be relative, and their critics are wrong if they suppose that such a point of reference is in some way in us or directly available to us. The logic of the concept of God, and the complex dialectic involved in every creaturely attempt to speak of the creator—to form a concept of that which stands as a critical norm over against every finite being and action (including the very attempt at analysis and understanding of these issues)—provide a model for the conception of such a comprehensive point of reference and of our relationship to it.

The debate between relativists and antirelativists is not about mere logical puzzles or sociological facts: these by themselves could hardly account for its being so unremitting and often so shrill. Far deeper (religious and philosophical) issues are at stake. The debate is really about the fundamental nature of the human, and about that over against the human in terms of which we define ourselves; it is about our finitude and its meaning, on the one hand, and that normative conception by means of which we grasp ourselves as finite, on the other. In Western thought it has been in reflection on what has been called "God," and on the relation of the human to "God," that these issues have been most clearly discriminated and refined.

The concept of God and the concept of human finitude (relativity) belong together and mutually inform each other. If we can work out the dialectic of this relationship in contemporary (secular) terms, we will be able better to understand both the import of our relativity and the significance that talk about "God" can have in contemporary life.

IV

In conclusion, I would like to comment on an anomaly that some of my readers must feel: theological positions are notoriously absolutistic, but here the claim is being made that the idea of God belongs properly with a thoroughgoing relativism (of everything finite); relativistic claims supposedly undercut every absolutism—above all, religious claims to absolute truth—but here it is being contended that relativism actually enshrines the traditional religious teaching that we are God's creatures. Is such an inversion of the ordinary conception of these issues really plausible?[9]

I have already attempted to show the way in which relativism specifies and articulates theological ideas about creatureliness and finitude, so I shall say no more about that matter here. Something must be said, however, about the reasons why Western religious thinking and institutions have often been absolutistic in the extreme when (according to my analysis) they should have been humbly relativistic. A full analysis of this problem would involve detailed historical work which certainly cannot be undertaken here, even were I competent to do so. I can mention only one major formal consideration which made it all too easy for those who believed in God to move in absolutistic—and thus in fact idolatrous—directions.

The older theology took for granted the misunderstanding (shared with much of the philosophical tradition) that human knowledge was based on some sort of immediate relationship to its putative object. Theology was the Queen of the Sciences because the knowledge it presented was that of the ultimate reality and goodness (God), and thus that in terms of which all else had to be understood and criticized. In a sense, then, even though it operated primarily in a material rather than a critical mode, theology (or theological metaphysics) was for many centuries the fundamental critical discipline: it was the last court of appeal for human understanding; its subject matter was that in terms of which all other subject matters were to be understood and assessed. But traditional theology was not *self-*critical, i.e., it did not understand itself as essentially criticism, but rather as the mediator of what was ultimately real and true. Theological knowledge was believed to rest on the direct revelation of God through the Bible, Jesus, and the church. What claims to knowledge could possibly be more authoritative than that? With such a role and dignity, is it any wonder that theology became essentially dogmatic (rather than critical), and that those who accepted the deliverances of theology as genuine knowledge became absolutistic in their convictions and imperialistic toward others? It was, then, by reference to this indisputable knowledge of reality that theology carried on its work of assessing and criticizing all other cognitive claims and enterprises.

From the point of view represented in this chapter, the lasting importance of theology is to be found not so much in these (dogmatic) claims to knowledge of God as in the insistence that all claims to knowledge—being made by finite humans, and having finite realities as their objects—be continuously subjected to critical analysis and assessment. It is no longer possible, of course, to carry out this critical program by direct reference to the reality or being of God, for it has long since become clear that God, and the knowledge of God, are not so immediately and simply available to us as earlier generations may have supposed. Indeed, as I have argued here, the concept of God itself —once its implications have been clearly understood— forbids any such assumption: God transcends our every insight and idea, and failure to take this seriously leads inevitably into idolatry—precisely the condition of much dogmatic theology. The concept of God, it turns out, is a highly dialectical one which forbids all easy and unproblematical assertions about its referent. Thus, because of the inner dynamism of its own central concept, theology is forced to give up its earlier dogmatic posture and to become essentially a critical discipline. Instead of being the symbol for that known ultimate reality in terms of which all else must be understood, "God" now becomes a symbol demanding continuous criticism of every claim to knowledge—including theological claims—and of every finite experience and concept.

It is true that some contemporary theologians might not agree that theology is essentially a critical discipline in the sense suggested here,[10] and certainly the theological tradition has not always understood itself in this way. For this reason the relevance of theology to modern (critical) knowledge has often been obscured, and such matters as the interdependence of the concept of God with the conception of the relativity of everything finite were not perceived. It is my opinion, however, that unless and until theology completes the move from a dogmatic posture to a critical one, its importance for the broader ranges of human life and culture will continue to decline.

PART TWO

CHRISTIAN
THEOLOGICAL
CONSTRUCTION

Modern men . . . have no longer the sense for the terribly superlative conception which was implied to an antique taste by the paradox of the formula, "God on the Cross." Hitherto there had never and nowhere been such boldness in inversion, nor anything at once so dreadful, questioning and questionable as this formula: it promised a transvaluation of all ancient values.

Friedrich Nietzsche

4 / The Christian Categorial Scheme

Christian theologians have long understood their task to be the uncovering and interpreting of the major concepts or doctrines of Christian faith and life—concepts such as God, humanity, Christ, sin, salvation, faith, church, sacraments, and the like. To this end they employed biblical and historical studies to gain understanding of earlier uses of these notions, some of which were usually regarded as normative; and they exercised their own imaginative powers to reformulate and reinterpret these concepts so they would be intelligible and meaningful in terms of the experience and problems of their own times. The task of theology was thus largely one of appropriating and handing on tradition—not, of course, in any rigid or legalistic way, but so reinterpreted as to be effective in shaping the life of each new generation. The assumption underlying this approach was that the truth about human existence and human destiny was to be found in and through the concepts and doctrines mediated by tradition, and the business of theology was to make that truth freshly available. This assumption was theologically undergirded by a doctrine of revelation which claimed that this truth was no mere product of human inquiry or speculation but had

Presidential address, American Theological Society, 1979.

been conveyed to humanity by God's own revelatory activity.

I do not believe this model of theological work is serviceable any longer. The movement of history in our time toward increasing interdependence of the several great human societies and civilizations, rapidly becoming a single unified world culture, forces us to think in world perspective about our common human existence instead of remaining with the parochial terms provided by our own particular cultural and religious past. And the increasingly insightful work of the social sciences, of the history of religions, and of the new explorations into human symbolism and language, provide us with theoretical means for understanding the origins and development of our religious ideas and practices and for seeing them in significant relationship to similar developments in other cultural traditions. In short, we are becoming aware that all religious phenomena, including those of our own tradition, are historical through and through. Humankind emerged very slowly from animality into consciousness and some measure of self-determination. Gradually, imaginative pictures of the world roundabout and of the nature of human existence were developed, and these provided some measure of orientation in the world and helped to give some order and direction to life. In the course of time some of these pictures and myths, handed on from generation to generation by poets and storytellers, came to have sufficient coherence and unity and persuasiveness to provide the basis for comprehensive and far-reaching interpretations of human life and its meaning. Out of these the several great religious traditions have grown. Each has developed and refined one or more comprehensive worldviews, in terms of which all human existence can be understood and in relation to which, it is claimed, it must be ordered and shaped if it is to find genuine fulfillment, i.e., if it is to find the "salvation" which the tradition promises its devotees.

The Christian tradition also has grown up in this way, and we who are Christians are especially fortunate—because of the early Hebraic interest in history—to possess records on the basis of which much of its historical development can be reconstructed. For the past two centuries much effort in the universities and the churches has been devoted to such historical labors, so we are in an unprecedented position for understanding our own religious inheritance historically. For a time—during the so-called neo-orthodox period—it was thought that the emphasis on historicity in the Jewish and Christian traditions provided a basis for claims to uniqueness and superiority among the great religious traditions of the world. But in such moves there was always much special pleading. We can now see that our religious traditions must be understood as one family among the many that have appeared in the course of human history, and any claims about their validity or significance must be made in awareness of and comparison with the other great religious and secular world-views which have come to inform human life and culture. I certainly cannot engage in such extensive and complex comparative work within the bounds of this chapter, but I can make a few remarks about the reconception and reorienting of Christian theology required if such work is to go forward.

Two steps are necessary. First, we must see clearly the implications of the fact that Christian faith is but one perspective, one world-view, among many vying for our attention and loyalty today. This may appear to be an obvious point, but its full significance for theological work has not often been candidly faced. When we apply the concept of "world-view" to our own tradition, in this way simultaneously distinguishing it from and relating it to other "world-views," we are both enabled and required to step back from unqualified commitment to it. Instead of simply presuming our tradition to be the sufficient source of ultimate saving truth for all humanity, we increasingly come to see that what we Christian theologians are essentially concerned with is the discernment and articulation of one particular perspective.

When this point becomes clear, we are already in a position to see the second move which Christian theology must take today. It must ask itself, How does one articulate a world-view, and specifically this one? My answer to that question is: through uncovering the fundamental categories, the basic conceptual and symbolic framework, which gives the world-view in question its structure and order and experiential flavor. The basic task to which Christian theology should now be addressing itself, thus, is articulating the fundamental Christian categorial scheme, the structure of concepts and symbols which gives the Christian world-view its distinctive character and significance. If and as that is done, we move into a position from which it is possible meaningfully and significantly to compare the Christian world-view with the other great religious and secular perspectives alive in our time.

A world-view, of course, is given its full character and meaning by a complex pattern of words and symbols, liturgical practices and moral claims, behavioral patterns and institutional structures, stories and myths which are handed on from generation to generation, shaping and interpreting the experience of those living within it. But not all these expressions and patterns and practices are of equal weight for our purposes. The basic structure and character of every world-view is determined by a few fundamental categories which give it shape and order. These are connected and interrelated in various ways by the larger vocabulary of terms and symbols used in liturgy, ideology, and story to provide concreteness and fill in details of an overall picture, or complex of pictures, which can accommodate and interpret the infinite variations and nuances of the experience of many generations. The basic configuration of defining terms of a world-view I call its categorial structure. Our task as theologians is to pene-

trate through the vast multiplicity of Christian institutions, practices, and liturgies, of Christian philosophies,
theologies, and myths, to the fundamental categorial
scheme that informs them all.

I

I can make only the barest sketch here of a partly his-
torico-typological, partly systematic, procedure for attempting this. Let us try to discern the structure of the
Christian categorial scheme by setting it over against
other typological alternatives in the environment from
which it emerged. In this way we can focus on the similarities and the differences in overall patterns of human life,
and of the interpretation of human life, thus avoiding, we
may hope, getting bogged down in the masses of detail
which fill out each perspective. Obviously, we will be making massive abstractions and generalizations here, all of
which are subject to criticism, dispute, and revision, but I
hope that our procedure will at least make clear how a
theology understood as articulation of the Christian world-
view could proceed.

It will hardly be contested, I suppose, if I begin with the
claim that the concept of God is one of the central categories of the Christian perspective. This is the concept, as
Paul put it, of a reality "from [which] and through [which]
and to [which] are all things" (Rom. 11:36); it is, that is, the
concept of what I call the "ultimate point of reference" in
terms of which all else is to be understood. In that respect
it provides the unifying focus or center which orders and
organizes the entire world-view. The significance of this
center can be discerned when this "radical monotheism"
(H. R. Niebuhr) is contrasted with two other more ancient
perspectives out of which it emerged during the Old Testament period.

The idea of one God seems to be a development and
concentration of certain motifs in ancient Near Eastern

polytheism. A polytheistic scheme gives divinity to many of the diverse powers that affect human existence: rainfall and harvest, fertility and love, wisdom and healing, warfare, the tribe, the nation. In each activity of life individuals and the community turn to the appropriate god or goddess in order to gain some mastery over it. A scheme like this obviously has its uses, but it helps not at all with the overall task of bringing order into the demands and exigencies of life as a whole: the gods and goddesses simply reflect the experienced impingement of diverse and uncontrollable powers. Moreover, since the deities are themselves pictured as members of a kind of social or political community, sometimes harmonious but frequently engaged in intense struggles or wars, what happens in the human sphere in consequence of the interaction of these powers is often unpredictable and even incomprehensible, a kind of fallout determined by the tensions and struggles in heaven. Human life is basically determined from above by powers which, though they can be partially appeased through proper sacrifice, are in many ways inscrutable and unapproachable. Obviously this sort of mythology provides a rather chaotic picture of the world within which human life transpires. It is a picture based on human experience—the experience of the chaotic, the irregular, the unpredictable in life—interpreted with the aid of metaphors and symbols drawn from the human experience of social and political tensions, struggles, and warfare. Just as the chaos in human affairs can be accounted for by recourse to the continuous struggle among human wills seeking to fulfill desires for sustenance, wealth, sex objects, position and power in society, so also the chaos and unpredictability in the world at large can be understood as resulting from the struggles among the great gods and goddesses which control it. It is easy to see that a polytheistic mythology tends to highlight the disorder and chaos in life; and for just this reason it gives little help in providing stable orientation for selves and communities.

The world of human experience, however, is not merely chaotic in character. There is also always a recognizable order which may impress itself as absolutely permanent and unchangeable: day follows day, each proceeding through morning, noon, evening, and night; the seasons succeed each other with absolute regularity; the cycles of birth, growth, death, and decay follow each other irrevocably among all plants and animals, and above all in the succession of human generations. All of the contingencies and struggles which polytheistic mythologies reflect and express in fact take place within this context of unchangeable order. It is not surprising, then, that in Babylon and in Greece, in India and China and elsewhere, conceptions of an overarching cosmic order developed, an order to which even the gods and goddesses were subject. When this side of human experience is emphasized in the elaboration of a world-view, conceptions of the regularity, the inevitability, the fatedness of all things and all events appear. Perhaps, then, tomorrow's events can be read in the stars, the perfect example of absolutely orderly movement: Babylonian astrology drew that conclusion. Perhaps it can be ascertained in some other way: through consulting an oracle, by reading animal entrails, by casting Urim and Thummim. In any case, there is a cosmic order that determines the inevitable sequence of events—the outcomes of battles, the fruitfulness of marital unions, the destiny of a newborn child.

In this scheme the understanding of the world and of human life moves in just the opposite direction from the mythology of chaos which polytheism expresses. But the important thing for us to note here is that the consequences of these two mythologies for human existence are in many ways the same. In neither case do humans have any significant control over their own affairs: they are ei-

ther in the hands of the gods or at the disposal of fate.
What happens in life is essentially determined by powers
on high. The best that humans can do in a world envisioned in terms like these is simply accept their situation,
fit themselves and their wishes and desires into the exter-
nally determined order of events as best they can. In these
ancient mythologies, I think, we can see the origins and
the bases for that deep-felt sense that the essence of religious piety is to be found in submissiveness, obedience,
humility—a religious sensibility that is still widespread in
modern times.

In contrast to these two ways of symbolizing or pictur-
ing the world, the context of human life, stands the radical
monotheism which emerged out of them and owes something to each. Israel's God, Yahweh, was apparently just
one of many Near Eastern gods, probably especially as-
sociated with Mt. Sinai in the desert. However, this god
started early (in our knowledge of him[1]) to make moves
beyond his original jurisdiction. He soon succeeded in
overpowering the gods of Egypt (at least so the Israelite
storytellers have it) as well as the gods of Canaan, giving
the Hebrew people a land of their own (at the expense, of
course, of these other peoples and gods). So this was a god
of unusual *power,* especially in warfare. The relationship
of the Hebrews to him was also unusual. It was a free
covenant made between Yahweh and the people: he
would be their god; they would be his people. It is important that we examine more fully the significance of these
two points, Yahweh's power, and the covenant relationship between Yahweh and Israel.

I have already noted that from our first awareness of
him Yahweh's power seems to grow. This continues
through the subsequent centuries of devotion, struggle,
and reflection until, after some considerable lapse of time,
Yahweh is taken to be the very creator of the heavens and
the earth and all their contents, including humans (Gen.
2:4ff.). By the time of the exile, six hundred years after the

exodus, Yahweh is believed to be the all-powerful lord of the universe who has created the world by the word of his mouth (Gen. 1) in absolutely lordly fashion, one whom Second Isaiah can proclaim as "the first and . . . the last; besides [whom] there is no god" (Isa. 44:6).

> I am Yahweh, and there is no other,
>   besides me there is no God;
>   I gird you, though you do not know me,
> that men may know, from the rising of the sun
>   and from the west, that there is none besides me;
>   I am Yahweh, and there is no other.
> I form light and create darkness,
>   I make weal and create woe,
>   I am Yahweh, who do all these things. . . .
> I made the earth,
>   and created man upon it;
> it was my hands that stretched out the heavens,
>   and I commanded all their host.
>   (Isa. 45:5–7, 12)

Yahweh's great and expansive power, first manifest at the exodus, here has become the sole and absolute power creating and governing the universe. The stars also, it may be noted with Babylonian astrology in mind, are here placed directly under Yahweh's personal command.

It is important that we take note of the difference between the world-view developing here and the earlier polytheistic and fatalistic mythologies. In contrast with the more or less chaotic picture of the human situation which polytheism presents, there is an absolute *order* here; in that respect this monotheistic perspective is like fatalism. However, unlike the impersonal determinism of fatalism, the order here is *personal* in origin and character; it is an order established by will and through purposive activity. In that respect this monotheism is reminiscent of the polytheism from which it emerged, where the gods, as personal and willful beings, were engaged in carrying through their own decisions and purposes. Moreover, being grounded directly in personal activity, this is an order within which finite personal beings (i.e., humans) can find a proper home. After telling us that God "created the heavens" and "formed the earth," Second Isaiah notes, "he did not create it a chaos, he formed it to be inhabited!" (Isa. 45:18). This world, thus, within which humans live, is neither the impersonal order of fate nor the chaotic consequence of the struggles and warfare of many gods. It is the deliberate product of the intentional activity of the single all-powerful God, who created it as the proper context for a meaningful and fruitful human life. Moreover, it is not a place in which God simply leaves humans to their own devices after creating them: as we saw with the exodus, if they fall on evil days, God acts as savior to rescue them and give them a new start.

Now what is the human relationship to this God? Eventually, as we have seen, God is held to be the creator of humanity, the absolute source of human existence. But that was a later realization as the conception of God was gradually reconstructed from the "mighty warrior" of the exodus period into the "creator of the heavens and the earth." The relationship between Yahweh and Israel was first grasped as one of covenant. That is, it was a *moral* relationship in which Yahweh bound himself to the people of Israel, and the people bound themselves to God. A covenant relationship is one that can obtain only between moral *wills,* i.e., between beings who are capable of making and keeping promises, beings who are capable of setting purposes for themselves and who can take responsibility for realizing those purposes, beings who are capable of determining themselves and their activities with respect to the future. In this sense a covenant can be made only between free agents. We should note here that the covenant between Yahweh and Israel implies that both God and humans are such moral agents: both make promises here, and both are expected to keep those promises responsibly. However much more powerful one party to the covenant may be, covenant depends on morally responsible action from both sides. Yahweh's failure to keep his side of the covenant—or the utterly incomprehensible way in which he did so—was to raise great problems for Hebrew faith later on, as we can see clearly in books like Habakkuk, Job, and Ecclesiastes. Israel's failure to keep its side of the covenant was to become the basis for an interpretation of the human disasters which later befell it; to explain these, a whole philosophy of history was gradually worked out by the Deuteronomists and others. So (in the world-view that is developing here) from the time of the exodus, the human, the ultimate reality with which humans have to do, and the relationship between these two are all portrayed as having an essentially moral character.

Later, when Yahweh becomes understood as the creator of all that is, this moral dimension will prove of decisive importance in shaping the understanding of human life and its context. For it will mean that the very existence of the universe and all that is in it, as the expression of God's decision and purposes, has moral—and thus human and humane—significance. The world is to be the context within which finite moral beings—human beings—along with many other finite creatures, can find an appropriate home.

II

We are now in a position to specify the basic structure of radical monotheism, to see what picture of human life and its context it portrays. The purpose of such a world-view—that for which it has been imaginatively, if unconsciously, constructed—is to provide orientation for human life. It will need to present, therefore, at the very least, a picture or conception of humanity, an interpretation of the context within which human life transpires, and a claim about the way human life is to be directed or oriented within this context. Accordingly, it is not surprising to find that there are three fundamental categories in this world-view: humanity, the world, and God. The entire world-view is worked out and given its structure and character through the development of these categories in relation to each other.

God is the ultimate point of reference in terms of which all else is to be interpreted; as we have seen, God is a moral agent, creator, and governor of all that is. This means that the other two categories, humanity and the world, cannot be understood simply in terms of themselves, what they in their own intrinsic character appear to be; they gain their being and their meaning from their relationship to God, and it is only in this connection that what they are, and what they should do and become, can be rightly grasped.

Humanity, the second category, enjoys a very special relationship to God. Like God, human beings have creative powers and are morally responsible: in the language of the tradition, they have been created "in God's image." They have the capacity to enter into covenant with God, therefore, and to align their wills and their activities with God's work in the world; through entering into this special relationship with God, they realize such fulfillment as is open to them (what the tradition has called "salvation"). As free and responsible beings, however, they also have the power to move in directions not in accord with the divine will; and human life and history is in fact marked everywhere by the existence and effects of such counter-productive and self-destructive activity, institutions, and practices (sin). So the human relationship to God is one of absolute dependence at one level; but at another level there is an autonomy and freedom of self-determination which makes possible both the tensions of sin and rebellion and the unique fulfillment of covenant and communion.

The world, our third category, refers to the context within which human life transpires; it includes within it-

self all creaturely existence. In the monotheistic perspective, human beings do not live simply suspended before
their creator, as it were, in direct and continuous face-to-
face interaction with God. Their existence as finite creatures could hardly be made intelligible in such terms.
Human life unfolds within the spatial and temporal context of a multitude of other creatures to which humans are
also related and on which they depend for their existence
and well-being in many ways.

All that we know or experience or can imagine can be
given a place proper for it within this threefold categorial
scheme. What we call "faith in God" is the standpoint
which experiences and reflects, thinks and imagines, de-
cides and acts in these terms.

The interpretation of human existence provided by radical monotheism is in many ways highly attractive. It provides a picture of the human as possessed of a significant
measure of freedom and creativity, and as placed within
a context where this can be exercised and meaningfully
developed. Although older deterministic attitudes, stem-
ming from fatalistic and polytheistic mythologies, have
sometimes reasserted themselves in Christian history in
doctrines of total predestination by an all-powerful God, in
principle the conception of a fundamentally moral relationship of covenant between God and humans overcomes such views; and humans have ordinarily been pictured as free moral agents who can in some significant
sense take responsibility for their own lives and actions
and determine their own destinies.

This freedom both from external determination (by fate
or the gods) and internal determination (by desires for
food and sex, for power, prestige, and glory) is achieved by
the special place and character given to the central category of this world-view, *God.* God functions not simply as
an external determining power impinging on the human,
but as a center or focus for devotion and orientation for
self and community. In the degree to which humans ori-

ent themselves on God, they come into full freedom and
fulfillment; in the measure that they orient themselves in
terms of other powers and values, they become enslaved
and debilitated in idolatries. This is no mere doctrinaire
point. Since God is visualized as a perfectly righteous and
loving will, devotion and obedience to God involve a disci-
plining of self and community in terms of such moral
qualities as righteousness, mercy, and faithfulness; so the
qualities emphasized in the concept or picture of God
become replicated in these selves and communities, and
morally responsible life and action become valued highly.
Through providing a center of devotion—God—which is
beyond both the world and the human, radical monotheism is able to overcome both the chaos of a polytheistic
world and the overly rigid order of fatalism, and is simultaneously able to encourage the historical development of
responsible human freedom. By devoting themselves to
the God who transcends both humanity and the world,
humans increasingly (over time) can discipline themselves
into morally responsible agents with powers of freedom
and self-determination similar to God's.

Of course, it is easy to reject this whole picture of human
life and its context either as simply false or as inappropriate to our actual human nature and condition. We may
believe, for example, that the fatalistic view that humans
are essentially pawns in the hands of unchanging cosmic
powers is both truer and more in accord with our sense of
human life: much scientistic interpretation of the human,
particularly a behaviorism such as B. F. Skinner's, tends to
express such a modern version of fatalism. Or the polytheistic view which emphasizes the unrestrained and
unordered pluralism of our motives, desires, and experiences and which decries all attempts to discipline the various impulses of life through developing morally responsible selfhood may seem a truer picture of human
possibilities and fulfillment: the widespread appeal of the
contemporary "human potential" movement, as symbol-

ized by Esalen, clearly has great power in contemporary American life, and it has found a theological voice in the "new polytheism" of David Miller. Fatalistic and polytheistic world-views have firm roots in perennial dimensions of human experience, and they will always be able to make credible cases for themselves. It should be clear that they represent strikingly different options from radical monotheism.

While monotheism has not been the only kind of Godtalk in the West, it has been the preeminent line, and the most distinctive and original line, emerging first in ancient Israel and dominating in different ways the theological reflection and construction of Israel's three progeny: Judaism, Christianity, and Islam. In all three of these religions the fundamental threefold categorial structure I have outlined provides the frame within which human existence and all else is experienced, understood, and interpreted. The first and primary category is God, the ultimate reality, the ultimate point of reference in terms of which all else must be understood, the ultimate point of devotion and orientation for human selves and communities. Second is the category of the world, which includes all reality other than God, the structured whole which is the context of all human experience and life. Finally, there is the category of humanity, ourselves, we who, with our capacities for reflection and self-awareness, are seeking an orientation in this world that will enable us to find some measure of meaning and fulfillment in life. Implicit in the way these three categories are defined and the way they function is the fundamental claim that human existence gains its true definition and thus finds its fulfillment only through orientation on God; to the extent that we define ourselves and orient ourselves simply in terms of the world—or in terms of any items within the world, including our own wishes and desires—we will be frustrated, stunted, diseased, ultimately destroyed, for all such attachments are idolatrous.

III

It would be useful to compare and contrast the ways in which Judaism, Islam, and Christianity have each worked out the threefold categorial scheme characteristic of radical monotheism, but I have neither the competence nor the time to attempt that here. We shall concern ourselves in the rest of these remarks with the peculiarities of the Christian version. Christian faith, life, and theology are distinguished from these other two traditions by the addition of a *fourth* category—Christ—to the framework of interpretation. This category, moreover, is just as fundamental and indispensable in defining and articulating the Christian world-view as are the other three. We must try, now, to see how this is possible and what it means.

The fundamental importance of the category of Christ was expressed in classical Christianity by claims about his deity; i.e., by claims that Christ can properly be understood only as somehow identical with God, identical with that ultimate reality which is the source and ground of all else, and, moreover, that God cannot be properly understood apart from Christ. Such claims already appear in the New Testament; some representative examples:

> No one has ever seen God; the only Son, who is in the bosom of the Father, he has made him known. (John 1:18)

> He is the image of the invisible God. (Col. 1:15)

> All things have been delivered to me by my Father; ... no one knows the Father except the Son and any one to whom the Son chooses to reveal him. (Matt. 11:27)

> I and the Father are one. (John 10:30)

Later on at Nicea (325) the mythic language of these New Testament passages was given a hard metaphysical interpretation: Jesus Christ was said to be "begotten of the

Father uniquely. . . . of the substance of the Father, God of God, Light of Light, true God of true God, begotten, not made [i.e., not a creature, not part of the world, not subsumable under either the category "world" or the category "human"], consubstantial with the Father."[2] I do not want to take up here all of the difficult metaphysical and theological questions—not to say problems of sheer credibility—which this language raises. I bring up these mythical and metaphysical formulations only to underline the one point that I am now making: from the very beginning Christians have insisted on the centrality and the importance of what I have called the fourth category of the Christian world-view, the category of Christ. Insistence on the indispensability of this category is what distinguishes and defines a perspective as "Christian."

In the modern period the centrality of this category for Christians has been underlined in another way. Some recent writers—for example, some of the "death of God" theologians and certain other "Christian humanists"—give great weight to "Christ" even though they have become dubious about the continuing viability of the category of God. In effect this reduces the standard fourfold Christian categorial scheme to three and proposes a strikingly different world-view from Christian monotheism, a view structured by the categories "world," "humanity," and "Christ." Whatever the merits of such a position, it is interesting in this context because it shows that the significance of the symbol Christ for human orientation and self-understanding is not derivative from God, i.e., it does not depend on the Christian dogmatic attempt to maintain Christ's divinity. On the contrary, the category of Christ clearly has its own intrinsic and independent meaning; and for this reason it has its own unique contribution to make to the Christian world-view, a contribution that cannot be reduced to or subsumed under any of the other three constitutive categories (God, world, human). It was the independent significance of this symbol for under-

standing human existence, the world, and God, that led
the early Christians to give Christ such a high place in
their lives and their reflection. The deifying of Christ—
whatever difficulties we may have with that notion—was
an expression of the early Christian sense of the unique
and incomparable importance for human self-understanding and orientation provided by this symbol. Christian
faith through the centuries has concurred in that view;
and it is for this reason that I am suggesting that we have
here a fourth category which functions on an equal footing
with the other three in giving structure to the Christian
world-view.

It is not immediately evident, however, how a fourth
category can be introduced into the scheme of radical
monotheism. I want to suggest that the category of Christ
does not function in precisely the same way as the other
three—so that we have a quadrilateral world-view here
instead of a trilateral one—but that instead it serves primarily to qualify in a definitive way the other categories,
particularly God and the human. On the one hand, the
church saw in Jesus the perfect or normative or true expression of what humanity is and should be; on the other,
he was the perfect, definitive, and final revelation of God.
So the normative understanding both of the human and of
God is to be gained only with reference to Christ. This
equipollent double-sidedness of the significance of Christ
was given dogmatic standing in the formula of Chalcedon
(451), where it was held that Christ has "two natures," a
divine and a human, which are perfectly united and bal-
anced. He is, thus, "perfect in Godhead . . . [and] perfect
in manhood, truly God and truly man, . . . consubstantial
with the Father in Godhead, and . . . consubstantial with
us in manhood."[3]

Once again, it is not necessary for us to buy into all of
the difficult metaphysical and theological problems as-
sociated with these formulations in order to see the central
conceptual point being made, a point accepted in virtually

[handwritten margin note: But Xt not on equal footing as other categories.]

all subsequent Christian reflection and thinking. The point is this: it is not possible to understand what is meant by "Christ" without reference to the concepts of God and of the human, but it is also not possible properly to understand either "God" or the "human" without reference to Christ. There is a complex dialectical interdependence among these three concepts in the Christian world-view, and this interconnection has decisive impact on the whole Christian frame of orientation. The symbols of God and of the human are not nearly as open as might otherwise have been supposed; each is now delimited in important ways, for the norms for their proper understanding are to be derived from Christ.

Let us look at the concept of God first. In the various religious traditions all sorts of claims about divine powers, gods, goddesses, demons, and the like have been made; many sorts of religious experience (often supposed to be of God or the gods) have been reported in human history —experiences of the holy, the awesome, the terrifying, experiences of grace and beatitude, of mystical vision; philosophers have had wide differences of opinion as to what notions of ultimate reality or of God are adequate, or whether it is appropriate to speak of God at all. Although this great pluralism of human experience and reflection is certainly to be acknowledged and consulted and learned from, for Christian thinking the definitive clue or key which brings it into order is *Christ:* "He is the image of the invisible God," as Colossians puts it. For Christian theology, that is to say, God is to be understood as Christlike: God may not be thought of as hateful, indifferent, even impersonal; rather, God is to be thought of as loving, forgiving, redemptive reality—as *moral* reality, concerned with the personal being and the personal fulfillment of human beings. Jesus is a criterion or model in terms of which we are to construct our idea of God.

The conception of the human in Christian theology is similarly constricted and concentrated by the concept of

Christ. Here also human history confronts us with an ex-
tremely wide range of possibilities: from the no-self doctrine of Buddhism to highly egocentric forms of individualism and solipsism to social theories of self-in-community;
from highly spiritualistic notions that the soul alone is real,
the body unimportant or an alien prison, to thoroughly
materialistic conceptions; from rigid moralisms to nihilis-
tic antinomianisms. Obviously not all the questions raised
by these diverse contentions can be settled simply by looking at Jesus. But for the Christian perspective Jesus is
taken as somehow defining or normative for deciding
what the human really is, what the central human problems are, and what human salvation is. Thus, exploitation
or oppression of others or excessive concern for personal
pleasure or the fulfillment of one's own desires, cynical
devaluing of the meaning in life or indifference to human
needs and suffering, prideful self-assertion accompanied
by the downgrading and humiliation of others—all these
(and many other) forms of human existence and activity
must be called into question from the Christian point of
view. In contrast, virtues like love, mercy, forgiveness,
service to others above self, working toward reconciliation
and community among humans, and the like, are here
regarded as expressing the authentically human. In all of
this, Jesus is a model, a normative picture, of what human
being really is and ought to be; and the concept of human
nature, its problems and its fulfillment, is worked out with
reference to that model.

How Jesus—or Christ—is to be understood has, of
course, been a much debated question in Christian history. I am not concerned here to argue for this or that
particular interpretation of Christ[4] but rather to make a
conceptual and methodological point: whatever the view
of Christ we as theologians wish to defend, it will decisively affect our understanding of God and of the human.
These three categories are dialectically interconnected in
the Christian conceptual scheme.[5]

I have said nothing thus far about the effect which the concept of Christ has on the category of world. That effect is somewhat more indirect than with God and the human, but it is no less significant. The terms of the monotheistic categorial scheme are not really detachable from each other in such a way that we can decisively modify one or two without affecting the third; any change in one of these categories reverberates throughout the whole scheme, transforming and reshaping the entire perspective. The introduction, thus, of the category of Christ, with its powerful effects on the notions of God and of humanity, is bound also to affect the conception of the world. We can see this already in the mythology of the earliest Christians. Christ is not understood only as the man Jesus of Nazareth, nor even as the savior of all humanity: he is the agent of the creation of the world, one who is continuously active in the world, sustaining and supporting it. John identifies Christ as the very "word of God" and holds that "all things were made through him, and without him was not anything made that was made" (John 1:3). In Colossians we read that "in him all things were created, in heaven and on earth, visible and invisible, . . . all things were created through him and for him. He is before all things, and in him all things hold together" (Col. 1:16–17).

However implausible these sorts of claims might seem, from the perspective of our conceptual analysis it should not be difficult to see why they were made. If God (the ultimate point of reference in terms of which all else is to be understood) must be interpreted in the light of Christ, and if humanity gains its normative definition from Christ, then surely the conception of the world—God's creation, and the context within which human life falls and without which it cannot be properly understood—will also be significantly affected when "Christ" is introduced into the categorial scheme. The world now must be understood as the sort *(a)* which this kind of God (defined with reference to Christ) might have created, and *(b)* which provides a suitable context for the support and sustenance of that mode of human existence which Jesus Christ definitively represents. Our understanding of what the world really is will thus also be decisively affected and shaped by introduction of the category of Christ. The world may not be thought of as simply an impersonal material order, nor as a rigidly determined fatalistic order, nor as a chancy ramshackle structure about to disintegrate into chaos; it is an order established by the loving God working out creative and redemptive purposes in and through the movement of history, an order which provides a proper context for the emergence and development of loving human beings living in faithful community with each other and with God. Thus, the world is to be conceived as the proper context for our humanization, our being brought to full humanity (the norm of which is Christ), and the this-worldly historical processes in which we are immersed and from which we have emerged are in fact the processes of our humanization.

These are all momentous claims which we may well want to question or dispute. I am not trying here to argue their truth. Rather, I am trying to make clear the dialectical interrelatedness and interconnectedness of the four principal terms of the Christian categorial scheme—at least as that scheme has come down to us today.

If that scheme is now relatively clear, and if my outline of it is generally persuasive, we have come into a position from which we can define the task of Christian theology today. It can be expressed in three points.

1. Christian theology must attempt to clarify further and to articulate more fully the four terms of its categorial scheme with the help of the extensive vocabulary resources that have been worked out in the course of Christian history. Such concepts as sin, fall, salvation, church, sacraments, atonement, faith, hope, love, trinity, history, eschaton, and the like, each discriminate nuances of Christian experience and reflection which give the categorial

scheme concreteness and thus make it meaningful for employment in human life.

2. The categorial scheme must be brought into relationship with contemporary human experience as articulated in our best scientific and historical knowledge and our most profound prophetic and poetic insight, in order to see whether a plausible and viable contemporary version of it can be constructed. It is a serious and important question whether it is possible meaningfully and appropriately to interpret modern experience and knowledge in terms of a world-view structured by the four principal categories, God, world, humanity, and Christ. Doubtless any attempt to construct a contemporary Christian worldview will involve criticism and reinterpretation of much of what goes for knowledge in today's world, as well as rather drastic reconception and reformulation of the four fundamental Christian categories.

3. At this point, and only at this point, can the question be raised as to whether the Christian fourfold categorial scheme is any longer viable or whether the time has come drastically to transform it. How does the Christian worldview stand up in comparison with Buddhist and Jewish, Marxist and liberal humanist and other perspectives? Has the time come to drop the category God or the category Christ—or both of them—from the fundamental places they occupy in the Christian scheme? Should they be replaced by other symbols with quite different metaphorical foundations and metaphysical implications; or should the categorial scheme be expanded beyond four to include important dimensions of life and reality which these categories cannot adequately accommodate? Or has the time come to dispense with the Christian categorial scheme altogether in favor of some more adequate framework for orienting human life? These and other similar questions must all be faced.

Indeed, as we all know, these questions are being daily raised in our culture, and they are frequently in the consciousness of most of us. I suggest that the procedure I have outlined here, of attempting to define clearly the Christian categorial scheme, and then examining its viability and fruitfulness for understanding and orienting contemporary human life—in comparison with other categorial schemes available to us—provides a systematic, thorough, and responsible way to address these issues confronting us all. These problems are also central to the struggles with which the contemporary church is engaged. If Christian theology is to continue to serve the most pressing needs of the church, therefore, it is imperative that it shift from its more traditional doctrinal and dogmatic patterns to approaches focusing on comprehensive assessment and reconstruction of the Christian worldview.

5/Toward a Contemporary
Interpretation of Jesus

PREFATORY NOTE. This chapter should not be regarded as an outline for a contemporary constructive christology. It focuses, as has much traditional christological reflection, on Jesus as the central figure in God's revelatory and salvific activity, but such an approach has serious limitations if taken as definitive for a christology. (1) It takes a single individual as paradigmatic for defining the human—and thus also the divine—and in this way tends toward conceiving human and divine reality in individualistic rather than communitarian terms. (2) Because no single individual can sum up and exemplify all sides and dimensions of human reality and experience, it tends toward one-sided emphasis on certain aspects of human life at the expense of other equally important and authentic features; and thus it may result in narrow and constrictive—and in certain circumstances highly repressive—views of human life and its norms. (3) This problem has become especially acute in the contemporary scene for many women, who find Jesus—as a male—hardly a liberating model for conceiving the paradigmatic human, and who believe Jesus' posture of self-sacrifice, held up to women and other repressed groups as normative, has been a vehicle of dehumanization and even enslavement. Thus, however important Jesus might be for contemporary christological reflection, an adequate interpretation of the normative human will need to go beyond him to more inclusive communitarian models. In this regard it is instructive to remember John Knox's contention that in the New Testament "Christ" designates not only the man Jesus; it also, on occasion, refers to the complex of salvific events surrounding Jesus' life and death, and to the early Christian community within which new dimensions of love and freedom were being experienced.[1] The present chapter only hints at these other dimensions of "the meaning of Christ"; it does not develop them at all. For this reason it should not be regarded as sketching out a full christology; at most it presents a "contemporary interpretation of Jesus."

———

Christian faith is most decisively distinguished from other life orientations by the centrality it gives to Jesus. Throughout much of Christian history this fact was expressed in the objectivist mode by mythical and metaphysical concepts believed to represent the actual structure of reality, the fundamental order of being: Jesus, an itinerant preacher and healer from Nazareth in Galilee who was crucified under the Roman procurator Pontius Pilate, was said to be the "Christ," the very "Son of God," the Second Person of the divine trinity who was of "the same essence" as God the Father Almighty, the "Lord" whom each believer worshiped and before whom finally "every knee [would] bow, in heaven and on earth and under the earth" (Phil. 2:10). With such conceptions promulgated by the church and accepted by believers as divine truth, it is hardly surprising that "Jesus Christ" was a symbol absolutely central for Christian faith. Even the liberal theology of the last two centuries has regarded Jesus as central and paradigmatic, revealing both the true nature of God and the real possibilities of our humanity; and when the symbol "God" became questionable for some Christians—as in the recent "death of God" theology— Jesus remained the point of reference for defining and understanding the authentically human. Though traditional dogma had been explicitly repudiated, its powerful historical momentum continued to make the symbol of Jesus Christ effective, even determinative, in the life and thought of almost everyone working within Christian traditions.

It is not justifiable, however, for a methodologically self-conscious theology simply to be carried by historical momentum. The task of such a theology is not simply reformulation of traditional claims in contemporary idiom; it is, rather, to build from the ground up (so far as that is possible) a conception of the human, of the world (the context of human existence), and of God (the ultimate point of reference for ordering human life), which can make sense of human experience and thought, human life and problems, today. Though such a project may sound pretentious, we dare not undertake anything less in theology once we have become aware that all our religious symbols are, and always have been, human constructs, and that, moreover, these symbols have often functioned in highly oppressive and destructive ways. It is no longer good enough simply to pass on the tradition, however weighty and meaningful and fruitful that tradition has been in the past or may still be. Every element that goes into our theological position must be critically scrutinized and, so far as possible, justified in terms of appropriate criteria. Whether or how "Jesus" can properly continue to be central in a contemporary theological position is something to be established, not something to be taken for granted. In view of the recent feminist critique of the almost exclusively masculine character of Western religious symbols, the centrality of Jesus—and the symbolism used to articulate that—become especially problematical.

The question, then, of who Jesus is (or was) and how we should interpret him theologically must be entirely and explicitly a matter of *our* decision. It is not something predetermined for us by tradition, neither the orthodox tradition that proclaims Jesus the Son of God nor the more recent academic tradition that regards Jesus as a historical *our theology our own constructive work*

figure from Nazareth. Each of these alternatives (and others) needs to be considered, but it is *we* who must decide which to use and how to interpret it (or them). Our theology must be our own constructive work.

It would be a mistake to overemphasize the novelty of what is being proposed here. Ordinary humans, looking at the Jesus presented to them in one tradition or another, have always been the ones who decided how Jesus should be regarded, what should be believed about him. Initially, for example, it was members of the church—or rather, members of certain segments of a highly disparate religious movement—that decided to regard Jesus as the "Christ," or the "son of man" or the "Son of God." Modern scholarship has shown conclusively that these were not titles Jesus used of himself and required his followers to accept.[2] Jesus preached the presence and coming of the "kingdom of God," and how he understood himself personally to be related to that apocalyptic event remains unclear. The authority of his message did not derive from some title ascribed to him, but rather, on the one hand, from the grip which the myth of God's powerful lordship over history had on Jesus and his hearers, and, on the other, from the power of word and deed with which Jesus persuaded his hearers that God was now moving to bring history to its long-expected dramatic climax. It was others responding to Jesus and to what was reported of him who characterized him in various ways from rabbi or prophet to Second Person of the trinity. Moreover, throughout church history believers and others have repeatedly interpreted and reinterpreted who Jesus was and in what his work consisted (e.g., in the various atonement theories developed over the centuries), always in accord with the needs and insights and meaningful symbolism of the time. (This includes the nineteenth century's quest for "the historical Jesus.") Each generation has decided for itself how it would understand and appropriate Jesus, even though this may often have involved largely taking over from tradition what were regarded as authoritative views instead of self-consciously deciding what was to be believed. If, now, we decide to make our own choice about how we will understand Jesus' significance, we are simply doing self-consciously and deliberately, and thus not thoughtlessly or accidentally, what has always been done. The proper question for a contemporary christology, therefore, is: not how has Jesus been regarded by this or that supposedly authoritative tradition (even the historians' tradition)? but rather: what criteria should we use in deciding how to regard and interpret Jesus?

But there is a prior question to be addressed: why concern ourselves with Jesus at all in contemporary theological construction? This question is not difficult to answer: it indicates a point where contemporary theology must—unavoidably—live out of tradition. The way in which the concepts of God and of humanity are framed in modern Western reflection—in terms of such notions as freedom, love, creativity, and the like—has been powerfully shaped by centuries of reflection on who or what Jesus Christ was (or is), what he did, what he taught, and what befell him. For much of Western history Jesus has been taken to be in some way normative for understanding both who God is and what we humans are, and this import has become constitutive for the very concepts with which we think about these matters. An examination of the significance of Jesus for our thinking about humanity and God will be, then, a necessary part of any truly critical theological work today. It is important that we be as self-conscious as we can of the significance Jesus has, or should have—or should not have!—in our theological reflection. That objective can be achieved only by attending directly to the questions about Jesus Christ with which our cultural and religious tradition confronts us. We may choose to reject any or all of the answers proposed by tradition to the question of Jesus, but the question itself may not be ignored if we are to understand as fully as possible what we are doing as theologians.

I

If theology is understood as deliberate *construction* of a viable contemporary understanding of humanity, the world, and God, as I am arguing that it must be,[3] we ourselves must take full responsibility for every element we build into our theological perspective. Hence, if Jesus Christ is to be given a significant position—or any position at all—in our theology, this will be because of needs and reasons which we ourselves, in our contemporary attempt at theological understanding and construction, find compelling. What might such reasons be?

I have argued above (Chapter 4) that the fundamental theistic categorial scheme has three terms: God, the world, and humanity. These terms, taken simply in and by themselves, are of the widest possible generality, and perform the almost entirely formal role of providing the principal points of reference, the structure, which every theistic scheme will display; they tell us nothing about the specific valuations that will be made within that scheme, about the styles of life implied by it, about the moral implications it might have or the social institutions or communal patterns it might demand. In short, these three categories taken simply by themselves provide us with no real guidance for human life, and thus they cannot significantly orient human existence. The category "human" is as wide as the infinite variety of forms that human life and culture have taken in the past, together with all the as yet unrealized possibilities that still open before us; the category "world" refers to and includes the structured interconnectedness of everything that has been, is now, or shall be, the overall context of human existence; and the category "God," vaguest and most general of all, indicates the ultimate point of reference in terms of which both of these, humanity and world, are finally to be understood. None of these terms, then—taken simply by themselves, in the abstract—gives us any basis for assessment of any state of affairs in the world or for preferring any particular form of human action or mode of human life: every reality and every possibility is included within their scope. This is of course no accident. If they were any less comprehensive and inclusive, they could not provide the categorial structure for a *world*-view, nor would they provide a base for comparative examination and evaluation of alternative conceptions of human life and of reality.

This categorial structure can provide orientation for human life—that is, can provide criteria and norms and values with which to guide human preferences and choices, with which to assess human actions and styles of life and institutions, with which to stimulate human imagination toward particular forms of creativity and to facilitate the cultivation of particular cultural and individual potentialities in preference to others—only if it is decisively qualified and given concrete normative content by some further term(s) or category(s). Some specific image or conception of the human must be set forth as normative, or there will be no way of judging which among all the possibilities that confront us are to be preferred, which are to be discouraged, and which (if any) are to be forbidden. Furthermore, unless it can be—and is—claimed that these preferred modes or styles of human existence and culture are peculiarly appropriate or fitting within life's overall context, i.e., unless it can be believed that the world is not simply an open structure of infinite possibilities but in some significant sense supports and sustains these particular ones, enables them to grow and to flourish, the normative image or conception of the human will not be able to perform a significant orienting function in *this world;* the world, thus, must be seen as the sort of context which facilitates, indeed makes possible, this form of human existence (in contrast, perhaps, with other less desirable forms), if the proposed paradigm of the human is to be taken seriously as normative for us here and now.[4] Finally, unless that which is taken to be the ultimate ground of all

that is can be grasped as actually grounding and sustaining
this whole complex—humanity (as depicted and defined)
within the world (seen as the appropriate context for this
humanity)—the conceptions and images of humanity and
the world will have no substantial metaphysical foundation, and thus they will not be able to command unqualified religious devotion; in short, their claims to provide proper and adequate guidance for the orientation of
life and thought will be questionable and their effectiveness always threatened. Thus, if the theistic categorial
scheme is actually to provide orientation for human life,
all three of its defining terms will need to be given material content and significance.

   In fact, of course, every actual religious tradition, every
world-view, always has such concrete content; without
this, it would have no particular shape and no conceivable
use. The interesting and important question thus
becomes: how are we to decide which material view of the
human, which particular understanding of the world,
which concrete image of God we should accept and develop in our own constructive work? How do or can we
move from a purely abstract and formal discussion of the
theistic categorial scheme to a concrete and particular
interpretation of humanity in the world under God, an
interpretation which makes normative claims on us, on
our actions and styles of life and on the social and cultural
institutions within which we live and which we will seek
to promote? In the long religious and cultural history of
humankind, many different pictures of the human have
been proposed as normative and many different conceptions of the world and of God have been set forth as valid
or true: how should we choose among them?

   Clearly, no absolute or definitive answers can be given
to these questions. We have no way of putting ourselves
into a neutral position from which we can "objectively"
assess alternative conceptions of the human and the
world, test them against the "actual facts" of human exis-

tence, and thus ascertain which ones are more true or valid. We already exist as formed humans, with particular commitments, particular interests and values and ways of seeing life and the world, and particular conceptions of human possibilities; we already participate in particular cultural patterns of life and social institutions. All of these predispose us to appreciate certain modes of life and expression and to ignore or discount or fail to understand others. There is no way for us to jump out of our skins in order to see what raw and unformed human nature might be. Inevitably, in our search for a viable and appropriate understanding of human existence in the world, we will begin with the perceptions and understandings and commitments and values which we already have, which already define the human and its possibilities for us, and working from that position and with that framework we will attempt to grasp the wide panorama of human life and possibility, holding to that which seems to us meaningful and valid.

We need not, of course, resign ourselves to a completely arbitrary subjectivity here. In the first place, our commitments and values do mean something to us; they are our way of grasping what it is to be human, and without them we would have no sense even of the sort of questions we are trying to ask. Though they bias us in certain directions and away from others, they also provide the indispensable base without which our inquiry could not proceed at all. Secondly, we are surrounded, both in our own pluralistic culture and certainly in the world at large, with others who experience their humanity quite differently, who have other interests and pursue other values, who participate in other quite different cultural patterns and social institutions and religious traditions, and who, thus, perceive and understand human existence and the world in strikingly different ways than we do. It is possible—indeed, almost unavoidable—to observe diverse human commitments and styles roundabout us; and we can enter into conversation with their representatives and can learn, thus, to appreciate forms of the human very different from our own. Doubtless the problems here are immense: barriers of language, cultural and religious traditions, class, social position, education, race, gender, and the like all contribute to making appreciation and understanding of alien institutions and forms of life very difficult. Nevertheless, some degree of openness toward the different and the strange is always possible, and given a desire to expand one's appreciation of human diversity and thus to deepen one's understanding of human nature, the constrictions and constraints of the customs and habits and commitments which form one's own mode of existence can be loosened in some respects and opened up to new perceptions and insights. Reading novels, studying history, traveling abroad, living for a time in an alien culture —humans have broadened themselves and their understanding in ways such as these from time immemorial. Though our actual commitments and values and idealized pictures form the base or point of departure for our understanding of human existence and the world, intercourse with others will broaden and deepen these as we develop capacities for sensitivity to and appreciation of human potentialities which would otherwise be completely unknown to us.

In the space of a short essay like this, I cannot, of course, explore all the diversity of human possibilities; I shall not even sketch out a procedure for accomplishing such an objective. But that is not necessary for our purposes here. These are, on the one hand, to see how it is possible and legitimate to give sufficient concreteness to the theistic categorial scheme to enable it to provide orientation for life; and, on the other hand, to make some proposals about the continuing theological significance of Jesus. These two objectives are closely interconnected, as we shall now see.

A principal way in which cultural and religious traditions convey to their adherents the configurations of human possibilities they regard as valuable and normative is through the story or image or picture of a person who exemplifies the desired dispositions, commitments, and values. It is not through abstract analysis and logical argumentation that we come to our basic discovery and understanding of what it is to be human. It is, rather, through the models which other humans provide for us—first of all, those with whom we are in direct contact in the family and immediate community; later (though also very early) those cultural and religious heroes whose stories are repeatedly related to us as exemplifying the attitudes and values which we are encouraged to make our own. Abraham Lincoln, Martin Luther King, Adolf Hitler, Mohandas Gandhi, Mao Tse-tung, Albert Einstein—or Socrates, Jesus, Mary, the Buddha—the stories of these and of many others have been related time and again, and have been meditated on and elaborated in countless ways, thus providing pictures or models which children early internalize and to which adults repeatedly return as they give form and shape to their own selves and communities. It is largely through such stories or pictures of the human that our conception of human existence, its possibilities and its problems, is formed within us and becomes a principal point of orientation for our lives and our reflection.[5] The question, then, of how we shall give concreteness and specificity to our categories of humanity, world, and God, is at least partly a question of which stories and pictures of human existence we should adopt as normative for our thinking and living.

Identification of the various significant images of the human available in our pluralistic culture and world, which might serve as concrete models in contemporary theological construction, and development of criteria for making a selection from among them, are among our most important theological tasks today. I cannot, however, undertake these here. Suffice it to say that when we adopt a model or an image of the human and make it normative in theological construction, we must be able plausibly to claim *(a)* that it "truly" or "accurately" expresses or represents human nature, its potentialities and its problems, and *(b)* that it can be intelligibly understood in the context of, and in significant interrelationship with, what we take to be the "real world." Obviously both of these matters will be susceptible to dispute, since they involve exceedingly complex phenomenological, scientific, epistemological, and metaphysical issues, and any attempt to sort them out and resolve them will be both difficult and controversial.[6] I wish to point out, however, that the Christian tradition, in working out its conception of Jesus as the Christ, has recognized both of these concerns as germane and has, in fact, developed its claims in terms of them. In the classical Chalcedonian formulation Jesus Christ is said to be "truly man" and "truly God." That is, Jesus is taken to be the perfect expression or representation of humanity—not in the abstract, but humanity in its proper relationship to its ultimate metaphysical foundation; and so Jesus is said to be the perfect expression or representation of God as well. It is because both the anthropological and the metaphysical are believed to come to a focus in Jesus that he can be the concrete image which provides orientation for human life in the world. Although classical christology was formulated in terms and categories in many respects alien to contemporary styles of expression and thought, it articulates concerns to which we today must still attend: any image or model proposed as the proper focus for orientation in life must be able to justify itself both anthropologically and metaphysically.

With these remarks about the formal importance of christology for a theistic world-view in mind, let us turn to a consideration of Jesus as focus for contemporary faith and devotion.

II

I suggest that traditional metaphysical doctrines such as the incarnation or the two natures of Christ, and traditional mythical claims that Jesus is the unique "Son of God" or the "son of man" who will ultimately return on the clouds of heaven, should not be interpreted as describing the peculiar makeup or character of the divine man, Jesus of Nazareth, but rather should be understood as a way of expressing the central conviction of much Christian faith: that in the man Jesus is to be found the normative paradigm or model for understanding who or what God is and what true humanity is, that Jesus is thus the proper focus for orientation in life. If Jesus is believed to have this kind of significance, it becomes of central importance to ask: Who or what is this Jesus? What can we know about him? How do we relate to him? What claims about Jesus are to be accepted? which rejected? It is well known that Jesus has been thought of in many ways in the Christian tradition: as an itinerant preacher and healer from Nazareth, as the only begotten Son of God, as one crucified under Pontius Pilate and raised on the third day, as King of kings and Lord of lords, as one with whom pious believers are in daily communion in prayer, as one whose body and blood are present on every altar where the mass is celebrated, as the great idealistic preacher of the Sermon on the Mount, and so forth. To which of these views should one subscribe, and which reject? And how does one decide such matters?

We can begin to address these issues by observing that, whatever else they may want to say or however much they may differ in their claims regarding what is of central importance here, all views of Jesus agree that he is *someone remembered.* He is a figure from out of the past who lived in Palestine, where he preached and healed and taught and was ultimately crucified under Pontius Pilate. He left marks on the history of his time, and these are still recoverable by us because the New Testament is extant (it contains virtually all our historically reliable reports about Jesus). In short, whatever else he may have been or is, Jesus was a man who lived and died in first-century Palestine. The creeds of the church so identify Jesus as do all the New Testament records, and this claim is concurred in by all non-Christian commentators (with the exception of the small circle who deny Jesus' historicity—a position for which there is very little historical support). As a starting point, then, in our exploration of the question, Who is Jesus Christ? we may say that he was a first-century preacher and healer who was publicly executed near Jerusalem under the Roman procurator Pontius Pilate.

It is a commonplace of contemporary scholarship that we do not have the necessary materials available to construct a detailed biography of Jesus or to uncover the hidden inner motives of his words and actions. This, however, is no handicap for the theological questions which we are here pursuing. Our interest in identifying who Jesus is or was arises because of the Christian claim that he is the proper model or paradigm to give specificity and concreteness to our otherwise abstract and purely formal conceptions of the human and of God; for this purpose what is needed is a portrait or picture of him as a distinctive person, not the many details of his life. What sort of man do we encounter in the words and actions and sufferings that have been preserved for us? What possibilities of the human did this Jesus actualize? Which did he de-emphasize? What sort of character do we see portrayed in our reports and records? If in and through the words and stories of the New Testament the portrait of a particular and distinctive person becomes etched in our consciousness, that is precisely what is needed for our purposes. Such a portrait can serve as the principal resource for working out a characterization of what may be regarded as authentic human existence; it can also provide the major reference point for developing a conception of the metaphysical foundations, the grounding in Reality, which would be required to make intelligible the claim that it is precisely this particular exemplification of the human and its potentialities that is to be regarded as normative. Whether such significance and such uses should be given to the portrait cannot, of course, be determined until it has actually been drawn.

As it happens, the New Testament presents us with just such a portrait of Jesus. It does so, of course, in its own first-century terms. The historical story which it has to tell of Jesus is clothed in a mythic story about a divine being come down from heaven and born miraculously to a virgin mother, or a divine spirit descending from heaven like a dove and entering into a man at his baptism. It is a story which comes to its climax with Jesus' resurrection from the dead and his return to the heavens from whence he originally came and from which he now rules both church and world as King of kings and Lord of lords.

Should we accept this mythicized portrait of Jesus as giving his proper identity? Or should we begin with something less—for example, the historical figure whom we can still discern behind the mythic picture? Before the nineteenth century did its historical and theological work, it was not necessary to ask that question. It could be taken for granted that the entire New Testament account—from the Fourth Gospel's claim that the *logos* of God "became flesh" in Jesus, to his resurrection from the dead and his ascension into heaven, where he now sits at God's right hand—presented a *history,* a succession of salvific events that actually happened. So the picture of Jesus in terms of which faith oriented itself and with which theology worked was essentially of this divine being come to earth, here to suffer and die and rise again from the dead. If Christ, then, was to be the paradigm for understanding the human and the divine, it would be this dying/rising god who would be the central focus for understanding both who God really is and what human existence is all

about. In the present century Karl Barth has gone the
farthest in trying to develop a theology expressing this
traditional understanding of Jesus Christ.[7] However subtle
and sophisticated Barth's working out of the details may
be, for him faith is understood essentially as buying into
and accepting this traditional Christian myth, and the
work of the theologian is directed largely to analyzing and
imaginatively elaborating the meaning of that myth for
our understanding of God and humanity.

Such a procedure, however, forces us to ground our
theological work on an arbitrary starting point which must
be accepted fideistically. In contrast, the theological
stance which I have been urging in this book calls for
different moves. Once it is recognized that theology is
(and always has been) an activity of human imaginative
construction, it is no longer acceptable to begin our theological work with an authoritarian starting point, however
venerable and revered that foundation may be. For that
is simply building on the imaginative work of earlier generations, accepted more or less uncritically, instead of
carefully, critically, and deliberately doing our own constructive work, thus taking full responsibility for ourselves
and our theology. To give the expressions and constructions of earlier generations such authoritative and uncriti-
cizable standing—once we have recognized that this is
what we are doing—is out-and-out idolatry, an intolerable
position for a theology seriously attempting to speak of
God. To be intellectually and religiously responsible we
must do our own theological thinking at every point; we
are never entitled simply to take over what tradition
teaches.

Fortunately, as a result of nineteenth- and twentieth-
century historical studies, it is no longer required—or
scarcely even possible—simply to take over the New Testament mythic portrait of Christ. We are now able, to a
large extent, to distinguish the mythic from the historical
elements in that picture in a way that earlier generations

could not.[8] This possibility forces us to face a question unknown to Christian theologians before the nineteenth century: Which dimensions of the New Testament portrait of Jesus—the mythic or the historical—should we regard as more fundamental in determining our understanding of who Jesus really is (was)? Jesus can be seen primarily as a figure in a *mythic* story, or primarily as a figure in *history.*

Unlike those earlier generations which did not make this distinction, we must make a choice between these alternatives since for modern thought myth and history have become differentiated from each other. A myth, in its depiction, interpretation, and explanation of the meaning and problems of human existence, finds it essential to make reference to *another world* than that of everyday life;[9] a modern historical account, however, must confine itself to relating and describing what actually happened *in this world,* so far as this can be determined on the basis of evidence available to the historian. Any fully developed Christian theology will doubtless contain both mythic (or metaphysical) and historical (or empirical) elements: the crucial question is how these are to be ordered to each other. It is important, if our theological work is to be methodologically self-conscious and critical, that the basis on which we develop our mythical or metaphysical frameworks be carefully examined and justified.

Modern historical scholarship enables us to see how the New Testament's mythic picture of Jesus developed. Before Jesus' followers thought of him as messiah or Son of God or the divine Logos come to earth, he was known to them as simply another human being, a carpenter, a preacher, a healer. Above all, Jesus was one who was publicly executed, and his scandalous death made it impossible to use any of these mythic notions—taken over from Jewish and Greek religious traditions—without drastically transforming and correcting them. Instead of a powerful messianic figure who would demonstrate the in-breaking

of God's rule through a dramatic overthrow of the Roman
military yoke, it was necessary to speak of a "suffering
messiah" who died on a cross. Instead of a heavenly "son
of man" who would call down legions of angels from
heaven to overthrow the evil rulers of this present age,
Jesus' followers were forced to accept a "son of man [who]
must suffer many things, and be rejected by the elders and
the chief priests and the scribes, and be killed" (Mark
8:31). The mythic pictures which portrayed heavenly
power and promised supernatural success had to be corrected by the earthly facts of Jesus' failure and death. The
historical facts of Jesus' life, and especially his death, thus
provided a kind of criterion for reconceiving the myths
and their meaning.[10]

It is interesting and important for us to note that despite
this theological priority which the historical had over the
mythic in early Christian faith, in many respects it was the
mythic consciousness which eventually won out in the
Christian tradition. This is perhaps because of the central
importance which stories of Jesus' "resurrection" had in
certain strands of the tradition. Though interest in Jesus'
sayings as a wisdom teacher, and memories of his healings
and his demeanor, would doubtless have survived his
death for some time, it was the connecting of all these with
the belief that Jesus had come back to life after his crucifixion, that he had been seen by his disciples and others, and
that these events were a divine attestation to Jesus and his
ministry (cf. Rom. 1:4), that enabled him to become such
a powerful historical figure. The resurrection of Jesus,
taken as a factual event following upon his crucifixion,
provided the impetus and link enabling Christians to understand the several moments of this myth of a dying and
rising god as a continuous historical account of salvific
events linking heaven and earth.

When Jesus' crucifixion is absorbed into and interpreted
through this mythic frame, it can easily lose the earlier

scandalous and paradoxical character which had so impressed, for example, a Paul:

> God chose what is foolish in the world to shame the
> wise,
> God chose what is weak in the world to shame the
> strong,
> God chose what is low and despised in the world, even
> things that are not,
> to bring to nothing things that are. . . .
> Christ crucified, a stumbling block to Jews and folly to
> Gentiles.
>
> (1 Cor. 1:27–28, 23)

Now Jesus' passion and crucifixion become but one episode in what is ultimately a glorious victory over the forces of evil and death wrought by divine supernatural power. And so, instead of the historical continuing to serve as a criterion for correcting and transforming the mythic, the mythic ultimately swallows up and even reverses the meaning of the historical. In the mythic picture we are presented, finally, not with a helpless Jesus dying on a cross, but with a divine being of great might who can overpower any and every enemy that comes up against him. Jesus has become the divine lord before whom every knee will ultimately bow, the divine judge who will separate the sheep from the goats at the last judgment, indeed the divine warrior who at the battle of Armageddon will finally overthrow all the forces of evil in a mighty display of his violent wrath. It should hardly surprise us, then, that followers of this mighty Lord of history have engaged through the centuries in violent crusades against the infidels, have condemned heretics to death by fire and drowning, have invented the tortures of the inquisition and participated in the imperialistic conquest of Asia and Africa. For their Lord was one who destroys the unrighteous in violence and wrath, not one who simply and meekly en-

dured the suffering and death thrust upon him by the
agents of political power.

III

It is, I believe, a mistake to make this mythic identification of Jesus our primary one; it has strayed too far from
the historical actuality from which it sprang and which
should serve as its criterion. Contemporary christology
will doubtless need to use mythical and/or metaphysical
language in working out its interpretation, but the metaphysics and myth should be disciplined and corrected by
the historical facts, so far as we can recover them. To the
extent it makes Jesus central for grasping the human and
the divine, it must build on the actual fact of who Jesus
was: what he did, what he taught, how his life came to that
climax in which he "was most fully himself" (Hans Frei).[11]
Otherwise it is simply a free creation of the imagination,
and no adequate justification can be given for attaching it
to Jesus.

We do not, of course, know many of the details of Jesus'
life; we have only what the early church preserved, and
even with that it is almost always difficult to discern what
is historically reliable. But it appears to be universally
agreed among historians that Jesus preached the "good
news" that the evils in this present life were about to be
overcome with the imminent in-breaking of the kingdom
of God; his own healings of suffering and sickness, and his
forgiveness of sins, were dramatic signs of the kingdom's
coming. There was an important ethical component to
Jesus' teachings, summarized in the double commandment to love God and to love our neighbors. Jesus understood this in a very radical sense: love involves the re-
peated forgiving of offenses against us ("seventy times
seven," he told Peter, Matt. 18:22), going out of our way
to help suffering fellow humans (the "good Samaritan,"
Luke 10:29–37), always turning "the other cheek" and

going "the second mile" (Matt. 5:39, 41), and all of this not only with friends but even with enemies (Matt. 5:43–47). Life in the kingdom of God, to which Jesus called his disciples, was a reversal of our present life, where power over others is reckoned as signifying one's importance and serving others is regarded as demeaning: "whoever would be great among you must be your servant, and whoever would be first among you must be slave of all" (Mark 10: 43–44). This overturning of ordinary human standards of significance or greatness in Jesus' teachings was brought to a burning focus in the final action of Jesus' life, in which he refused to defend or protect himself against his enemies and accepted meekly their whips and curses and finally a violent death on a cross. Since the cross epitomized all that Jesus did and taught and stood for, it is not surprising that it has become the central symbol of Christian faith; this was the moment which decisively revealed him for what he was.

It is well known that the Synoptic Gospels give practically no information about the first thirty years of Jesus' life. They concentrate almost entirely on his ministry, and they focus much of that on the concluding weeks, when Jesus knows that he is heading toward death; an extraordinarily large amount of space is given to the last few hours of his life. Some, wishing to know about other aspects and periods of Jesus' life as well, have regretted this disproportionate focusing on his death. But that is a mistaken attitude, suggesting that the quantity of information is what is important in our knowledge of Jesus. On the contrary, as we have seen, the theological significance of Jesus is to be found in what his life and death reveal, or can reveal, about the nature of the human and the possibilities of the human. And for this purpose we have all that we need. The picture of Jesus which we can reconstruct historically gives us a very striking image of the human: when this is made paradigmatic, authentic human existence is seen to be life given in service to others, life of unqualified *agape.* Here is a human being entirely consistent with himself—teachings, actions, final martyr's death: a life oriented entirely on self-giving, never self-aggrandizement.

In some respects this picture of Jesus giving himself up completely in the prime of his life may impress us as unbelievable; and yet Jesus is not really portrayed as superhuman or as a demigod. As he faces his fate in Gethsemane, he must struggle with himself, as would anyone else, to obey God's will. The mode of existence paradigmatically exemplified in Jesus is certainly one-sided, and it takes heroic resolve to carry it through, but it has been historically replicated in various degrees and ways subsequently —in a St. Francis, a John Woolman, a Mohandas Gandhi, a Martin Luther King, a Mother Teresa. It is clearly a form which human life can take in history, and it is, moreover, one that has a certain appeal in our world, governed as it is by the lust for wealth and power, success and physical comfort. The vivid portrait of Jesus given in the Gospel accounts can lay upon us a powerful claim, that here is presented the very norm of authentic human existence.

As we have noted, to the degree and in the respects that Jesus impresses us as the proper paradigm for grasping the normatively human, he can also serve as a concrete model for working out our conception of God; here we move directly to explicit metaphysical claims. The ultimate point of reference in terms of which all else is to be understood is now to be conceived in terms which render intelligible the claim that true humanity is epitomized in Jesus: there must be something in the foundation of things, in the ultimate grounding of all that exists, that drives toward expression in precisely this mode of (human) existence. If Jesus expresses the authentically human, his sort of self-sacrificing love should not be regarded as merely a historical accident: it must be grounded in and expressive of an *agape* at the deepest levels of Reality.[12] From this point of view we can understand why the church felt impelled to say that Jesus was the "revelation" of God, or even "the image of the invisible God" (Col. 1:15). When, then, we give ourselves in and to this same self-giving love, we are allowing the deepest Reality with which we can be in touch to come to full realization in our own being. In more traditional terms, we are allowing God's will to be done in and through us.

Obviously, all such statements or claims are expressions of a *faith*, i.e., expressions of commitment to this figure, Jesus, as the paradigm of the truly human and the ultimately real. Other quite different commitments are possible for us; other paradigms of the human may seem much more plausible. Julius Caesar, Socrates, Buddha, Henry Ford, Mozart, Henry Miller—any of these may seem to reveal the truly human more adequately, and we may choose to commit ourselves to one of these paradigms, or to some other, or to none so individualistically defined; for example, we may regard images of community as more appropriate for defining and representing the normatively human than any image of an individual can ever be. Arguments can be given for and against each of these possibilities. Human reality is not fully determined by its biological propensities, but completes itself with the assistance of ideal notions or pictures which it holds before itself and seeks to realize. What is distinctive about the Christian understanding of the human and the humane is that it significantly determines itself by the portrait of the historical figure Jesus, as that figure impresses itself in and through the New Testament.

Let me summarize this discussion with two observations about the place of biblical materials in the work of contemporary constructive theology.

1. We have noted that Christian faith has constructed and responded to many different Jesuses, in the course of its history; that there are many ways to interpret the New Testament picture(s) of Jesus. I am arguing here that both the logic of the Christian claims themselves (as found in the New Testament, where historical facts forced revision

of mythic motifs), and also the methodological demands of
a responsible constructive theology, require us to give the
historical elements in the New Testament materials priority over the mythic. When we systematically follow this
principle, the New Testament portrait of Jesus, so far as it
emphasizes the story of a preexistent divine being who
comes to earth and later returns to heaven, must be signifi- *
cantly revised. Thus, the New Testament cannot be taken
as simply and straightforwardly authoritative for contemporary theological work, even in what it says of Jesus or
God. Hermeneutical principles derived from contemporary theological reflection and historical study must be
brought to the biblical materials, and their application
may well result in significant modifications of traditional
views.

2. Nevertheless, the Bible is clearly an indispensable
foundation for Christian reflection on Jesus. All of the
knowledge that we have about the historical Jesus is
gained in and through the biblical materials. Without the
New Testament there would be no Jesus at all who could
serve as a paradigm making concrete and specific the understanding of the normatively human. Without the Old
Testament there would be no way adequately to understand the context of faith and life within which Jesus appeared and which provided him with his own orientation
in life; more specifically, the full dimensions of the image/
concept of God to which Jesus was devoted, and which
served as the symbolic foundation on which a distinctively
Christian conception of God would gradually be constructed after his death, would not be known. We would
understand little of what devotion to this God meant: total
and undivided loyalty, the whole of life ordered according
to the divine will. And thus the very thing that made Jesus'
message and life so impressive as a paradigm of authentic
human existence—its radical theocentrism and self-giving
—would be neither intelligible nor compelling. The Bible,
thus, will be indispensable to Christian faith and Christian

theology, as long as God remains the central focus of devotion and orientation and Jesus the central paradigm for grasping who God is.

IV

I have been arguing in these chapters that the image/concept of God is a center or focus for consciousness which is claimed (believed) to bring orientation to life—and thus genuine fulfillment—for human selves and communities. If such a focus is to live up to the claims made for it, three desiderata must be met: *(a)* The image/concept must be sufficiently unified and clear so that we are aware both when we are attending to it and what it is to which we are attending, and so that interest and affection can be directed toward it; that is, we must be able to turn ourselves toward God and know that we are doing so. *(b)* There must be a sense of the reality or truth of what the image/concept stands for and directs us toward; that is, we must be able to believe that what is called "God" is *real,* and not just a product of our fancy. *(c)* We must be persuaded that it is precisely this reality, attended to in and through the image/concept of God, that provides full and adequate—not partial and incomplete or even misleading—orientation in life for human beings; that is, we must be convinced that here we are in touch with the true grounding of our existence, that this is *God,* not an idol. We need to consider now whether and in what respects an image/concept of God constructed on the basis of the paradigm or model of Jesus (developed in terms of the historical rather than the mythic picture) meets these desiderata.

There should be no problem on the first point. The picture of the man Jesus in the New Testament, even though set in a mythic frame, is sharp and clear. Jesus appears as a dramatic and, in his own way, powerful figure, attractive in many respects, however difficult it might be for us to emulate him. Many persons over the centuries

[margin handwriting: Concept of God must point to the Real, + do so adequately]

have found him to be the most significant and attractive model of the human of which they knew. The fact that such persons—along with others influenced in varying degrees by the Christian perspective—have felt they ought themselves to be loving, forgiving, and self-sacrificing, devoted to the well-being of others, is testimony to the effectiveness with which the image of Jesus has imprinted itself on human consciousness as exemplifying authentic human life. Moreover, Jesus has not only been a model or example in terms of which persons and communities judge themselves; he has also been the focus of affection and devotion, and, in the Christian cultus, even of worship. We have here, then, an image that is sharp enough, dramatic enough, and attractive enough to serve effectively as the center or focus for orienting personal and communal life; the symbol "God," when represented by this image, is given definite specificity and concreteness.

This does not mean, of course, that the problems of life are solved when one devotes oneself to Jesus (or the God represented by Jesus), nor even that they are lessened. On the contrary, they may become much more difficult, certainly more morally demanding. What devotion to Jesus might mean for life in twentieth-century America is not immediately apparent; nor can we assume that it is easy to give oneself to this figure. But that the image of Jesus lays a powerful demand on those who take him seriously, and what the general character or quality of that demand is—overturning as it does many of our ordinary wants and desires and standards of value—is surely evident. There is little question that this image is capable of inspiring tremendous devotion when it actually orders the lives of individuals and communities. Our first desideratum, then, having to do with the clarity, sharpness, and effectiveness of the image of God when that is understood in terms of the concrete figure of Christ, appears to be adequately met.

This would not be possible were not the second

desideratum in some significant degree also met. For those who respond to the figure of Jesus with affection and devotion there is undoubtedly a powerful sense of the *reality* of what is present and mediated here; something true and valid and very significant for human life comes to vivid focus in him. One may argue, with Nietzsche, Freud, and others, that the overriding emphasis on absolute self-giving love, as it is portrayed in Jesus, is a trap which is really destructive of important dimensions of human life and important human possibilities. Or one may argue, with Luther, that this vision applies only to personal relations and not to the sociopolitical order. Or one may agree with many that we are presented here with a beautiful and heroic but totally impractical ideal, and if we are going to orient ourselves effectively in the real world in which we live, we must adopt other standards and values. Nevertheless, this figure does make some claim upon us—many of us—and in doing so he impresses us with a sense of that claim's significance or validity. The notions of self-giving, of vicarious suffering, of loving one's enemies, however difficult or impractical, do seem to point toward something profoundly true about the human spirit and human relations. We may not want to give them the absoluteness which they appear to have in the image of Jesus, but their powerful appeal means that this image symbolizes and focuses for us something genuine and real about the human and how the human must comport itself. The question is not whether reality is present in this symbol and mediated to us through it, but whether it is *ultimate reality* that comes to us here, whether this is that reality in terms of which life must be oriented if it is to find fulfillment, whether this is God. And that brings us to our third desideratum, which is the crucial one.

However true it may be that Jesus represents a significant—even a magnificent—possibility of human life, by what right could one claim that this is more than just one of the many possible modes of the human, that this is the true or normative or defining image of the human? What justification could be given for holding that the cosmic and evolutionary movement, which has produced and which continues to sustain the human, reveals itself most fully and definitively at just this point? In the older mythic language: why might one hold that here *God* is uniquely revealing Godself?

I have suggested (in Chapter 1) that God, metaphysically viewed, is to be understood as that "cosmic movement" in the ultimate ground of all that is, which expresses itself in the evolutionary-historical process that eventuates in the production of humanity, of humaneness. That is, by "God" we mean our creator, that in which our humanity, and any tensions within us toward a fuller realization of humaneness, are ultimately grounded. The question, then, whether commitment to Jesus is not idolatrous but is directed toward (the true) God—put mythically: whether Jesus is truly God's "revelation"—is really the question whether in Jesus *(a)* we encounter that which properly represents or exemplifies that which is truly or authentically human, and *(b)* we encounter that, devotion to which creates and further enhances genuinely humane order in human life and community.

The answer to these two questions will obviously depend on our conception of Jesus, our conception of what is "truly humane," and our conception of what is required to create or bring about the truly humane. For example, if we take Jesus to be "humble, meek and mild," one who simply sacrifices himself to his enemies, but we believe that overthrow, possibly including violence, of the oppressive powers of evil is required to bring about a humane social order, then devotion to Jesus will not seem of much help in forwarding the historical process through which humanity is created, i.e., it will not bring us into touch with that divine creative power that underlies and is moving us toward authentic human existence. Or, if we take human salvation (fulfillment) to be a supernatural life with

God after death, and regard Jesus as a divine being come down from heaven to attract our devotion and loyalty away from the "things of this world," then committing ourselves to him will have little significance for overcoming the structures of evil and oppression here on earth, will have little to do with establishing a more humane order here. Or again, if we believe that a properly ordered human society is essentially hierarchical, with ordinary folk serving and obeying those with power, wealth, intelligence, and talent who rightly command the elite positions at the top, then devotion to Jesus—who blesses the poor and condemns the rich, who calls publicans and sinners to be his followers and rebukes the "solid citizens" of his time, whose birth is celebrated with a song about putting down "the mighty from their thrones, and exalt[ing] those of low degree" (Luke 1:52)—will hardly be regarded as conducive to bringing about a better ordered human society.

Obviously, there is room for difference of opinion on all these points, and the varieties of Christian theology are witness to the many different interpretations that have been given in the past. My own view of these matters is as follows. First, Jesus is to be seen as one who was essentially self-giving, who taught that we should love both neighbor and enemy, who finally gave himself over to his own enemies without resistance and died on a cross at their hands. Second, the "authentically human" may be seen as reaching its maximum in just this sort of self-sacrificial love for and forgiveness of others, especially if we understand such love, not as simply individual passivity or self-abnegation, but as that self-giving activity which is essential to the creation and sustenance of communities of love and freedom, communities in which, as Paul put it, "there is neither Jew nor Greek, there is neither slave nor free, there is neither male nor female; for you are all one in Christ Jesus" (Gal. 3:28). It is in terms of such communities of genuine equality, freedom, and love, in which each person has his or her own proper place and dignity and none are masters dominating or oppressing the others, that I would define the truly human. Third, such communities will hardly be successfully established through the violent exercise of power attempting to overthrow evil and oppressive structures. Rather, they can be created only through transforming the human spirit so it will no longer be self-aggrandizing—and that means transforming the fundamental communal ethos and institutional structures within which that spirit is nourished, so that these no longer give rise to unmanageable anxieties and so that basic human needs for sustenance and security as well as for love and respect are met. From this point of view Jesus' self-sacrifice and death, giving rise—after his death —to a new community of love and forgiveness and freedom, is a model of the sort of creative action required to transform human situations of hostility, alienation, and evil. Vicarious sacrifice may make possible the birth of new communities of freedom and love among humans— but likely not for those who make the sacrifice: only for future generations are the new possibilities opened up. Violent direct attack on the evils of society only seems to beget more violence and more evil. To break the vicious circle of estrangement and enmity in human affairs, effecting genuine reconciliation, requires radical love and forgiveness and sacrifice, even for and to one's enemies.

I do not mean to suggest here some easy or simplistic answer to all the problems of humankind, that all we need do to solve our massive problems is "love our neighbors and our enemies." I am suggesting, though, that it is in communities of love and freedom and creativity that human fulfillment (salvation) is to be found, and that what is needed, therefore, to forward our humanization are "ministries of reconciliation" (cf. 2 Cor. 5:18), i.e., communities and vocations which are directed toward breaking down the barriers of hatred, enmity, and distrust between   peoples   and   establishing   communication, cooperation, mutual respect, justice, and eventually love. Such a spirit of self-sacrifice, reconciliation, and the building up of community among persons is well exemplified in Jesus' ministry, teachings, and death (if that is not understood as legalistically requiring certain very specific modes of self-denial in every situation), and it is picked up again in the self-understanding of the early church, seeking to express in its own life that "mind . . . which [was] . . . in Christ Jesus, who . . . emptied himself, taking the form of a servant" (Phil. 2:5–7).[13] However much this vision has been compromised or lost, it has remained the norm in terms of which Christians have continued to see authentic human existence and have judged themselves and their world. In our own time of dissension and division and a new awareness of the diversity of human religious, cultural, and political life, it remains a vision of mutual openness and community that is desperately needed.[14]

The claim that we should take the figure of Jesus as a paradigm for understanding both the human and the divine, ourselves and those cosmic and historical forces working toward our humanization, though it may not be fully persuasive, is, when carefully interpreted, at least intelligible. Such a position presents a coherent, meaningful, and in certain respects a compelling, picture of human existence and destiny, and of the human place and task in the world. Obviously, it is not the only picture available; there are other quite different ways, both religious and secular, of understanding human existence and its problems. Buddhist and Hindu, Freudian and Marxist perspectives, for example, can each present convincing cases and should be taken seriously. I have not maintained here that Christian perspectives are the only ones with legitimate claims on our attention or plausible claims to truth; only that they can be given an intelligible interpretation in the light of what we otherwise (believe we) know about our world, about human existence, about the course of evolution and history, about the problems of contemporary life.

They, thus, present a picture of human life and the world which contemporary persons can and should take seriously as they decide to what they will commit themselves, what image(s) or value(s) they will make central in loyalty and devotion, what God(s) they will worship.

There is no compelling proof that an image/concept constructed on the model of Jesus Christ presents the True God, not an idol. But we can see why claims might be made for that assertion. This God combines great powers both to *humanize* us, to transform us into genuinely humane beings, and to *relativize* us, judging our every achievement in the light of a very demanding norm. As I argued above (Chapters 1 and 3) and shall stress again later (Chapters 9 and 10), it is just this power to humanize and to relativize that distinguishes the True God (i.e., what we mean by *God*) from all idols.

Criteria for the truth of God
1) humanize
2) Relativize

It must be recognized, of course, that precisely the moment we claim to worship the True God, we must beware. Such a claim is largely a means of promoting ourselves: that *our* beliefs are the true ones (in contrast with those Freudians and secularists and Hindus), that *our* community is God's elect, that *our* activities are specially guided by the Holy Spirit. Instead of expressing the humanizing and reconciling Spirit at work in history, such a claim manifests an idolatry of our own beliefs and practices. Our lives can be said to be genuinely oriented on Jesus, and on the God who comes to expression in and through Jesus, not when we make grandiose claims, but only when a humanizing and relativizing Spirit actually works through us and our communities, breaking down barriers between humans and building up a universal community of love and freedom and justice.

A claim for truth —

whose faith is judged by openness to other virtues? paradox? No — Rather a corruption of God.

V

It would be possible to go on from here, filling out the Christian categorial scheme—with help from the major

Christian doctrines—into a full world-view. I shall not do that, however. Let me conclude this chapter by summarizing what I have tried to accomplish.

1. I have attempted to show that every conception or doctrine of God will have to draw on some concrete experience(s) or image(s) if it is to avoid being completely formal and abstract, that is, if it is to be able actually to provide a focus for orientation in life. It is important for a critical theology both that this be recognized and that some attempt be made to formulate acceptable criteria for selecting the particular model(s) or paradigm(s) on the basis of which the concept of God is built up.

2. I have suggested here two sets of criteria for theological construction that are implicit in much recent (as well as older) theological work, and which, it seems to me, it is important to make explicit, even though this can be done in only a very preliminary way here. First, coming at the problem from the side of the concrete image(s) or paradigm(s) to be used in constructing the concept of God, I have suggested three desiderata to which we need to attend: *(a)* sharpness and clarity of the focus for devotion and orientation; *(b)* plausibility of the claim that this is a significant reality, not an illusion or mere fabrication of the imagination; *(c)* persuasiveness of the contention that what is present and given here may properly be regarded as metaphysically ultimate, i.e., that this is God, not an idol, that it can give an orientation to human existence which leads to fulfillment of its potential, not to frustration, failure, and finally destruction. Second, coming at the problem from what is intended by the notion of God, I have suggested two criteria to be employed to distinguish the True God from all idolatrous claims: *(a)* that the reality claimed to be God must be that, devotion to which will truly *humanize* us, enable us to come to fulfillment of our human potential; and *(b)* that this reality must at the same time truly *relativize* us, call into check our tendencies toward an-

thropocentrism, hubris, and self-aggrandizement, our tendencies to make ourselves into gods instead of accepting our proper place within the creaturely order. These two sets of criteria are obviously interconnected, but I have made no attempt here to discuss this.

3. Finally, I have attempted to employ these criteria as I briefly sketched the way in which Jesus Christ can be used as the defining model or paradigm in constructing the image/concept of God. This move is complicated, we noted, by the fact that there are many different interpretations of who or what "Jesus Christ" is, and it becomes necessary to develop further criteria to make possible critical and justifiable choice among the several options. I proposed that careful attention to the distinction between mythic and historical elements in the New Testament provides us with a basis for constructing an image of Jesus which can be theologically justified, and I attempted to sketch briefly the outlines of that image and to suggest some of the features which a concept of God constructed with reference to it would have. Other chapters of this book (especially Chapters 1, 4, and 7) amplify in various ways some of the suggestions made at this point.

In sum, in this chapter I have attempted to show briefly why Jesus Christ is still significant for Christian theology and how a contemporary constructive theology might proceed in its reflection on Jesus. As I have suggested, a full christology—that is, a full interpretation of the normatively human and the paradigm of the divine—would need to go considerably beyond such reflection on the figure of the individual Jesus to elaboration of a picture or conception of human community. The historical roots for such an understanding are to be found in the early Christian church and its vision of communal existence. Any full interpretation of "the Christ-event" would need to undertake a much fuller examination and assessment of these than has been possible in this chapter.

6/Evil and Salvation:
An Anthropological Approach

Every theological position must deal with the questions of evil and salvation. It could be maintained, in fact, that these are the central issues in human life which generate the religious consciousness and which every religious position seeks to address. If we wish to develop a critical and carefully constructed theology, it is important, therefore, that we consider how our notions of evil and salvation are built up and what justification might be offered for holding them. In the following remarks I offer some reflections on the concepts of evil and salvation, followed by a proposal of the sort of theological anthropology which could provide foundations for developing a contemporary Christian interpretation of these matters.

I

In considering our consciousness of such broad yet central theological issues, we should take care to distinguish the conceptual and interpretive images and frameworks which we employ from the raw existential and experiential data to which they give form and meaning. It is of course never possible to disentangle these dimensions of experience completely—even such designations as "evil" and "salvation" are already complex interpretations of something much more primitive experientially—but if we are to be alert to the way in which our linguistic and religious traditions are shaping our apprehensions of these matters, we must at least attempt to address the issue as sensitively and critically as we can. This is especially important with the questions of evil and salvation, because here, presumably, we are attempting to formulate, on the one hand, something close to the root or core of the human predicament, and, on the other, the "way out" of or the solution to this problem. Since we are trying to get at what is universally true of human existence, it is especially important that we not too quickly or naively buy into the linguistic and conceptual apparatus supplied by our own (doubtlessly somewhat parochial) religious and philosophical tradition. Though there is no way for us to jump out of our own skins, it is well that we try, so far as possible, to discern just what sorts of skins we have.

I shall begin with the conceptual and interpretive aspect of this problem simply because it is impossible to begin anywhere else—there is no way for us to consider or discuss these matters without doing so in and with some concepts and terms. The terms we are examining here, "evil" and "salvation," fall within, and gain their specific meaning in relationship to, configurations of other similar terms, such as "pain," "suffering," "sin," "destruction," "despair," "guilt," "disease," "catastrophe," "horror," and the like, on the one hand; and "fulfillment," "meaningfulness," "redemption," "joy," "peace," "happiness," "hope," "health," "ecstasy," "beauty," "goodness," and "God," on the other. An adequate analysis of what is meant by "evil" and "salvation" would require careful mapping of the interrelations and interdependence of these various terms with each other and with other similar concepts, enabling us to come to a clearer understanding of the structure of this region of our common language. It would be useful to compare this mapping with similar mappings of terms and concepts drawn from other religious and linguistic traditions, for only in this way can we become aware of the hidden limitations and biases of the tradition within which we are working and become open to other possibilities of experience and consciousness which might decisively illuminate and transform our problems. None of this, however, can be done within the compass of these brief remarks, even had I the competence to do it.

I shall limit myself, then, to some general characterizations. First, it is to be observed that, with reference to the human, one of the configurations noted above is positive, the other negative. Human disaster or failure and human well-being and fulfillment seem to be the points of reference in terms of which the configurations surrounding "evil" and "salvation" first get generated: thus the framework of such valuation is, initially at least, anthropocentric. (One wonders whether it could be otherwise: since all these terms are *our* terms, generated in response to problems *we* face to enable us better to deal with our world and our experience, is it not inevitable that our most primitive or foundational valuations would be in terms of what fulfills or what frustrates our human existence and its projects?) The acts of generalization involved in developing these complexes of terms, however, move toward transcendence of their anthropocentric beginning points. "Health" and "beauty" as well as "pain" and "disease" and "catastrophe" may be applied quite as well to other beings than human; and with the conception of "God"—though "God" means initially, perhaps, that reality which is ultimately salvific of the human—there is clearly an attempt to gain a point of reference entirely objective to the human, a point of reference in terms of which all else (including the human) can be assessed and judged. Thus, in a theistic scheme evil ultimately is defined with reference to God's will and judgment, not ours, and our originally anthropocentric apprehension of evil must be reconstructed in the light of what we take God to require. Similarly with "salvation": though this doubtless was originally a largely anthropocentric conception, defined by what *we* would recognize as fulfilling or salvific, in a radically monotheistic world-view it is God alone who knows and determines what is truly saving of the human, and this may go counter to our own instincts, perceptions, and desires. The notions of evil and salvation which we in the West have inherited have been shaped decisively by monotheistic religious traditions. It is important that we be critically aware of the way in which this colors our perceptions and interpretations.

I am suggesting here that, although the primitive experiences out of which language about evil and salvation developed must have been largely anthropocentric, because of conceptual developments in our language and religion—the generating of an increasingly wider and more general conceptual framework or world-view, particularly as centered in "God"—this anthropocentrism was gradually overcome. The movement toward the transcendence of anthropocentrism was, thus, largely *conceptual* in character, and it becomes an exceedingly interesting question why and how such conceptual developments occurred and can occur. It would be useful to see what sort of analogous conceptual developments occurred and occur in other religious traditions.

Although sketchy, this discussion makes increasingly insistent the question of the existential elements underlying these conceptual developments. Since there is no way to abstract completely from all interpretive concepts, it is very difficult to address this issue. What seems to be called for is a movement in the opposite direction from the one of increasing generality and objectivity sketched above. If that is correct, I suggest that the existential root of the experience of "evil" lies in the organism's feeling of *pain*, a feeling that (unlike all the other modes of negative consciousness mentioned above) does not necessarily include a conceptual element—though for most instances of higher-level (human) consciousness, some conceptual dimensions would almost certainly be present. The feeling

of pain is the mode in which a threat of danger or destruction most primitively impresses itself on an organism; I
suggest that it is this sensing of potential destruction, and
then the awareness of power(s) capable of and bent on
such destruction, that is the germ of the concept of evil.
Thus, there appear to be at least three emergent levels of
awareness, each built upon the preceding, underlying the
consciousness of "evil": awareness of pain, of the danger
of destruction, of powers working such destruction. Consciousness of salvation would seem to be a reactive or
second-order consciousness involving one or more of these
three levels: it is an awareness of being rescued from pain,
from the danger of destruction, and from those powers
which are bringing about such destruction.

In the religious consciousness of evil and of salvation
these primitive roots may, of course, be generalized and
objectified to the point where—as in a radical monotheism
—the original awareness of evil as bound up with one's
own pain and destruction is completely concealed or even
reversed (cf. the Calvinist triumphant willingness to be
"damned for the glory of God"). Such is the power of an
effective symbolical and conceptual frame. When this happens, contradictory moments and tensions become incor-
porated into the very heart of the notions of evil and of
salvation, and they develop an internal dynamic pushing
toward greater and greater depths. In this way these notions, although often in a highly paradoxical fashion, become vehicles of profound religious and human insight
(e.g., in concepts of the significance of ordinary suffering,
of vicarious suffering, of self-sacrifice, of martyrdom, and
the like). Obviously the Christian consciousness has drunk
deeply from this well.

It would seem, then, that the conceptual elements in
the consciousness of evil and salvation are more important
to theological construction than the existential ones, for
they determine how the existential data will be understood and interpreted, even how they will be "ex-

perienced." If that is the case, then an outstanding question for any theological approach to such questions will be how or why certain conceptual frameworks or configurations of symbols are to be preferred to others. It will not do, in seeking to answer that question, to say simply that they better or more accurately reflect or interpret experience: for it is just the question of the grounds for claiming this that is at issue. We need to move "below" the level of experience to the question of the human nature that is doing the experiencing, if we are to be able to address this issue. That is, we have to develop a theological anthropology. I wish now to suggest how this question can be approached.

II

Doctrines of evil and salvation present beliefs or assertions about some kind of rescue from "bondage" or healing of "disease" on the one hand, and/or about human fulfillment or realization on the other. Neither of these can be stated clearly apart from an understanding of what the human is. The negative notions of bondage and sickness gain their meaning by dialectical contrast with positive conceptions of freedom and health; the positive notions of realization and fulfillment presuppose some understanding of the range of human possibilities, as well as a normative conception of those configurations of possibilities that distort or skew human being in contrast with those which complete or satisfy its inner tendencies, needs, and capacities. A theological interpretation of evil and salvation, then, can be developed only in terms of a conception of the human which grasps and articulates human possibilities and problems as we experience and understand them today. How can we begin to focus on such wide-ranging issues?

Any satisfactory contemporary approach to these questions will need to take account, on the one hand, of the full

significance of the plurality of religious and cultural traditions of which we are conscious today, and, on the other,
of modern philosophical, biological, and social scientific
theories of the human; it cannot, therefore, be simply a
direct extension of traditional views and concepts.

Modern historical and comparative-religion studies reveal human religiousness, including Christian religiousness, to have developed in a variety of ways in different
parts of the world. Each of the great religious and cultural
traditions has gradually come to define certain human capacities as normative, and has developed techniques of
training and education which help inculcate and heighten
these capacities while at the same time devaluing and
diminishing others. In consequence, in the different traditions we see spread before us a panorama of ways of being
human and of understandings of the human. In addition,
within each tradition there have been vast differences
between the roles played and self-understandings held by
persons of different races, classes, and genders. The various Christian claims and styles of life must be understood
within the context of this great variety of patterns.

Our modern awareness that Christian patterns, like all
the others, are socially and historically relative in many
respects, together with our recognition that other traditions and viewpoints have achieved insights into and possibilities of the human overlooked or denigrated in Western Christian reflection, requires us to work out a
theological anthropology in broader and more comprehensive terms than our tradition had envisioned. It was
never supposed, of course, that such notions as "reason" or
"freedom," *"imago Dei"* or "sin," applied only to Christians; they were appropriate designations for all human
beings. Nevertheless, they were inevitably understood in
terms of Western Christian experience and were so
defined and interpreted. We can now see that these notions are themselves historically relative and may or may
not be adequate for understanding the variegated experi-

ence—and thus the capacities and possibilities—of all
human beings. That question must be left open, as we
attempt to take seriously the ways in which other traditions and perspectives have defined and understood our
human nature and condition. We do not know as yet in
what respects or to what degree traditional Christian notions will need to be modified as we take account of insights drawn from other points of view. For this reason an
adequate contemporary Christian conception of the
human must build into itself an openness to unfamiliar
experiences and conceptions and be willing to be self-
critical at any and every point. Such an anthropology obviously cannot be developed in simple extension or extrapolation of traditional concepts. It will require a "stepping
back" from those concepts to a "meta-position" which will
allow examination and assessment of traditional Christian
metaphors, images, and notions alongside others which
seem to merit close scrutiny and possible adoption.

I think that the theological anthropology which we need
here can be developed in terms of the conception of humans as essentially *historical* or *sociocultural* beings.
Many modern studies—for example, anthropological studies of the varieties of human life and culture, contemporary psychological and sociological studies of the sociocultural nature of selfhood, philosophical reflection on the
power of language and symbolism to give form to our
experience and to define our very perceptions, work in
modern genetics and sociobiology, and new discoveries
about the chemical foundations of human consciousness
and experience (in both their ordinary and extraordinary
ranges)—seem to be converging toward an understanding
of the human as a peculiar animal so biologically "unfin-
ished" at birth as to require the imposition of elaborate
artificial cultural patterns if it is to be viable. Such a conception of the human as biologically founded and yet open
to far-reaching cultural and historical development is able
to interpret the variety, differentiation, and complexity

which human existence has come to have around the globe. Moreover, through its emphasis on the way in which cultures develop historically, it can give an account of how the several great cultural and religious traditions emerged and grew to their present character and proportions. In this conception, then, we have an understanding of the human which does justice to the historical and scientific facts as we know them today and at the same time provides a meta-position from which the development of the various religious and philosophical claims about the human can be grasped and evaluated.

It must be acknowledged, of course, that this sort of interpretation of humans, as essentially sociocultural or historical animals, itself grew up in the West and owes much to Jewish and Christian traditions. However, it is no simple extrapolation of traditional claims. On the contrary, it represents a meta-position beyond those claims precisely because *(a)* it attempts to take full account of (and to give a full account of) the claims of other traditions and viewpoints as well as those of Western religion, including social scientific and biological studies that bear on our understanding of the human, and *(b)* it provides a standpoint from which traditional Western religious and philosophical claims about the human can themselves be criticized and assessed.

No doubt representatives of other faiths and traditions and points of view would not regard such a conception as neutral or unbiased; they might, therefore, wish to call it into question in various ways and propose alternative meta-notions of their own. That is, of course, their right and their responsibility. Such moves by others could only help to advance the effort to work out a truly universal conception of the human, an effort that is gradually emerging today as the several great cultures and civilizations converge toward one interconnected worldwide humanity. Pending the development of any real consensus on these matters, however, it is important to press forward with such provisional concepts and hypotheses as are available to us, always remaining open to criticism and correction by advocates of other positions. In my view the modern Western conception of humans as sociocultural or historical beings provides the most promising base at present on which to develop a comprehensive understanding of human existence.

III

We are now in a position to see why the question of salvation arises for humans. As living organisms—animals —humans are in continuous interaction with their environment in pursuit of certain necessities without which they would cease to exist; the threat of destruction always hangs over them. The most elemental of human needs are biological, and physical pain signals biological need. But, as we have noted, humans are as much sociocultural beings as they are biological, and our consciousness is structured and stocked by language, acquired in social interaction. Accordingly, most of our felt needs are culturally defined and culturally relative. Even needs directly rooted in our biological makeup, for example for food, always come to consciousness in a culturally defined form: we hunger for steak and ice cream but are repelled by items that in another culture may be regarded as delicacies. The conceptions of evil and of salvation, then, for a sociocultural animal—i.e., conceptions of that which most fundamentally threatens human existence and that which overcomes the threat—have double roots, biological and cultural.

The understanding of the human which comes to dominate a culture defines which needs should be met and how they should be met; thus distinctive value preferences develop and eventually are given institutional and ideological expression. "Evil" is understood as that which goes counter to or threatens the most fundamental value confi-

gurations; "salvation" is that which makes possible escape
from or overcoming the powers of evil. Although rooted
biologically in the striving of the organism to maintain
itself in a threatening world, evil and salvation—by the
time they become ingredients in a religious consciousness
—have developed an integrity and almost autonomous
meaning of their own, as I suggested above. In many religious schemes, in fact, biological survival is no longer a
primary value; rather, "devotion to God," "loyalty to the
community," "love of neighbor," "devotion to truth,"
"keeping the faith," come to be of central significance for
most humans, and they are willing to sacrifice their lives,
if need be, for such "spiritual values." The double-sided
makeup of human nature allows for a wide range of possible conceptions both of evil and of salvation, and in consequence a great variety of religious and moral orientations
have appeared in the course of human history. Doubtless
such value orientations contribute in many ways toward
the enhancement of human life and the preservation of
human communities—indeed, they define the distinctively human as over against the merely animal—but in
some extreme forms they may also be disruptive of human
community and destructive of the biological basis of
human existence.

These facts put us into a position to move our anthropological reflections from descriptive to normative concerns.
The understanding of the human which I am sketching
here defines it most fundamentally by its power to transform and transcend its prior animality through creating
those complexes of symbols and institutions, values and
ideologies, which we call cultures. For this view the well-
being of humanity depends absolutely on the enhancement of the sociopsychological activities and processes
and institutions which promote such creativity for all humans. This suggests a normative principle which can be
used in assessing the diverse views of evil and salvation
which have appeared in history: whatever tends to en-

hance and strengthen those culture-creating processes
through which our original animality is transformed into
humanity is good; whatever tends to corrupt, block, or
destroy these processes of humanization—for any human
beings, regardless of race, class, or sex—is evil; whatever
rescues us from or otherwise overcomes such evil processes, powers, or events is salvific.

We have a principle here—let us call it the criterion of
humanization—by means of which the most diverse aspects of human life and culture may be assessed: family
patterns and child-rearing practices; social institutions and
class structures; methods of socialization and processes of
social interaction; patterns and conceptions of community
and of individuality; political and economic and educational institutions and practices; scientific and technological developments and institutions; moral and religious values, institutions, and ideologies. Every dimension of social,
cultural, and personal life has its direct or indirect effects,
positive or negative, on the processes of humanization.
Doubtless we still know very little about these matters, but
relevant wisdom is to be found in all the great religious
traditions as well as in modern secular humanism (as
represented by such figures as Marx, Nietzsche, Freud,
Dewey, Piaget, and others).

Though the criterion of humanization, and thus of authentic human existence, solves no problems in itself, it
provides a critical perspective for assessing the claims of
the several religious and secular traditions and enables
clearer perceptions of the major human problems to
which we must address ourselves. It is a criterion already
accepted and used in many circles. In contemporary
Christian thought, for example, the criticism of traditional
Christian institutions, beliefs, and practices by liberation
theologians (whether black, female, or "third world") is
based largely on what I am here calling the criterion of
humanization. But interest in this criterion is in no way
limited to Christians: the worldwide demand for more

humane social institutions, for greater economic justice and equality, for liberation from every sort of oppression, is evidence of an emerging consciousness of the criterion of humanization in many different settings.

This criterion can be understood as a secularization and universalization of certain fundamental Judeo-Christian themes. The goodness of creation as a whole and specifically of human existence, the significance of history and of what transpires within history, the importance of human communal existence and of just social institutions, a high valuation on morally responsible selfhood and on such virtues as mercy, forgiveness, love, faithfulness, and the like —these all have been central emphases of Jewish and Christian faith. They have led to forms of community and selfhood, and to institutions and ideologies, which have regarded human historical existence as of central importance, as something, therefore, for which humans must take full responsibility. "God"—the ultimate point of reference for these traditions and the ultimate ground of all legitimation—was understood to be the creator of the world and of these human physical selves which inhabit it, and God was also believed to be continuously involved with worldly history, moving it toward a consummation of perfect justice and freedom. The serious concern with human social institutions, with possibilities of realization for every individual, and with the quality of interpersonal relations, to which the criterion of humanization directs us, can thus be seen as representing a configuration of valuations very similar to, if not derived from, the Judeo-Christian understanding of human life in the world and of the ultimate reality on which human existence is to be oriented. Jewish and Christian talk about ultimate reality as "God" expresses a belief that both the striving of all persons toward genuine humanization, and those worldly processes which promote and enhance that humanization, have an ultimate metaphysical foundation, i.e., a foundation in that Reality which grounds all that is (see Chapter

1). And the Christian affirmation that "Christ" is at once "true humanity" and "true divinity" expresses a belief that the paradigmatically human has appeared in history, and thus we have an image both of what is genuinely humanizing and also of that which ultimately grounds our humanization (God)—the image of Jesus (see Chapter 5). It is the task of Christian theology to show that and how these central symbols of Christian faith—"God" as revealed in or defined by "Jesus Christ"—are still important today, or even indispensable, for specifying and clarifying what humanization is and, thus, where our true salvation is to be found.

Of course one can be committed to the criterion of humanization without accepting these claims about Jesus and about God; there are other forms of humanism than Christian. But the Christian claim about what is normatively human and thus truly humanizing is surely one that all who have a serious interest in these matters should consider.

IV

These brief remarks are far from constituting a Christian theological view of evil and salvation, but they do sketch what seems to me a promising approach to this question. To work out this approach in detail, one would need to explore the relevance and richness of a number of important traditional Christian notions not explicated here, for example, "vicarious suffering" and "original sin," the theories of Christ's "person" and "work," certain eschatological themes and images, and so on. One would expect these Christian concepts and perspectives to bring to light issues and insights not otherwise visible to our anthropological analysis and construction. However, since the traditional Christian theories and concepts do not formulate matters directly in terms of the notion of humanization, they would doubtless need to be reconceived in important ways.

The approach sketched here makes it possible to keep theological reflection on human existence and salvation open to conversation with and insights from other religious and secular traditions and viewpoints, and brings it into close connection with the understanding of the human that is developing in the modern social sciences, history, and biology. Thus, it takes account of major extra-Christian dimensions of our modern consciousness and experience of the human, even while shaping its principal claims about the human, about salvation, and about God in terms of central Christian emphases. It suggests a way, therefore, that—as one sought to work the fourfold Christian categorial scheme into a full contemporary theological interpretation of life and its problems—the category of the human might be developed.

The human as category among the 4.

7 / Christian Theology and the Modernization of the Religions

From the very beginning Christians were so impressed by the power and significance of salvation through Jesus Christ that they were led to make highly exclusivistic claims: ". . . there is salvation in no one else [than Jesus Christ], for there is no other name under heaven given among men by which we must be saved" (Acts 4:12); ". . . no one knows the Father except the Son and any one to whom the Son chooses to reveal him" (Matt. 11:27); "I am the way, and the truth, and the life; no one comes to the Father, but by me" (John 14:6). The implication was that saving truth was known to Christians alone, and the church was not long in drawing the conclusion that "outside the church there is no salvation" (Cyprian). The problem of the "righteous pagan" has always been recognized in the church, of course, but such individuals have usually been understood more as exceptions that proved the general rule. The possibility that other religions, communions, or traditions have access to saving truth was hardly given serious consideration through most of the church's history.

First published in *Bangalore Theological Forum* (1976), 8: 81–118. I am indebted to M. M. Thomas' little book, *Man and the Universe of Faiths* (Bangalore: Christian Institute for the Study of Religion and Society, 1975), for some of the fundamental insights without which the position set forth in this essay could not have been developed.

Even Judaism, from whom Christians received both their fundamental understanding of God and also their first scriptures, was believed to have forfeited its special place in God's economy through rejecting God's Messiah. In Christian faith alone was genuine salvation for humans to be found.

Through much of its history the church has been able to maintain variations of this exclusivistic position, and Christian theology has confidently regarded itself as resting on the absolutely secure foundation of God's special revelation, a foundation unavailable to any other religious tradition. But during the past two centuries a steadily increasing pressure from the other great world religions has been felt by Christian theologians. As non-Western cultures became better known, and it was discovered that profound conceptions of human life were harbored within very different religious traditions, it no longer seemed plausible to regard other religions as totally and completely in error. How, then, was their truth to be understood? How could the finality of salvation through Christ, and of Christian truth, be preserved if it were admitted that other religious orientations knowing nothing of Christ also knew a significant salvation and truth?

A number of approaches to this question have been suggested, none of them entirely satisfactory. Perhaps the most widely accepted view—with origins going back at least to the second century and variations formulated by such leading and diverse modern figures as Hegel, Schleiermacher, and Barth—is the contention that final religious truth lies only within Christian faith, but approximations to or preparations for that truth are found in varying degrees in other religions. This has the advantage of saving the absoluteness or finality of Christian claims, while at the same time acknowledging a certain validity to other religious perspectives. But it is an intrinsically unstable position. Exposure to the subtlety and sophistication of religious reflection in, for example, Hinduism or Buddhism, makes very pressing the question whether the Christian claim to ultimate superiority over others is not simply special pleading. Moreover, when one examines carefully the interpretation of human life and its fulfillment provided in these other traditions, it becomes increasingly difficult to understand in what sense they really are approximations to the Christian position; instead they seem to express significantly different conceptions of the human condition and its salvation, conceptions which, in their profoundest formulations, seem to be radical alternatives to Christian faith more than a direct preparation for it.

The outcome of this perception is often some version of religious relativism, such as that formulated by Ernst Troeltsch. According to Troeltsch, the great religions each express the profound and lasting insights into human life and its meaning which have come to light in a particular cultural tradition; each, therefore, is appropriate to its own culture, but none can claim finality for all of humankind. Christianity expresses and communicates that truth which is ultimate and saving for Westerners, but it has no right, any longer, to claim that it is the mediator of religious truth for all humanity. We live in a culturally pluralistic world, and only a diversity of religious orientations can be fully appropriate to that fact.

This solution to the problem has not proved much more satisfactory than the other. Not only did it deny the proud claims of Christian faith; it went so far as to despair of an ultimate unity of religious truth—and this raised very pressing questions about whether the religions could any longer legitimately claim that *truth* was that with which they were most fundamentally concerned. Thus, relativistic acid ate away at one of the deepest and most precious religious contentions, and in this way further weakened the authority of religion—all forms of religion—in what was already a rising tide of secularism and skepticism.

Is there not some way to acknowledge the cultural relativity of each religious tradition, but still maintain that in and through the great religions ultimate truth is to be found? Could one not hold that each of the religions represents but a partial and relative insight into the ultimate reality and truth for which all are reaching but which none successfully or adequately formulates? A third position maintains that each of the great religions in its own way is attempting to express and cultivate a taste for "transcendence" or the "absolute," for the "infinite" or "God"; rejecting the exclusivistic and imperialistic claims of each, we can and we must learn from them all. On this view, religious relativism does not prove the falsity of the religious enterprise, as skeptical secularism claims; rather, it demonstrates the real magnificence and profundity of the religious quest for an ultimate that always finally escapes us. Humanity is deeply religious in its very nature, and it is in religious fulfillment that true human fulfillment lies. Although this position seems to have its roots in Hinduism, especially as articulated by such writers as Vivekananda and Radhakrishnan, it appears to be increasingly appealing to Christian writers, particularly those, like W. C. Smith and John Hick, who are especially concerned about the rising tide of secularism in the modern world. This position, of course, implicitly gives up all claims to the finality or definitiveness of specifically Christian faith.

All these positions, it seems to me, suffer from a common defect: they attempt to resolve an essentially *historical* issue—the problem of properly understanding the claims and tensions and interrelations of various religious faiths with each other—in static or structural, instead of dynamic, terms. In so doing they implicitly presuppose that history has already come to its end, at least as far as the problem of the relation of the various religious faiths to each other is concerned, and that it is possible, therefore, to see *now in the present* what the proper and permanent structure of those relationships is. Whether the claim is that Christian faith is the realization or fulfillment of that to which the other religions are only approximations, or that each religion is to be understood as essentially a function of and thus relative to a particular culture, or that humanity is essentially religious in nature and all religion, therefore, is reaching for a transcendent reality which escapes every tradition, the approach is the same: each of these theories presents us with an interpretation which claims (at least implicitly) to lay bare the permanent and essential structure of human religiousness, and possibly of human nature. But if human existence is essentially historical, and religion, like human nature itself, emerges only gradually in history and changes continuously in history, it is a mistake to look for any such permanent structural solution to the problem of the relations of the various religions to each other. Rather, our attempts at understanding here—whether philosophical or theological, secular or religious—should be historical in character, in keeping with the reality and the problems which we are seeking to grasp. That is, we should see the tensions and the interrelations of the various religions (including, of course, Christianity) as a historical development—a process in which the issues are not always the same and the relationships not always constant—a development which has come to a certain focus in the modern period and which can be expected to move in new ways in the future.

Our task of understanding is to lay hold as well as we can on the direction and the nature of this movement into the future. As with any massive historical development, the attempt to understand what is going on in the present involves some conception of the direction in which the movement is going and thus some conjecture about the future which the whole process seems to be approaching. All understanding of present historical realities is in this sense predictive or prophetic in character—perhaps even eschatological, so far as there is a claim or a hope that genuine or true understanding of what is happening is to be attained—and it is a mistake to think that pure empirical or phenomenological description of historical realities is sufficient, or even a real possibility. If it is true that the great religious traditions are historical realities, and that their encounter and struggle with each other is also historical, then it is surely a mistake in principle to attempt to grasp this encounter in static-structural terms, as in all the approaches mentioned above. Rather, we must attempt to grasp the dynamic of the historical movement in which these faiths are involved; if we are attempting to develop a theology of religious pluralism, we shall have to try to interpret and understand precisely that movement theologically.

The premise

I

What constitutes a theological interpretation of a historical movement? How is a theological interpretation to be distinguished from some other sort of interpretation, say, a "philosophical" one, or simply a "historical" interpretation? Is there any justification for going beyond a strictly historical analysis and projection to a theological interpretation of the matter?

One answer to these questions would be to hold that a theological interpretation of something is prepared for a specific group of persons, for example, Christians: it is an interpretation of the pertinent facts in terms of basic Christian beliefs. The purpose of theological interpretation, from this point of view, would be to show what the facts under consideration mean from a Christian point of view, as well as how Christian beliefs are illuminated by those facts. Since many people have Christian commitments, theology would be performing a service by helping to make intelligible to those persons the present historical encounter of the great religions.

This conception of theology and its purposes is certainly not to be despised, but it has some limitations. In the first place, it makes theology into a parochial discipline, an activity of interest only to Christians. Any claims of theology to be dealing with matters of universal human concern or with general human truth seem to be implicitly given up, and this cuts the intellectual nerve which gives life to the theological enterprise. Secondly, to regard theology as largely an exposition of the beliefs of Christians or some other particular group, and the application of those beliefs to a special set of problems or a particular situation, is to assume that the beliefs of religious groups are relatively fixed and stable, that they are readily ascertainable, and, above all, that they are not themselves to be subjected to critical appraisal and reconstruction but are simply to be accepted as the basis for the "theological interpretation." Certainly it is possible to proceed in this fashion, but doing so only further compromises the intellectual character of theology.

However important it may be for religious groups like the Christian churches to engage in interpretive and indoctrinative work of the sort I have just been describing, this is not the conception of theology with which I wish to approach the problem of the present encounter of the great religions. It is, I believe, an approach that the present movement of religious history is rendering out of date and misconceived. For it seems to take for granted that religious groupings today are fairly stable and easily definable, and that they hold to static and fixed bodies of belief which can be readily ascertained. But none of these assumptions is true at the present time, certainly not for the Christian churches. If anything is clear, it is that there is little agreement about what Christian faith involves today and what constitutes proper Christian belief. It might be possible—though difficult—to come to some agreement, through careful historical study, on what defined the several major branches of Christianity in the past, at least in some periods of the past; but almost all such patterns and conceptions are under strong attack in one quarter or another today. Of course, it is always possible to regard some practices and beliefs out of the past as "normatively Christian," and to insist that any deviation from these is a movement away from Christian faith—and every religiously conservative party makes just such a claim—but it is clear that all such contentions are in the last analysis simply arbitrary preferences. Who is to decide what is the "classical" or "normative" form of Christian faith or the Christian church? Why should any particular decision of that sort be acknowledged as authoritative and binding? If anything characterizes the present situation, it is the breakdown of all such authoritative claims about the true nature of Christian faith and the Christian church; even in Roman Catholicism, which had gone the farthest among the Christian churches in clearly specifying how the church and the church's faith may be definitively ascertained and defined, the authority of the magisterium seems to be decisively broken and Catholic priests and laity everywhere are "making up their own minds" about what they believe and what they shall do.

Conservatives in every Christian body may still wish to maintain that it is possible and necessary to give an authoritative and binding definition of Christian beliefs and praxis, and that theologians should proceed on that basis, but such a position is a kind of romanticism about how things used to be. History has moved the Christian faith beyond that sort of possibility, willy-nilly, and any theology alert to its own historical situation can no longer proceed on such an assumption. Theology has been cut loose from what seemed to earlier generations to be its secure moorings, to fend for itself in a rapidly changing world. Theology—and that means each theologian in his or her work—can no longer take it for granted that there is a fixed body of belief which is simply to be interpreted and explained. On the contrary, the central task of theology in the present situation is to ascertain just what beliefs or concepts inherited from the tradition are still viable, and to determine in what ways they should be reconstructed so that they will continue to serve human intellectual and religious needs. Thus, to do their work properly today, theologians must estimate what is in fact going on in the world, what directions the history of the churches and the history of religious reflection are moving, and must seek to make their work relevant to and appropriate for that movement. Theology can no longer look simply to authoritative or normative decisions or situations in the past for its principal guidance; it must orient itself toward that future into which we are rapidly moving, a future which is open and indeterminate in many respects.

How shall we proceed in our attempt to attain a standpoint from which to give a theological interpretation of the present encounters and movements of the world's religions? If everything is in question, where do we gain a footing? As I have suggested, any proposed foundation will rest more on an estimate of what is going to happen in the future than what has proved immovable in the past. Of course all our conjectures about the future will be rooted in experience and wisdom gained in the past. Moreover, it is on the basis of what has been going on, and what we believe to be going on now, that we estimate what will go on in the future. So it would be foolish to attempt to cut ourselves completely loose from that past out of which we have come. Rather, we must guess, as well as we can, what trends and tendencies in the present historical turbulence are a clue to the future, and attempt to develop a theological position that will make sense of and be founded on the significance of those developments.

When making a journey through difficult and uncharted territories, one ought to travel light, taking along only essentials which will be needed on the journey. What are the theological essentials? What theological concepts or doctrines have such usefulness and importance to our movement into an open and unknown future that—in the light of our present understanding of things—we dare not leave them behind? There will be no unanimity, of course, in the answers to these questions; here I can only give my own assessment of the situation in the hope that it will be illuminating also for others. It seems to me that, as we have been propelled with greater and greater rapidity into an uncertain future, humans everywhere have increasingly raised the question whether it is a genuinely humane world that we are producing. We are worried about contamination of the environment in which we live; we are concerned about the terrible human misery in which large portions of humanity are presently living; we are haunted by the specter of mass starvation if population growth cannot be satisfactorily controlled; we wonder whether the basic necessities for a decent human life can be attained for the larger part of humanity without such a rigidly planned social and economic order as to destroy individual rights and liberties; we fear that the clash of ideologies in the world today, all of which claim to have as their deepest concern human and humane values—or even just a kind of unseemly accident or happenstance—may lead to a nuclear holocaust where everything is lost; we sympathize with the desires of oppressed and underprivileged people of all sorts and descriptions to gain new freedoms, to take full responsibility for themselves and their lives, and to become genuinely self-determining, and yet we who enjoy such privileges fear the massive social and political and economic revolutions that such changes must inevitably bring. Throughout the world there appears to be a growing passion to reconstruct the present order into one more truly humane. That is the great aspiration of our time—underlying much of the unrest in our world—whether we are Christians or Buddhists, Americans or members of the so-called third world, communists or adherents to Western-style democracy. How shall we build a new and more humane world for all of the peoples of the world? That is our most important question.

With this focus and aspiration as our point of departure, let us consider the function of theological beliefs and conceptions. What role or task do, or can, such beliefs have in the search for a new human order? Do some theological concepts or doctrines have such usefulness or importance for our movement into an open and unknown future that we dare not leave them behind? Can the worldwide struggle for a more humane society provide us with a criterion for doing theological work today?

Before trying to answer those questions, let me make explicit what is involved in this approach to the theological task. This approach involves a frank acknowledgment that religious believing and theological analysis and reflection are *human* activities, engaged in for human reasons to achieve certain human ends. This may seem obvious enough when so baldly stated, but it has seldom guided the self-understanding of theologians in the past as they went about their work. For the better part of its history Christian theology has understood itself to be presenting the truth about God and humanity and the world, whatever might be the uses of that truth. No doubt it was taken for granted that this truth had important—indeed indispensable—uses for humans: it was the truth about our actual human nature and our ultimate human destiny; it was the truth indispensable to our eternal salvation. Without question the truth with which theology was concerned had an ultimate utility and significance. Yet this traditional understanding of theology articulates a considerably different approach than that of my proposal that theological beliefs and reflection should serve the aspiration for a new and more humane order. The difference can be put this way: instead of *theological claims* about some extraworldly or ultimate "salvation" being made the criterion of what we should believe and practice in this world, I am proposing that what is necessary or required to build a humane order in this world should be made the criterion for assessing our theological beliefs and for determining the character of the theological task. Theology is done by living human beings in this present world, and it should serve their lives and their aspirations. Only such a theology can be justified in the present human crisis and massive human striving. To the extent, then, that theology serves and facilitates our further humanization, it has an important task in the present juncture of history; to the extent that it distracts us from this massive effort for a more humane order, by talk of another world and of other realities that are more important than addressing the issues faced in the present worldwide historical crisis, theological beliefs and theological reflection are not worthy of our serious attention.

Such a humanistic and this-worldly criterion for theological work will seem much too nearsighted and restrictive to many. If theologians give up their longer view of what is happening to humanity—a view that takes into account and is focused by our eternal destiny—have we not lost the ultimate reference point for deciding what we shall do here and now? Are we not left in the flux and turmoil of conflicting relativities in which there is no ultimately guiding beacon? Yes, that is indeed the case. But is not that just our actual present situation? Is not just this ultimate uncertainty the meaning of the breakdown of all authoritative conceptions and norms which we earlier noted? In the past, church and Bible and tradition enjoyed a special authoritativeness for Christian belief and theology because they were assumed to hold within themselves, in some sense or in some way, the ultimate truth for humankind and for salvation. The breakdown of the authority and the normativeness in Christian beliefs and institutions, which we earlier noted, signals a growing doubt about these claims to truth and claims about what is of ultimate importance to humanity, and a growing conviction that we ought to order our lives in terms of the problems that face us here and now in this world, rather than in terms of some alleged otherworldly destiny. It is certainly possible to deplore this widespread change of orientation in human consciousness, and it is possible to refuse to accept it as a basis for theological work, to insist that Christian theology must remain oriented, as it was in the past, on a relatively stable structure of beliefs and in the service of an institution believed to be clearly defined and divinely ordained. But such an orientation on, and definition in terms of, the past, we have already rejected for our purposes here. Theology must be done in terms of the awareness that that past is slipping away and we are rapidly moving into a new and quite different future. For such a theology the old benchmarks are gone—or are rapidly disappearing—and it becomes necessary to steer our course in terms of such insights and understanding of human needs and human values as we can discern and formulate here and now. This is a fearful and frightening task, but there seems no other course open to us, if we forthrightly acknowledge what seems to be happening in ourselves and our world. The central problem facing the present generation is the construction of a genuinely humane order—lest we destroy ourselves completely. If theological reflection is to be justifiable in this crisis, it must contribute to this work. A theology that makes an essential contribution to our humanization is the only sort we can afford today. But if theology has important contributions to make to our further humanization, it is well worth doing.

II

We cannot explore here the full reaches of Christian theology, or the Christian system of symbols, to see where and in what respects they can contribute to the present task of humanization. We must confine ourselves to the two central symbols of the Christian tradition, "God" and "Christ," and what is said about them will be quite brief. However, these two symbols are especially relevant for our consideration of the relation of Christianity to other religious traditions, because together they express both the intention of universality in Christian faith (God) and also the particularity or distinctiveness that sets Christianity over against other religious orientations (Jesus Christ). If we can discover a significance in these two symbols, then, which can contribute to the further humanization of our world, we will be on the way to an understanding of an appropriate stance and task for Christian faith and Christian theology in the face of contemporary religious pluralism.

We begin with "God." "God" is the highest and most universal of the Christian symbols, and the significance of "Christ" is derivative from and dependent upon "God." It is because it is believed that *"God* was in Christ reconciling the world to himself" (2 Cor. 5:19), or that Christ is *God's* definitive revelation, that Christ has the centrality he does in Christianity.[1] Hence, if we are to understand the meaning and importance of Christ, we shall first have to get clear what is meant by "God." This involves us immediately in the most problematical and difficult issues with which the contemporary mind confronts the Christian tradition. "God-talk" has become highly questionable for many today, including Christian believers and theologians, and there are those who think it can and should be dropped as excess and outmoded baggage. That question is not something that should be decided simply on the basis of our intuitions, however: according to the criterion we are considering, our assessment of the continuing significance and relevance of the symbol "God" will depend on the degree and the way in which that symbol can contribute in the present struggle for further humanization.

What, now, is meant by "God"? God is said to be the creator of the heavens and the earth and the lord of history, the foundation or source of all that is, the Alpha and the Omega, "that than which nothing greater can be conceived" (Anselm); God is said to be the only proper object of supreme adoration and devotion, the one whose service is perfect freedom, the one who has created us humans and who also works to rescue us from the evils of our present existence; only through giving ourselves to God and to the service of God, we are told, is human salvation —that is genuine human fulfillment—possible. What can all this mean? Is this all largely mythology, to which we might adhere if we have a poetic or romantic turn of mind, or is there a significance in this symbol which is indispensable for the contemporary life and struggles of us all?

Certainly some of what is being claimed here is intelligible enough. We are reminded that unless we live in accord with that on which our human existence is grounded, we shall destroy ourselves; to think we can do anything we please, that we can make ourselves into whatever we will, is foolhardy. There are limits set to our beings and our enterprises which we must honor and respect if a truly humane existence on this earth is to be possible. In this emphasis, that we are ultimately responsible not merely to ourselves but to orders and structures which sustain us and which we violate at our peril, the ancient theological tradition was formulating fundamental human wisdom which modern ecology is rediscovering. But the ancient tradition had an important advantage over the more recent secular formulations. It did not need to rest its case, for ordering human life beyond itself, exclusively on an appeal to rational self-interest: it portrayed a reality of such supreme goodness and beauty and glory that humans would be drawn to give themselves to it without reservation. The image of a loving and forgiving God, one who is both our creator (the source of our humanity) and our redeemer (the fulfiller of our humanity), and who personally cares for us and sacrifices self for our sakes, is able to evoke a kind of gratitude and devotion that breaks the circle of self-centeredness and opens the self to wider moral and humane demands upon it, directing it toward a life characterized by a similar love and self-giving, a life that can help build a new humanity.

Since God is believed to be the creator of all, and one

who wills salvation—fulfillment—for all, true devotion to God requires breaking down the walls that separate and segregate selves and communities, and opening ourselves to that universal community that encompasses all and provides for the fulfillment of all. I do not claim, of course, that the symbol "God" has in fact always functioned this way in the past: we all know too well the perversions to which it has been subject, making possible the grossest forms of inhumanity in inquisitions and torture chambers, concentration camps and holy wars. I do claim that the symbol of God as the creator, sustainer, and perfector of our humanity through love and forgiveness provides a very powerful and significant object of devotion for such a cause. In comparison with the potential of this symbol, the ecologist's appeal to our deepest rational self-interest as the basis for overcoming our selfishness and self-centeredness seems feeble indeed, and ultimately inconsistent. We need a center of devotion outside the self, a center powerful enough to draw the self out of its own narcissism, if our self-centeredness and our ethno-centeredness and our anthropo-centeredness are to be overcome. The symbol "God" can provide such a focus for human devotion.

But the symbol "God" will function in this way, truly promoting our further humanization, only if it is conceived properly. Many different conceptions of God have been proposed in the past, many different sorts of gods have been worshiped, and certainly not all of them have conduced to the further humanization of our species. A god conceived as an arbitrary tyrant who "has mercy upon whomever he wills, and [who] hardens the heart of whomever he wills" (Rom. 9:18), will hardly inspire in devotees respect for and care of all their fellow creatures; a god portrayed as manifesting fearful and all-destructive wrath against all who violate the divine will, will hardly inspire patience with or forgiveness of those who offend us or with whom we thoroughly disagree. God has often been conceived as an all-powerful demon to whom we must devote

ourselves out of fear of everlasting torment: such a god
calls forth an "authoritarian personality" (Adorno), a spirit
which is cowering and obsequious before authority but a
braggart and bully when dealing with those who are
weaker or of lower social status, hardly a truly free spirit,
humane and just and loving. From the point of view of our
further humanization, some images of God—including
some with roots in the Bible and in certain strands of
Christian tradition—are exceedingly dangerous, and worship of such gods will only further human depravity. It is
not enough, then, to advocate devotion to God, if humanization is our concern; devotion to some conceptions of
God is dehumanizing, and it is little wonder that many
great humanitarian reformers in past and present have
found it necessary to dissociate themselves from traditional Christian beliefs and to take an agnostic or atheistic
position. We must be prepared radically to criticize and
reconstruct traditional ideas of God, if God is to continue
to serve as an appropriate object of devotion for our time,
one who truly mediates to us salvation (humanization).

What should be the basis of our criticism and reconstruction? Are we cut adrift here in a sea of vagaries and opin-
ions, each person constructing whatever image of God
seems fit to her or him and bowing down in worship? If
this were to be our conclusion, it is doubtful that theological reflection would be worth the effort. For the gods
which we would construct could not move us a single step
beyond our present insights and ideals, of which they
would be simply personifications. And we would be the
crassest of idol-worshipers, bowing down before that
which our own hands and minds have wrought. Such relativistic and parochial idols could hardly help move us toward a more universal community inclusive of all men and
women.

It is at this point that we can see the continuing importance of the other great symbol of Christian faith, "Jesus
Christ." The Christian imperative has not been simply

that we should worship God, God-in-general, just any God. On the contrary, it has been much more specific than that, contending that the true God, the one who truly brings fulfillment to humanity, is not directly available and known in every image or action but has been revealed in and through Jesus: "He is the image of the invisible God," declares the author of the letter to the Colossians (1:15); "No one has ever seen God," says the writer of the Fourth Gospel; "the only Son, who is in the bosom of the Father, he has made him known" (John 1:18). Christians themselves have not often taken with full seriousness these central declarations of their faith and have constructed their ideas of God from images and models other than that of the suffering Jesus. "Christ crucified" as an appropriate image for understanding who God really is has been as much a "stumbling block" to the Christian church as it was to the Jews of whom Paul wrote (1 Cor. 1:23), for Christians, like most others, have preferred to worship a God of power and glory rather than one humbled before the powerful, one suffering, weak, and dying. So, although there has always been a stress on God's love and mercy and forgiveness in Christian teaching, the *image* in terms of which God has been conceived—and thus the real center of devotion for Christian faith—has most often been the dazzling glory of almighty power. And to maintain that God in any way suffers or is even capable of suffering, to deny God's impassibility, was regarded as heresy. Not surprisingly, it was in the service of this God of might and glory that the worst horrors of Christian history were committed.

We should not go that way any longer, however. Modern historical studies, together with the growing secularism of our time, have enabled us to recognize that the Bible and the Christian tradition are largely products of human creativity in the face of changing historical exigencies, just as the other great religious traditions; we need no longer, therefore—indeed, we dare not—simply accept all

biblical or traditional images or conceptions of God as
authoritative or binding. To allow ourselves to be bound
in that arbitrary way by our past is to be crippled and
shackled as we try to deal with the immense problems
humanity today faces. The only God we are willing or able
to worship today—the only God we can afford to worship
—is the God who will truly further our humanization, the
God who will help to make possible the creation of a universal and humane community.

NB
rue
criterion
This would
drive
Gustafson
crazy

The crisis of our situation, therefore, frees us to consider
radically reconstructing the Christian conception of God
into a conception founded directly on the image of the
suffering Jesus. This God would be one who does not act
violently in the face of opposition but who lovingly and
patiently suffers the evil men and women inflict in the
hope of thus winning a free and loving response from
them, suffers crucifixion at their hands in hope of the resurrection of a new community of love and forgiveness in
their midst. It would be a God who seeks to build community among humans not by power of nuclear terror but by
evoking a spirit of free vicarious suffering for others. It
would be a God for whom human fulfillment could not
properly be understood in terms of a "kingdom" in which
all commands from on high were carried through in legalistic perfection and detail, but rather as a community of
free spirits living and working together in productiveness
and love. It would not be a God, therefore, who exercised
any heteronomous or compulsive authority over humans,
but rather one who encouraged and created truly free and
autonomous spirits, and who recognized that community
among such spirits is possible only if they manifest self-
giving and love toward each other and a willingness to
forgive and suffer for each other.

I do not claim that devotion to such a God would bring
utopia tomorrow; I certainly do not maintain that it would
solve all our problems, either easily or quickly. The problems which we face today are massive, and how they are

to be solved—if they can be solved at all—remains obscure to us all. If we are the free beings which this God is supposedly in the process of creating, it is we who will have to take upon ourselves the responsibility of finding a way through to a solution of these issues without destroying ourselves in the process. And that means moving forward step by step with a faith and a hope that some solution is truly possible, and a new and universal community—with new and better men and women to make up that community—can be created.

Such an awareness of full responsibility in our freedom, and hope for our future, could be engendered by faith in a God constructed in the image of Jesus Christ, and by the service of such a God. Such a faith and such a God, therefore, could serve well our further humanization in today's troubled world. Indeed, if such a truly humane God does not displace the gods of parochial groups and interests, the gods of prejudice and the blind conviction of right in the pursuit of power—whether by revolutionaries or reactionaries—there seems little real hope for our future at all.

III

I have been suggesting very briefly the way the criterion of humanization might guide our reconstruction of Christian belief. Let us turn now to consider the relevance of our criterion to the great non-Christian traditions. Here too: that which will further humanization as we move into the future is to be regarded as justifiable and good; that which is dehumanizing, or which is seriously distracting in the struggle to build a humane society, must be judged negatively. It is clear that the acceptance of this criterion involves some important preferences and decisions. We have already noted in our consideration of Christian theology, the way in which our criterion gives the urgency of present problems and needs precedence over the claims of tradition, particularly those claims about a supernatural

order or "other world" which might distract attention
from the urgent problems of this life. There is certainly
warrant for this emphasis in the prophetic strands of the
Hebraic-Christian tradition, with their contention that the
requirements of justice and mercy in meeting present
social problems weigh more heavily with God than religious ritual. But the sharp way in which I have formulated
the matter goes considerably beyond this traditional lean-
ing in the direction of secularistic claims, for I have argued
that the very idea of God itself is to be criticized and
reconstructed (or rejected) in the light of the requirements of this humanistic criterion. All claims to truth
made simply on the grounds of religious authority are in
question: theological truth-claims are to be assessed
strictly in terms of our present needs and our present
moral insight (educated, as much as possible, of course, by
past experience and by tradition). It can be claimed that
a moral-humanistic criterion of this sort has been implicitly invoked in religious criticism and theological reconstruction from the time of the eighth-century prophets,
but it has seldom been stated this unequivocally, so that its
theological significance and consequences could be clearly
seen. Thus, though this criterion has a Christian heritage
and background, it may have very radical consequences
when applied seriously to the central traditional Christian
claims themselves.

Whatever may be the historical roots of our criterion, I
have invoked it here because it seems to me to express the
deepest longings and hopes of contemporary men and
women the world over, a growing consensus around the
world—particularly among the oppressed and underprivileged—that the time has come at last to rebuild our
human world into an order genuinely humane. It is a criterion, therefore, which can properly be applied not only to
Western religious practices and thought but to other traditions and institutions as well. There is a tremendous thrust
toward modernization and humanization going on

throughout the world today, and all the great religious traditions must come to terms with it. Our criterion simply pinpoints this issue. It will not be surprising, of course, if some of the traditions fare better at its hands than others.

I am not competent to examine any of the great non-Christian traditions in detail or to make judgments about what is happening there. All of the great traditions manifest much variation and diversity, and the tensions and strains in them all are immense in the present struggle for modernization and humanization throughout Africa, Asia, and Latin America. I must limit myself, therefore, to some general comments about what seems to be occurring and the meaning this has for a theological interpretation of religious pluralism.

Anyone from the West who has lived among some of the peoples of the so-called less developed nations cannot fail to be impressed with the way in which dehumanizing social institutions, superstitious beliefs, and religious sanctions are thoroughly intertwined, mutually reinforcing each other. In India, for example, the caste system, which assigns persons a role and a destiny simply and completely on the basis of birth, and makes it difficult if not impossible for low-caste or out-caste persons to move out of a life which is very degrading, is sustained and supported by the belief in karma and reincarnation, the belief that one's present condition is the necessary and entirely just outcome of one's deeds in previous incarnations, and therefore simply must be accepted; to struggle against one's situation would be to rebel against the very order of righteousness and justice which governs the universe. Within this general framework special afflictions of disease or other misery are often thought to be caused by demons or evil spirits who act erratically and in ways not subject to human control. To persons living within this conceptual world, the whole order of life, and the major events of life, seem imposed from without and cannot be significantly reshaped by human efforts in the present. Religious and superstitious beliefs of this sort, thoroughly accepted by and acceptable to vast numbers of ordinary people, greatly hamper efforts toward humanizing life in India and help to maintain inhuman living conditions for many millions. For this reason the leadership of modern India from Nehru on has been intent on breaking the hold of just such superstitions and has insisted on building a new secular India in which the inhuman living conditions of the masses could and would be overcome. So a great struggle is presently going on in India against some of the deepest-lying and most fundamental religious beliefs and practices that have shaped that civilization for millennia. What I have called the criterion of humanization is being invoked in a thoroughgoing attempt to criticize and reconstruct the traditional order and its religious sanctions.

Similar sorts of things could be said about the modernization of China, where totalitarian power has been used to wipe out as far as possible the old order and build a "new humanity"; about Latin America, where the Christian churches are coming to a new awakening with regard to the way in which the church has helped to legitimize and support massive injustice, and many church leaders are now in the forefront of revolutionary activity; and about Africa. Among all these peoples modernization and humanization are the watchwords of the leadership, however crude or ineffective or brutal their efforts may sometimes be. Of course in all of this there is also a tremendous ambivalence, for modernity—especially in its technological aspects, but also in many of its social practices and institutions, and in its beliefs about human nature, about justice and equality, about human possibilities of making and remaking the world—has been imported largely from the West and requires tremendous modification of traditional religious and cultural beliefs and practices. Whether modernization is to be achieved through political democracy or through Marxist institutions, its inspiration and basic ideology has been derived from Western sources. So

feelings of immense dissatisfaction with, even contempt
for, one's own cultural and religious past, are combined
with deep feelings of uncertainty and guilt about being
disloyal and unfaithful to all that had once been held so
dear. Deep desires to appropriate Western technology together with much of Western ideology and praxis are
mixed with feelings of revulsion toward crass Western
pragmatism and materialism, hatred of Western power
and dominance, and a deep affection for much in one's
own cultural and religious tradition. The contradictions
and tensions must be almost unbearable. Though Western
political imperialism may be coming to an end, economic
and cultural imperialism are far from over, and they are
the more deeply resented just because they must be so
fully accepted if a truly new order is to be built.

What is to be our attitude in the face of these tensions
and struggles? Surely a Troeltschian or sociological relativism will not do, however humane and correct it might
have seemed to a previous generation. Not so many years
ago it was possible (and no doubt correct) to think in terms
of a number of great world civilizations, each with a distinctiveness and integrity of its own. That the values, institutions, styles of life in each should be cherished and re-
spected, and that missionary and imperialistic activity on
the part of Christendom was a highly questionable intru-
sion on societies which should be granted their own autonomy, seemed a humane and highly persuasive thesis. It
could even be extended—and was—to apply to primitive
tribal cultures, whose values and autonomy, it was held,
should not be interfered with by the so-called "more ad-
vanced" societies. "Nothing human is alien to me" was the
motto, and that slogan still has great appeal. We should
glory in the fullness of our pluralism.

Such an attitude as that was surely an advance over the
stuffy imperialistic pride with which Westerners had been
colonizing and ruling the world for the previous two centuries, convinced that their culture and their religion

represented all that was high and good and true, and that all others should either be converted to Western views and practices or deserved to be dominated by the West, politically and economically. But a relativistic position is really no longer appropriate to the realities of today's world. We are no longer a group of relatively independent great cultures, each with its own integrity and dignity, each to be preserved in and through its own great traditional institutions, ideologies, and values. We are in the midst of tremendous transformations and tensions and turmoil, through which the multiplicity of integral human cultures is very rapidly being transformed into a single interconnected fabric of human civilization, the many constituent parts of which are culturally and socially and spiritually interdependent and interrelated in countless ways. We are still a pluralistic world, and we will remain so for a long time, but humanity no longer consists of several great independent societies or cultures. Our pluralism increasingly exists within and is formed by the powerful thrust toward modernization everywhere. It is not a question any longer of whether that is a good thing or a bad thing, whether it should be encouraged or resisted. It is a tide that is transforming all of human life on this globe and will continue to do so for the foreseeable future. It is the basic form and fact of our lives, of our moment in human history, and we do well, therefore, to order our existence accordingly.

If we return to our criterion of humanization, we will quickly see that for Christian faith a relativistic aloofness toward other cultures and religions is no more appropriate to the contemporary human situation than a patronizing paternalism. We must attempt, rather, to work in and through all the forces of modernization presently at work in the world (both in the East and the West) toward the establishment of a genuinely humane worldwide civilization. We must assist the modernizing process, in whatever way we can, to be a humanizing process. This certainly should not be used as a warrant for further Western cultural and religious imperialism; but at the same time it means we should not deplore, out of some romantic notion about the glory and the integrity of every human culture, the eroding away and ultimate destruction of old and outmoded values and institutions which now can be seen to be seriously dehumanizing. On the contrary, we should do all we can to help make the transition through which the cultures of the world are going—both our own culture and others—less painful and difficult. We should seek the overcoming of outmoded religious and cultural institutions and beliefs in other cultures just as truly and just as fully as in our own, for we are rapidly all becoming one humanity. To be a Christian—indeed, to be a modern human being —is no longer to participate simply or primarily in one cultural tradition; it is to be participant with and involved in the worldwide struggle for a fuller and more humane social order, a struggle in and through which older religious institutions and practices everywhere will have to pass away, as new and more humane ones are created.

Our criterion of humanization, thus, does not permit us any longer to take up a monolithic attitude toward other cultures and religious traditions, either attempting to conquer them completely or allowing them to stand in the integrity of what they have been in the past. We must be discriminating and selective, supporting that which furthers a more humane order, opposing that which is dehumanizing. Though it is true that the humanistic criterion which I have been sketching is fundamentally descendant from Western religious and cultural traditions, to invoke it is not simply to further Western spiritual imperialism in the old style. For it is a criterion which, as we have seen, requires radical reconstruction of our Western religious traditions quite as much as of Eastern traditions; moreover, it has already been implicitly accepted as a proper basis of judgment in much of the modern (non-Western) world, and is therefore not being imposed from without;

above all, it is a universalistic criterion, directed toward
the true fulfillment of all human beings and all societies no
matter what their cultural or religious traditions and commitments. It is centered on the humans concerned and
their needs, and is not the imperialism of an ideology.

It will be protested, of course, that this focusing of attention on human needs and welfare in this life is itself simply
one more ideology competing with all the others; and
from one point of view that is true. But the implied conclusion, that therefore no greater warrant for this position
can be offered than for any other, that we are caught in
a relativism of ideologies among which no justifiable dis-
criminations can be made, is very misleading. As we noted
earlier in this chapter, all ideas, ideologies, claims to truth,
faiths, are held by human beings for human purposes.
Their ultimate *raison d'être* is to serve certain human
needs or intentions. It is impossible to break out of an
ultimate relativism of viewpoints so long as we continue
simply to weigh one truth-claim against another, since
each proceeds from different premises and is coherent
and reasonable in terms of the overall world-view which
it presupposes and expresses; here there is an unending
warfare of religious, cultural, and philosophical positions
which can never be rationally settled because each position invokes its own criteria in assessing its own and others'
claims, and there are no universal criteria for arbitrating
the disagreements. Once we recognize, however, that
each of these perspectives is really a *human* position—
even though divine revelation may be claimed as its foundation—serving certain human needs and promoting certain forms of human life while inhibiting others, it
becomes possible to find a way through the relativistic
impasse and to begin to assess the alternatives. One can
ask which human needs are met by each position, which
forms of human life sustained and enhanced, which down-
graded or suppressed. One can, in short, ask about the
human meaning and significance of each religious claim

or each world-view, and one can ask if that human significance and consequence is indeed humanly desirable or
justifiable.

Every religious tradition promises salvation in some
form or other, i.e., promises true human fulfillment, or at
least rescue from the pit into which we humans have
fallen. Every religious tradition thus implicitly invokes a
human or humane criterion to justify its existence and its
claims. My proposal that we make humanization our explicit criterion for evaluating the several religious traditions
and their claims is thus based on a recognition of something implicit in them all. In this sense, a humanistic orientation of the sort described here should not be regarded
as just one more ideology among others: it can claim a
certain universality that none of the others can. For it can
claim both to be implicit in all the others and also to offer
a perspective on the great diversity of religious life and
truth which makes possible truly significant—that is, *humanly* significant—comparison and evaluation. Once we
recognize that every position is, after all, a human position, and can and should therefore be assessed in terms of
its human significance, we have a criterion that can give
us guidance in the present religious pluralism.

It must be admitted that there is little agreement
among religious traditions on conceptions of the human or
on the understanding of what constitutes human fulfillment. But the formulation I am proposing makes that an
issue which can now be directly debated and argued, each
party invoking in its own support whatever experiential
and other evidence is available publicly in our present
human existence. Each disputant will have to show why
his or her interpretation of the human is most adequate to
the actual realities of this life, and therefore can most
properly lay claim to our allegiance in this life. Admittedly
this discriminates against the appeals to supernatural or
otherworldly sanctions which all the religions (except
some forms of Buddhism?) have traditionally made for

their claims. But, as we have seen, it is just in the appeal
to some (mythic) sanction or authority outside our ordinary human reach that the unlimited diversity of religious
interpretations is found; and just because of this diversity
in their ultimate courts of appeal, and with respect to it,
the different religions are very difficult to compare, and
impartial judgments among them are virtually impossible.
What is needed in this circumstance is to abstract from this
diversity and relativity to the common point of interest in
the human which all the religions share. This can provide
a basis for comparison and evaluation.

In insisting that each tradition give its interpretation of
human existence and human fulfillment in terms of what
is directly and publicly available to all, rather than in
terms of its own ideology of some supernatural or otherwise hidden reality, we are only laying down ground rules
without which the debate could not proceed. Nevertheless, they are ground rules which clearly disadvantage all
contestants that are accustomed to basing their claims on
esoteric revelations or on other sorts of special privileged
authority. But that, of course, is precisely what the present
worldwide cry for humanization is all about: breaking out
of our bondage to structures of authority and power which
are not subject to open and impartial inspection and
which thus are in the nature of the case dehumanizing.
The question is: Do we recognize the validity of this cry
against the inhuman and this appeal to that which genuinely fulfills the human? If we do, then we have an arbiter
before whom each of the religious traditions can quite
properly be asked to justify its claims.

IV

I shall not attempt here any assessment of the claims of
the several great religious traditions in terms of the criterion of humaneness and humanization. That is a task
which is already being carried out around the world, as

each culture faces the problems of modernization, and which, in any case, others are much better equipped to carry out. Rather, I want to turn now to a question that some must feel has been becoming increasingly urgent in these pages: whatever pragmatic value the criterion of humanization may have in thinking about the place of religion in the modern world, can it be justified as properly Christian, and not just humanistic? Can one legitimately claim that a position which gives such prominence to this criterion is theologically adequate?

From a traditional point of view the interpretation of Christian symbolism which I have sketched with the aid of the criterion of humanization would undoubtedly be regarded as very spare. Nothing was said about human entrapment in sin, or about the atoning work of the cross; there was no explicit doctrine of the deity of Christ, nor of the church and the sacraments; even the question whether God was to be regarded as a heavenly being or infinite person who intervenes in human affairs remained undiscussed.

Though it would be possible, and appropriate, to develop positions on all these and other traditional questions, they were not discussed here because we were interested in formulating a conception that could put Christian faith into a position to enter into significant conversation with the other great religious traditions presently undergoing radical modernization and (we hope) humanization. It is precisely at the points where Christians make special claims about the divinity of Christ or about God's special attention to believers that such dialogue becomes difficult if not impossible. Such claims involve an exclusivistic view of Christianity, setting it apart from other religious and secular positions and implying a definite superiority over them all. Obviously it is possible to make such claims—perhaps every religion has in the past—but they are of the sort that really are not rationally arguable in the public arena, for they are based upon the assumed adequacy and truth of the very Christian mythology and symbolism which is under consideration. In short, they *presuppose* Christian faith rather than present it for careful consideration and evaluation. Such a presentation one can only take or leave: its interest is in conversion, not open-ended dialogue on equal terms with other partners. Evangelism has of course been the typical traditional objective in presenting the Christian position to others, and I have no intention of criticizing the appropriateness of such activity for certain situations. I do not, however, think such a stance either appropriate or useful in the present world struggle to overcome all authoritarianism and to reorder society in ways which grant each person and each community its own proper dignity. In such a situation and with such concerns we simply may not begin by asserting, or even just implying, our superiority to all partners or potential partners in dialogue. Rather we must enter into conversation as equals, hoping to be able to contribute something of significance to our common objective of building a more humane society, expecting also to learn much of significance from the other parties to the conversation, hoping and expecting all the while that we all will grow into deeper community with and respect for each other as we converse together. Surely such an approach to dialogue is the only truly human and humanizing one.

It is because of this interest in genuine dialogue with other religious and nonreligious positions that I have presented this somewhat spare or minimalist interpretation of Christian beliefs. I want to maintain, however, that this has not involved me in shortchanging or "selling out" Christianity in any fundamental way. On the contrary, it is strictly in accord with the deepest interests and concerns of Christian faith itself and gets to the heart of the Christian contentions. Here we come to a great divide in the understanding of what Christian faith really is. Is the central concern of Christianity the presentation of certain indispensable *truth(s)* to humanity so that "whoever believes . . . should not perish but have eternal life" (John 3:16); or is it primarily a "ministry of reconciliation" among all humankind inspired by the love of God manifested in Christ (2 Cor. 5:17–20)? Most Christians have maintained that it is both these things, though in their actual lives they may have emphasized one more than the other. I want to contend that it is important that a choice be made as to which is to be given ultimate priority and centrality, and which is secondary.

If the business of Christianity is most fundamentally to present truth-claims about God and Christ and ourselves, then our stance toward those others with whom we are speaking will be basically argumentative and combative; we will be concerned to persuade them to accept what we understand to be the truth, the unchanging truth, let the chips fall where they may. However, if the fundamental business of Christianity is a ministry of reconciliation among humans, building community where there is dissension, promoting understanding and acceptance where there has been estrangement and rejection—because the God to whom we are devoted is one who loves and forgives and reconciles—then our stance will have to be different. Our concern will be first and foremost to enter into community with those others with whom we are speaking, and where estrangement or separation exists to seek reconciliation with them. It will be, in short, not to make claims for ourselves or our truth against our neighbors, but to love and accept our neighbors as ourselves.

Downgrading the importance of the more peculiar and controversial traditional Christian truth-claims, as I have done, and highlighting the ministry of love and reconciliation which builds community among humans and thus contributes toward the establishment of a more humane existence, does not involve compromising the essentials of Christian faith but is directly expressive of those essentials. The Christian concern for the salvation of all men and women is primarily a concern for their full humanization.

At this point the contemporary worldwide struggle for a truly humane social order coincides completely with the central thrust of Christian faith, and there is no reason for Christians to set themselves apart, or to stand aloof, from those major forces presently at work in the other religious traditions and in secular society. Indeed, from a Christian point of view, precisely this thrust toward humanization should be regarded as the preeminent activity of God— the source and the fulfiller of our humanness—in the contemporary world.

The theological stance I have been briefly sketching here involves a modernization of Christianity appropriate to and correlative both with the modernization of the other great religious traditions in the direction of fuller humanization and also with those powerful movements in contemporary secular society toward the same end. It provides an interpretation of Christian faith, and the Christian God, which will facilitate and encourage the full yet critical participation of Christians in all the struggles for a more humane social order which are so widespread in the world today; it provides a basis for encounter on equal terms with the other great religious traditions, and for discriminating and intelligent dialogue with them about what is truly humanly significant in the several faiths of humankind; and it gives an intelligible interpretation to the central and enduring Christian claim, the claim about God and about the significance for our time of faith in this God who is conceived and defined in terms of the person, ministry, and death of the man Jesus—the God of love and mercy and self-sacrifice. I am contending that devotion to this God, and action in accord with the "will" of this God, are not only wholly appropriate to the life and struggles of our time, but that they have a significant—perhaps indispensable—contribution to make to our lives in the midst of these struggles.

I am not claiming thereby that the other great religious and secular traditions do not also have important, perhaps indispensable, contributions to make toward the fuller humanization of us all. That is for their adherents to determine and to explain, and we will gladly listen to what they have to say and will learn from them whatever we can. Doubtless Buddhism can teach us much about the overcoming of human suffering, and about the relativity of all our religious symbols and conceptions and the dangers of their hypostatization and literalization. And Hinduism will have claims to make about the importance of spiritual discipline and insight and the dangers of devotion to a too anthropomorphically conceived God. Judaism and Islam have significant testimonies to make with regard to God's incomparable uniqueness and the unqualified demands upon us which faith in God requires—insights which, as both of these traditions have long realized, suggest that most Christian talk about Jesus as divine or "Jesus as God and savior" is idolatrous. Secular humanism has much to teach us all about what constitutes true freedom in human society, and Marxism can enable us to understand better what economic and social requirements must be met if there is to be genuine justice and equality; both these forms of humanism can alert us to some of the profound dangers to which every form of human religiousness is subject. In this many-sided conversation Christians may dare to hope, perhaps, that faith in and devotion to the God who is working to "make human life more human" (Lehmann) may commend itself as right and proper and good to many who had oriented themselves and their activities principally in terms of a secular humanism or some other religious tradition.

The coming new age of a single worldwide humanity must build upon the best insights and disciplines of all our long and varied human experience, as conserved for us in the many religious and cultural traditions alive and meaningful today. We must be open to all, in conversaton with all, seeking reconciliation with all. But we dare not be uncritically receptive to every claim that is made, whether by perspectives strange to us or by the traditions we hold most dear ourselves. Each must be brought before the bar of the criterion of humanization and there made to prove itself. It is the task of theology, and of the corresponding modes of reflection on what is ultimately significant and on the nature of the human which are found in the other traditions, to define and clarify and interpret the criterion of humanization, to engage in reflection and discussion leading to deeper and fuller understanding of its significance and import, and to attempt to measure and assess in its terms the great claims and emphases about human life and destiny made by the various religious and cultural traditions of humankind. Thus, each of the great religious traditions should find its proper role in the coming world culture, and Christianity also will be able to show forth its own true significance for humanity.

PART THREE

SOME META-THEOLOGICAL ISSUES

Theology means taking rational trouble over the mystery. . . . If we are unwilling to take the trouble, neither shall we know what we mean when we say that here we are dealing with God's mystery.

Karl Barth

8/Theology
and the Concept of Nature

The growing general awareness that the order of nature within which humanity lives is a delicate ecological balance—a balance which cannot be indiscriminately exploited by humans much longer without destroying the continuing possibility of human life—has not been without repercussions among theologians. There is an increasing attentiveness to nature as a theological problem and an interest in developing theologies of ecology and conservation. In addition, there appears to be a growing belief that the theological focus on "history" in recent years has been extravagant or even entirely misplaced: it has turned attention in theology away from the natural world, which is "our real home"; it has led to a theological ignoring of the natural sciences and has thus helped to isolate theology from some of the most important and influential streams of human learning in modern culture; and it has contributed to and mightily reinforced the human sense of self-importance and insularity, for history is preeminently the human story, and the "God of history" seems principally involved in transactions with human communities and individuals (although of course God is said to be the creator and father of all). What we need, we are told, is a

---

Originally published in *Harvard Theological Review* (1972), 65:337–366. Copyright 1972 by the President and Fellows of Harvard College. Used by permission.

"theology of nature" that will enable us to understand the orders of life and being within which we live and of which we are part, and even a "natural theology" that will illuminate for us, and teach us properly to worship, the God implicit in nature.[1] The growing interest in religious experience as normal and natural to human beings, and as the primary foundation and resource for theological reflection; the attention to Eastern religious traditions which have been much more oriented toward nature than history; the widespread experimenting with consciousness-expanding drugs and other ways to supersede the range of ordinary human experience; the loud polemics against the "puritanical" restrictiveness of certain modes and variations of behavior and experience (especially sexual) in much of the Christian past—all of these testify to a sharp change of theological interest and attention.

It is not my purpose here either to applaud or oppose these developments. Before that can be done responsibly, another sort of task is called for. We need to examine rather closely the terms in which we are now being invited to think, so that we can use them circumspectly and precisely, and not be victimized by hidden nuances and unforeseen implications. What do we mean by "nature"? What is theologically at stake in the alleged contrast of "nature" with "history"? How is the present theological interest in the "natural" related to the long tradition of "natural theology"? Are there connotations of the concept of nature which make its theological employment questionable or even risky? These are immensely complicated issues, and I cannot claim more here than to scratch their surface. What I shall attempt in this chapter is to get clearer the structure, connections, and implications of the concept of nature as these bear on its theological employment. I shall not attempt to reconstruct the concept or to propose ways of redefining it so as to meet some of the issues which it raises for theology. This is partly because I am not clear about what kind of reconstruction is required, partly because I am dubious that arbitrary redefinitions can alter much the dominant tendencies already at work in and expressed through concepts as pervasive in the culture as this one. I hope this attempt at clarification and unpacking of some of these tendencies and tensions will help facilitate some measure of sophistication in what is bound to be an increasing theological interest in and use of the concept of nature in coming years.

I

Our terms "nature" and "natural" bear exceedingly complex structures of meaning. The Oxford English Dictionary lists eighteen distinct meanings for "natural" and fifteen for "nature." Moreover, in addition to their many common uses these terms have played important technical roles in philosophical and theological reflection and, in certain phrases and combinations, bear whole traditions of meaning and interpretation within themselves—for example, "natural law" (two kinds: scientific and moral), "nature and grace," "nature and supernature," *"natura naturans* and *natura naturata,"* "the natural man and the spiritual man."

The English word "nature," derived from the Latin *natura* (Greek: *physis*) from whence it gains many of its complex meanings and uses, originally meant birth or origin, parentage, original stock.[2] The inborn or inherent qualities or characteristics of a person or thing were thus "natural" to it (as opposed to artificially added to it or imposed upon it); these, taken to be its essential qualities or properties, came to be called its "nature," i.e., what was "native" to it. An object's or a person's nature was thus that which constituted it or him or her as that particular (kind of) object or person, appearing and behaving as it (he or she) does, having just those qualities and characteristics. Eventually, especially in philosophical reflection, the concept was generalized to refer to the totality of powers and processes of the world (especially the material world) conceived as a unified system and sometimes personified as female.

With this all too brief sketch of the etymology of the word in mind, we can understand something of the interconnections of meaning in the otherwise confusing array of uses, such as:

The contrast of the natural and the artificial

The contrast of nature with grace

The claim that certain sorts of behavior, e.g., homosexuality, are unnatural and thus wrong

The claim that freedom is the true nature of human beings, and that by it they transcend and overcome ordinary nature and create culture (here the "artificial" or "unnatural" is generally regarded as good or desirable or even "natural" for humans)

The view of nature as the totality, all that there is, the universe

The contrast of nature as the unspoiled beautiful wilderness with the ugly and polluted city

The notion of a "natural child" and Paul's notion of the "natural man"

Natural sciences as opposed to social or behavioral sciences

Nature (as the totality of the nonhuman) in contrast with history or culture

The contrast between natural theology and revealed theology or natural religion and revealed religion

Though it would undoubtedly be interesting and useful to attempt to set out in detail the history of the term "nature" in such a way as to develop a detailed map of its many interrelated meanings, I shall not proceed any farther down that road (even were I competent to do so). I hope what I have said gives a sufficient sense of the complexity of meanings here, so that we can turn directly to the question of the theological usefulness of the term.

II

It will not be possible here to examine all uses and meanings of the term "nature" which are, or have been, of theological importance. I shall confine myself to one focus or configuration of meaning(s) which seems to me to be at the heart of the growing current interest. This is the use of the term in such phrases as the "order of nature" or "the natural world," where the intention appears to be, on the one hand, to refer to the totality of processes and powers that make up the universe and, on the other, to suggest that which exists independently of all human artifice—it being both the context within which human activities are carried out and the source of raw material which human historical work transforms into culture.

It will be evident at once that this use of the term is ambiguous. For how is humanity, and all that is distinctively human, understood here? Is humanity a part of nature or over against nature? On the one side, so far as nature is held to include all powers and processes in the world, humans would seem to be included within nature. Certainly the material and vital dimensions of our being are directly rooted in natural processes and must be regarded as natural. Moreover, since our mental and spiritual existence is inextricably interlocked with our physical and organic being, it is difficult to see why it should not also be regarded as part of nature in this wide and all-inclusive sense. To see humanity in this way as fundamentally and perhaps totally a part of nature is the direction in which we are being pushed by many currents in contemporary science and culture. Human existence is a moment in a complex ecological balance without which it could not exist and to which it contributes. This ecological system is the presupposition of every dimension of our life; it is the context within which human life and culture becomes a possibility, and it is, in a real sense, the source and basis of our existence. This natural order, then, is the most fundamental reality (apart from God—if it is not itself to be viewed as the only viable referent for the word "God") with which we have to do.

But there is a problem here. We are being admonished to take this natural order more seriously than we have in the past, to recognize that since it is the indispensable context and basis of our life, we dare not upset the balance but must maintain it with great circumspection. Moreover, we are being told that in our attempts to gain technological mastery of our world and of the ills that afflict humankind, we may have already so polluted our environment and upset the delicate balances which sustain life here on earth as to be destroying ourselves. We must control the population explosion; we must clean up our rivers and atmosphere; we must stop the kind of economic and technological expansion that uses up resources at exponentially growing rates; we must stop using "artificial" insecticides and fertilizers, which have unknown disastrous long-term effects, and return to "natural" procedures; we must protect those species of life now in danger of extinction; we must set aside and preserve those few remaining pieces of "natural" wilderness and not allow them to be in any way marred by roads, power plants, transmission lines, and the like; in short, we must stop our wanton destruction of nature. All such admonitions and injunctions, of course, imply, first, that humans *have* done much to and with the order of nature and, second, that they *can* do something now to help restore the balance which in their ignorance and rapacity they have disrupted. That is, they imply that humans are not, after all, simply a part of nature, one more function of the processes and powers that make up the natural world, but that they stand in some sense apart from all these and can and do work on them and transform them. It is through human artifice, human culture, that the present ecological crisis has been brought upon us, and (it is hoped) through a further and more sophisticated application of that same artifice the crisis may eventually be abated. Insofar as "nature" here is viewed as distinct from the "artificial" activities of human beings which modify it and use it for raw material in the creation of culture, it is obvious that nature cannot be understood simply as that system which includes all powers and processes in the universe. Nature and culture are set over against each other in polar relation, and humanity is somehow in both, as both are in us humans.

This ambiguity in the concept of nature—nature as the totality of all processes and beings, and nature as polar counterpart to culture—cannot be dissolved simply by deciding to use the term "nature" in only one of these two ways, reserving some other term for the other concept; nor can it be clarified much by designating one of the two meanings as "nature$_1$" and the other as "nature$_2$". For the problem does not arise out of a simple confusion in our linguistic usage which a new notation can rectify. It is, rather, in the complexity of the thing itself, that which we are trying to designate with our word "nature," and the difficulty of specifying how that other very complex reality, humanity, is to be related to it. For in a very real sense humans are natural beings, are a part of nature and sustained by it, and cannot be conceived apart from the natural order in which they are ensconced; and yet humans are able to distance themselves from nature sufficiently to conceive it as something over against them which they perceive and on which they can work, which they transform through their activity into the "artificial" or "unnatural" reality which we call "culture." Nature, that is to say, is not simply an objective system of processes and powers; it is a system sufficiently complex that some of the processes and powers within it can come to self-conscious and deliberate activity which is then directed toward transforming the otherwise (apparently) unconscious order of nature toward the realization of their own ends. Nature appears to be a nonteleological, nonaxiological order within which emerges purposive and valuing activity. Nature is a material order[3] which gives birth to life and ultimately spirit, and within which these have their "natural" home.

We may be able to bring out some of the complexities of our concept of nature by comparing it with a related notion, *world*. It may be thought that inasmuch as "nature" refers to the totality of all powers and processes, it functions essentially like the notion of world. This latter concept serves as an ordering principle or "regulative idea" (Kant) by means of which we bring all the individual and particular objects and events of experience into relation with each other within a unified whole. *World* is never an object of perception or of experience: it can never "come into view" or be in any way directly experienced. It is, rather, the backdrop against which or context within which we have all our experience and within which we know ourselves to be situated.

If we treat the concept of world as fundamentally like other concepts which refer to or represent objects (which are identifiable in experience), we get into insoluble antinomies. This is not only because, as Kant held, of the impossibility of conceiving clearly, not to say experiencing, spatial and temporal absolute limits. It is also because the world includes within itself all space and time (as its abstract structure), and thus all events occur within the world. But it is obvious that not all events are occurring simultaneously: some have occurred and are over with; some are yet to come. The world, then, which includes them all within itself, never "exists" *as* world; only certain features of the world exist at any one time. Thus, it is not merely that we never do in fact perceive or experience the world as an object: in principle that would be impossible, for "world" is a concept for which no object (in that sense) exists (at any one time) at all. The notion of world is a construct created by the human imagination as a heuristic device to make possible the ordering and relating of all our other concepts of objects and events. It is thus indispensable to our thinking and even to the orderliness of our experience—and in every culture we find some sort of (often mythical) notions of this widest context within which human life transpires—but it is itself not an object of experience; it is a fundamental presupposition of experience.

The concept "nature" in many respects functions like the concept "world." It can stand, as we have seen, for the totality of all events and objects, the whole within which all fall and of which they are part. In this aspect nature is no more perceivable than the world: it is a construct of the mind. But nature is concrete in a way that world is not. Whereas "world" refers simply to the totality, the whole, and thus to nothing directly experienceable, "nature" refers in addition to particular dimensions or qualities within the whole, to structures and events which can be perceived and experienced. We would never say a tree is "worldly," but there are no problems at all in regarding it as "natural"; whereas to speak of "laws of the world" (i.e., of the cosmos) sounds exceedingly abstract and obscure, by "laws of nature" we designate everyday experienceable regularities in, for example, light, sound, and gravitation; for one to wish to immerse oneself in nature seems comprehensible enough, but what would it be to immerse oneself in the world? The relative concreteness which the concept of nature betrays in such expressions, in contrast with the concept of world, derives from the ambiguity we previously noted in it: "nature" refers not only to the totality but also, in contrast with "culture" or the "artificial," to certain features or qualities within the world, namely, to that which exists and functions independently of human contrivance or interference, that which is other than the human, over against the human, sharply distinct from culture. Thus, although nature (like the world) is the overall context within which all that we are and experience has its being, it has an immediacy and experiential concreteness for us which the world does not and cannot have. Nature is experienceable as well as conceivable; world is only a concept. It is for this reason, perhaps, that nature can be regarded as the source and ground of all being and life ("Mother Nature") in a way hardly imaginable for the world. And so nature can come to have a kind of religious meaning and become the object of religious devotion—and a direct rival to God—in a way not possible for the world.

We can now draw together some of the threads of this discussion. The concept of nature, as it functions in much contemporary discussion, appears to draw its meaning from two rather distinct roots: on the one hand there is the experience of that which is "natural" as contrasted with that made by human contrivance, the wilderness over against the city, plant and animal life in contrast with human culture; on the other hand there is the totality of all powers and processes conceived as a systematic whole. Nature is both of these: it is the totality viewed as "natural process" (not artifice); it is the widest context of human life, and thus our most fundamental home, viewed as wilderness ("untouched by human hand") rather than on some analogy or image drawn from the teleological and meaning-filled orders of society and culture.

In this respect the concept of nature raises very difficult theological issues. For it proposes a conception of the over-all context for human life which does not have built into it the dimensions of purpose, value, and meaning,[4] all of which concepts are drawn from the human experience of linguistic and cultural institutions and activity. The notion of God, on the other hand, as an agent characterized by freedom and purposiveness and love, is based on the model of human freedom and agency as experienced within society and culture. It was possible to relate these two—nature and God—by means of the concept of creation, as long as the world was viewed as a finite order brought into being by the infinite God, and destined to serve God's purposes. But when, with Giordano Bruno and others, nature itself became viewed as infinite, there was no longer any independent role for (the concept of) God to play; all metaphysical needs could be fulfilled by nature. So in Spinoza, God and nature became identified with each other—it not being possible to conceive of two infinites—but the identification occurred under the imagery of the concept of nature (i.e., natural process) rather than the concept of God (i.e., free agent).[5] What had been two ontologically distinct realities *(God* and *creation)* ordered toward each other in a very specific and distinctive way, so as to preserve the ultimate reality and importance of God, now became one reality (nature) viewed under two different aspects *(natura naturans* and *natura naturata).* And God no longer had an unusurpable place in humanity's understanding of itself and of the context within which human life falls; indeed, it is not clear that God any longer had (could be conceived to have) any distinctive place at all.[6]

The concept of nature, I am suggesting, as it is used in much contemporary discussion both within religious circles and without, has concealed within it an implicit metaphysic. It is a concept seemingly broad and inclusive enough to take up into itself and find place for every aspect or dimension of experience, and it provides an interpretation and ordering of all those features of experience in a particular or definite way, the paradigm or model for which is natural process. Thus it is now clear that the "ambiguity" which we earlier noted in the concept—as to whether human culture is a part of nature or is its polar counterpart—decisively determines its fundamental meaning and really cannot be removed or overcome. "Nature" is a metaphysical concept and involves an understanding of what is (ultimately) real. But like all metaphysical concepts, it is based on certain experiential models taken as clue or key to the real: "natural" powers and processes (as contrasted with "artificial" or "cultural") provide the paradigm.[7] The *double entendre* of "nature" is thus indispensable to its (contemporary) meaning and use.

I do not mean to suggest, of course, that everyone who uses the word "nature," or everyone who is engaged in current ecological campaigns, is a secret believer in naturalism as a philosophy and is conducting an evangelistic campaign under that banner; most are probably quite unaware of these metaphysical tendencies and implications, and many would explicitly disavow them. I am arguing, however, that for those concerned about the question of our fundamental stance in the world, our deepest convictions about what is real and true and good, our understanding of what human life is all about and what is the broadest context within which it is lived—in short, for theologians—the concept will have to be subjected to careful scrutiny and used only with the greatest care. For the metaphysical tendencies implicit in it are not obviously congruent with those of Christian faith.

III

This may not be to the detriment of the concept of nature, however, for Christian faith in certain of its implications has probably seriously misled us in our quest for orientation in life and the world. A number have argued that the Christian understanding of the world as God's creation governed by divine law, with humans its divinely appointed overlords, was an important presupposition of the development of modern experimental natural science, and thus of our modern understanding of nature.[8] But it can also be argued that this same complex of presuppositions must bear considerable responsibility for the unrestricted exploitation of nature which now threatens to destroy the delicate ecological balances that sustain all life.[9] Therefore it cannot be regarded as self-evident that the traditional Christian view is either adequate or appropriate any longer to provide orientation in life. We must examine its features more closely.

The principal terms of the Christian metaphysical scheme are three: God, humanity, and the world. All else takes place within a framework supplied by those terms. Even Jesus Christ, whom some might wish to give priority over these others, is defined as the "God-man": his being is thus grasped and made intelligible in terms of the more fundamental notions of God and humanity (however much, as Karl Barth has argued, it eventually comes to qualify those notions). It is in fact these two terms, "God" and "humanity," which provide the basic framework within which the Christian drama is worked out; the notion of "world" ("heavens and earth") remains vague and largely undefined, referring to the context within which, or the stage upon which, the drama of salvation is worked out, but not itself having a significant role within that drama.[10]

It is Yahweh and Israel, God and humanity—or even, as in the later individualism of much Western Christendom, God and the soul (Augustine)—that are the realities of central interest and concern.[11] Though humanity may be created out of the "dust from the ground" (Gen. 2:7) and could not exist apart from a context provided by heaven and earth and the multitude of other living creatures on the earth (Gen. 1), it is clearly the climax of God's creative activity. Created in God's own image (1:27), human beings are the ones for whom all other beings were made and to whose will they must be subject (1:28–29; 2:18–20, 15). Humankind, moreover, is the (only) creature in which God himself becomes incarnate. Although the incarnation has significance for all creation, the divine-human relation is clearly the axis around which all else revolves. In the end when God creates "new heavens and a new earth" (Isa. 65:17; Rev. 21:1), in which the fierce struggle in all life will be overcome ("The wolf and the lamb shall feed together, [and] the lion shall eat straw like the ox" [Isa. 65:25]), this is primarily for the sake of the "new Jerusalem," where

222 *The Theological Imagination*

humans can live with God in peace and all human suffering, pain, and misery will be overcome (Isa. 65:18–24; Rev. 21:2–4). The great words of the Christian vocabulary—sin, salvation, forgiveness, repentance, hope, faith, love, righteousness—have to do primarily with human realities and with the human relation to God and to fellow humans, and the principal conceptual work of Christian theology has been devoted to elaboration of profound interpretations of our human nature and predicament and of the idea of God. The rest of creation, though always recognized and sometimes acknowledged and even reflected upon, simply was not of central theological interest or importance, and (with the exception of the angels) never became the subject of any technical theological vocabulary or doctrines.

Moreover, the two central terms, "God" and "humanity," were understood to refer to realities which had a certain fundamental kinship with or likeness to each other, not shared by any other beings: human beings were created "in God's image," and God was principally conceived in terms of the human images of lord, king, warrior, judge, father, and the like. The ultimate reality which was the source and foundation of all else, that is to say, was thought of anthropomorphically, and humanity was believed to be at the very center of this reality's interest and affection. Indeed, God so loved rebellious humankind that "he gave his only Son" (John 3:16) for our salvation. Human beings, thus, have a kinship with and connection to the ultimate metaphysical reality not shared by anything else in all creation. It was hardly inappropriate, then, that for many Christian centuries the rest of the created order was seen to have its principal significance in the ways in which it symbolized or mirrored various aspects of the human problem or the divine-human relationship, having little or no significance in its own right.[12]

This theological attention to God and humanity and their relationship, and the relative disregard for nature or the world, was not an accident. An inner logic or consistency in Western religious traditions was being worked out here. A concept of God (or of the gods) is a means by which humans give ultimate metaphysical significance to the moral and personal side of their being, for it involves doctrines which interpret ultimate reality as moral and personal in character. This is not completely clear in polytheistic mythologies where the gods war with each other and often engage in activities which would be regarded as illegitimate for men and women. But in the movement to monotheism, where all (ultimate) power and value becomes centered in one being who thus becomes the focus of all devotion and loyalty, it becomes increasingly difficult to think of God as deficient in any respect. It is possible of course—and this has happened in some religious traditions—to attain a unity of world-view similar to that which monotheism achieves by moving toward pantheistic conceptions which tend to level moral distinctions and depreciate the personal side of our being. But this did not happen in Israel. Instead, Yahweh became increasingly viewed as the very epitome of moral righteousness, one whose judgments and actions, even though often incomprehensible to human moral sensibilities (Habakkuk, Job), were finally to be accepted as ultimately right and good. Since the ultimate reality with which men and women had to do, the source of their being, was preeminently a personal and moral agent who required of devotees not only absolute devotion but also moral rectitude, the moral side of human existence was, in this orientation, given the profoundest kind of metaphysical sanction possible, and true human existence became understood in terms of action, of willing and doing. Yahweh was one who acts, a personal and moral being, and so was the creature who had been made in Yahweh's image. Thus, both human beings and that which was taken to be ultimately real were understood in terms of those features of our nature which most sharply distinguish us from other creatures, namely, the abilities to act, to decide, to order behavior by reference to preconceived and deliberately chosen ends, to devote ourselves to such values as righteousness, mercy, and love. It is not surprising, then, that the images in terms of which the cosmic context of human life was understood were not primarily organic or material but rather political: all of existence was God's kingdom over which God ruled as an oriental potentate. Wind and wave, Leviathan and lamb, as well as women and men—all were created by God's will and word and obeyed God's command as God's will was worked out through all creation. The fundamental order in the world, thus, was seen as moral and personal and political, and all else was to be understood as in some sense an expression of this (distinctly anthropomorphic) view of the world.[13]

With this sort of orientation in life certain consequences follow directly. On the one hand, that which distinguishes men and women from the rest of creation—especially our volitional and moral capacities—will be emphasized as that which is the truly human, and humans, thus, will increasingly see themselves as active beings, free and creative, able to take responsibility for themselves and their world, capable of knowing something of the supreme Actor who rules the world and of becoming the loyal subjects of that Actor. The rest of creation, on the other hand, so far as it does not consist of free moral agents like us, is primarily material for the creator's (and our) purposes. It is the context within which God and humans are working, and it provides materials for their work. It has no will or purposes of its own; it knows no moral values and has no freedom of choice. It is there, thus, simply to be used by God and by humans as they carry through their purposes. (Cf. Kant: only persons, with their rational wills, are ends in themselves.) It is true, of course, that in the respect in which they perfectly fulfill the creator's will for them, the birds and flowers can serve as a sort of moral and religious example to us (Matt. 6:26–30), but this is because we, un-

like precisely those same flowers and birds, are beings
capable of moral discrimination, beings who have some
power to transform ourselves in accord with the examples
set before us: one does not admonish an oak or a robin
moralistically. The natural world, thus, is of an ontologically different order from humankind. Though humans
are a part of nature and have been made from natural
materials, they are lifted far above the rest of nature by
their moral and personal character: they are, indeed, the
very image of nature's creator and absolute lord.

Thus, the conceptions of God and humanity, as they
have developed in Western religious traditions, work
hand in hand toward the distinguishing of humankind
from (the rest of) nature. Nature is not conceived primarily as our proper home and the very source and sustenance
of our being, but rather as the context of and material for
teleological activity by our (nonnatural) wills working
upon and in it.[14] It is not really surprising that this kind of
orientation and stance, given certain other historical conditions, could eventuate in a tremendous technological
explosion in which the earth and its resources would be
increasingly subjected to human purposes; it is also not
surprising that such an attitude would tend to overlook
and neglect the question whether certain "natural bound-
aries" were being trespassed and certain "natural balances" upset. If nature was created by (God's) will for the
sake of further volitional activity, how could (human) will
be threatened simply by its strenuous exercise in nature?

The picture I have been painting here is, of course,
overdrawn. From the very beginning of Western religious
consciousness there has been an awareness that the earth
is not here for men and women to do with simply as they
please: it is, after all, God's garden, and humans are here
only to "till it and keep it" (Gen. 2:15), not transform it into
whatever they wish. At best they are only stewards within
God's creation. I have no desire to deny these motifs or
their importance: it is undoubtedly with notions of this

sort that theological reconstruction will have to work, at
least in part. However—this is my central point here—the
theological problem of nature is not simply one of rearranging emphases or details, lifting up certain motifs in
the tradition which may have been neglected. It goes far
deeper than that, into the logic of the central concepts of
our religious tradition. The very ideas of God and humanity, as they have gradually been worked out over millennia, are so framed as to blur or even conceal our embeddedness in the natural order as we now are
increasingly conceiving it. The great religious struggle between Israel and Canaan was over the question of the
relative metaphysical importance of natural power and
process on the one hand and personal moral will on the
other. When Yahweh won that struggle it meant that the
object of ultimate loyalty and devotion for humans in the
West would be conceived increasingly in terms of models
rooted in our moral and personal experience, not in our
sense of dependence upon and unity with the orders and
processes of nature. Thus the very concept of God itself—
as that concept has developed in the West—has built into
it a depreciation of the metaphysical, and certainly the
religious, significance of nature.

If we are to make theological use of the modern notion
of nature—and how can we any longer avoid it, since all
our thinking and experience is so heavily shaped by it?—
we shall have to engage in theological reconstruction
going down to the deepest roots of the Western religious
sensibility and vocabulary. The idea of God as preeminently active moral will must be reexamined, as well as the
correlative conception of humans as fundamentally moral
and personal beings, a conception to which this idea of
God gives metaphysical support. What the outcome, or
even the main direction, of such far-reaching reconstruction might be, I cannot say, but there is little question in
my mind that it will transform Christian faith (as we now
know it) in far more profound ways than seem to be imag-

ined by many who now blithely call for a theology of nature or for ecological theology.

IV

I have been arguing in this chapter that the concept of nature, as that concept is used in much contemporary discussion, and the Christian conception of God (and humanity), as that notion has developed historically, are not easily compatible. Each makes claims about the fundamental order in reality and proposes images in terms of which that order is to be understood; each thus contains within itself an implicit metaphysic. These metaphysical schemes disagree with each other at many points, not only in the paradigms or models by means of which ultimate reality is conceived but also in their conceptions of the human and of our place among other finite beings; their implications for religion and for ethics also sharply diverge at crucial points. In short, we seem to be confronted with two quite different world-views, not easily reconciled with each other.

This conclusion, however, may not seem particularly persuasive to some. After all, Christian theology has always had categories for the interpretation of other finite beings. Is it really obvious that these can no longer do service? Even though we may be hesitant about the continuing viability of such a traditional contrast as that between nature and supernature—the latter seeming to be a kind of unwarranted mythic redoubling of the former— why can the present problems not be handled in terms of such concepts as nature/grace and creator/creation? These conceptual pairs seem to be constructed specially for the purpose of grasping the relation of the total finite order—not only humanity—to God; moreover, they seek to do so in a way that preserves the proper integrity of each. Nature-creation has an order and structure which gives it its unique character and which is the proper subject of the sciences; humans are not gods but are part of this created order, bound to it in every dimension of their being.

It is true that the interconnection and interdependence of human existence with the rest of finite being was not, perhaps, as profoundly grasped in earlier centuries as is possible today with the help of the sciences. It may even have been held that the human soul was a direct gift of God, not part of our natural creaturely inheritance like our body. We today might wish to alter such judgments and regard women and men in their total personal existence as so bound up with the organic and physical orders which sustain and significantly constitute them as not to be conceivable in separation from them; and thus we might wish to drop the doctrine of the "soul" (as distinct from and contrasted with the "body") and speak instead simply of persons or selves. But surely such adjustments can be taken care of within the basic framework of Christian theology and need not be regarded as threatening the concept of God as the creator (and redeemer) of humanity and the world.

Are the difficulties raised in the foregoing sections of this chapter, then, not largely pseudo-problems? If "nature" is understood to refer to "creation," cannot these problems all be resolved, provided appropriate adjustments are made to bring the interpretation of creation into accord with our modern knowledge of nature? If so, there is nothing to prevent us from maintaining the structure of the traditional Christian world-view in its most fundamental and important features, however much we may alter the details of our understanding of the world.

This is, of course, the move that always comes to mind first when contentions are made that seem to threaten the deepest reaches of Christian faith; and it is a move worth exploring with great care. I certainly would not deny that it is possible in this way to give a theological interpretation to current scientific and historical knowledge which shows that our fundamental Christian concepts and doctrines have both the flexibility and the comprehensiveness to take up into themselves the most contemporary ideas and theories and incorporate them within an overall Christian perspective.[15] However, such moves are not as simple as many appear to suppose. It is exceedingly difficult, for example, to specify what such a notion as God's *grace*—a personal-moral conception—could actually refer to in a world understood primarily as *nature* (in the modern sense), i.e., in a world understood to be pervaded and structured by fundamentally impersonal forms of order. This is because, as I have been arguing, the concept of nature is not in fact an entirely "innocent" or neutral notion but makes definite metaphysical claims. This common theological response, then—that we need only reinterpret or adjust a few concepts or doctrines—really begs the most significant issues. For it is based on the assumption that the fundamental Christian categories are adequate to grasp and interpret virtually any issue or problem which they may confront—i.e., the assumption that the fundamental Christian claims are true in some irrevocable sense—and that the task of the theologian, therefore, is simply to find ways of adapting and adjusting and perhaps transforming these concepts and doctrines, so that they can continue to do their work. It is certainly possible, and from certain points of view appropriate, to proceed from such a stance. But that conception of the task of theology precludes ever raising seriously the question about the truth of the basic Christian claims themselves, and thus also the question of the continuing appropriateness and viability of the principal Christian categories. This sort of question can be seriously explored only if we are willing to entertain and examine perspectives sharply different from the Christian, to see whether other conceptual frameworks, perhaps, might not more adequately comprehend and interpret certain facets of experience and features of the world.

It is an issue of this widest and most fundamental sort, I am suggesting, with which Christian theology is confronted by the concept of nature. Although we may be inclined to treat this issue intramurally, it would be a mistake to do so. For resolving the problem of nature and of our immersion within nature simply through subsuming it under the traditional category of creation would result only in papering over and temporarily concealing from ourselves the deepest issues which this concept raises, namely, the question about the fundamental metaphysical models and paradigms with which Christian theology has ordinarily worked. Are these personalistic and political metaphors and concepts—including especially, of course, the concept of God—really appropriate or adequate any longer to do justice to our experience of ourselves as natural beings and our knowledge of the world as a complex of natural orders? Is not the notion of nature, as the systematic interconnection of all (natural) powers and processes and the foundation and source of all finite beings and events, a conception more nearly congruent with both our modern experience of ourselves and our modern knowledge of the world? I am not here arguing that an affirmative answer to this latter question is in fact true; I am arguing, however, that this is the real question for theology which the modern concept of nature poses, and this question, therefore, is the one to which we ought to give our attention. We should not obscure from ourselves the magnitude or importance of this issue by (relatively easy) demonstrations that the Christian conceptual scheme can still be made to work by a little stretching here and a little hauling there, and then congratulating ourselves on our modernity. We serve Christian faith best by facing with open eyes the full dimensions of the challenge posed by contemporary naturalism and secularism even though this involves a radical reassessment of the most basic Christian beliefs.

V

Having noted certain problems for Christian thinking raised by the modern understanding of human rootedness in nature, it is important to observe that there are equally serious difficulties confronting the (metaphysical) use of the concept of nature itself, difficulties also connected with the problem of the understanding of the human. I have been arguing that the characteristic metaphysical procedure of the Western religious tradition, culminating in explicit theological reflection and analysis, has been to take that which is distinctively human—our moral and personal being and experience—as paradigmatic for understanding the fundamental context of human life (God's purposes and acts) and the ultimate reality with which we have to do (God). There is an intimate connection, therefore, between our awareness of ourselves as personal and moral beings and the theological understanding of humans as creatures and subjects in God's kingdom, and the latter provides what is obviously an especially appropriate metaphysical underpinning and reinforcement for the former. As we have seen, however, our immersion in and dependence upon the rest of nature—i.e., our existence as fundamentally natural beings—raises serious problems for these basically anthropocentric procedures of the theological tradition and for the basically anthropomorphic metaphysic in which they eventuate. We must look now at the reverse face of these correlations: is the concept of humans as simply natural beings, and of nature as ultimate reality, able to do (metaphysical) justice to the personal and moral sides of our being, to that which constitutes our distinctiveness? There are very serious problems here for naturalism which do not admit of any easy solution.

It may seem at first that there should be no real problem here, for the concept of nature (like the concept of world) intends a reality which includes within itself all finite beings, and thus of course humans. It is clear that humankind is simply a complex development out of lower forms of life and could not exist apart from continuous interrelation with other living forms and with the physical environment provided by earth. Humanity has modified its environment in many ways, but this is also true of all other forms of life, though perhaps not to so great a degree. Every feature of human behavior has its analogy in animal existence; the highest spiritual aspirations of humans, their most rational processes of thought, their deepest religious convictions can (must) all be understood as rooted in natural biological and physical processes. Though we are highly complex natural beings, ones who enter into relationship with the rest of nature on levels and in ways perhaps not duplicated by any other, we are surely to be understood as fully included within nature.

There are several problems with this commonsense approach. In the first place it assumes that nature is a kind of thing, an object, that includes within itself all other objects or things of which humanity is one. But, as we have seen (in our consideration of the concept "world"), there is and can be no all-inclusive object of this sort at all. "Nature" is a concept by means of which we order our thinking in certain important respects: what kind of "object" it actually refers to we have no way, and could in principle have no way, of knowing (or even of imagining). It is a concept with which we seek to comprehend and relate all the objects of experience as ordered in space and time; and humans also, of course, so far as they are conceived as objects of experience, interrelated in various spatial and temporal and organic ways with other objects of experience, quite properly are thought of as "within" nature. But what about humans conceived as those who are thinking this whole system of concepts and experiencing this world of objects? How are they to be conceived both as thinkers and experiencers and at the same time as among the objects of thought and of experience?

The problems to which I am pointing here are not new

—they have been thoroughly investigated by the philosophical idealists—but they are very serious. They indicate, as Hegel particularly brought out, that the self is that peculiar kind of being (unlike any other of which we have experience) that is reflexive upon itself in such a way that it can become object to itself. Or better, as subject (not object) it is aware of itself as subject while it is simultaneously aware of the objects confronting it. "Nature," however, is among those objects (of thought), however all-comprehensive an object it may be. The self or subject is never an object in this sense, is never experienced as one, and it is a serious category mistake to attempt to conceive it as one. How then is it (logically) possible to conceive selves as "included within" nature, the realm of objects of experience and thought? It can be done only if (with Hegel) we conceive nature as in some ultimate sense itself Subject,[16] i.e., as self-reflexive being and thus able to take up other modes of self-reflexiveness within itself. But to do this would be precisely to reject the fundamental paradigm in terms of which our concept of nature is built up —natural powers and processes in the complex interrelations in which we experience them and think them in the sciences—and it would be to substitute as our metaphysical paradigm a model based on the concept of the self. This latter kind of move, as we have seen, is the basis for the concept of God: to move in this way would be to substitute a (formally) theistic for a naturalistic metaphysic.

The concept of nature, thus, can be supposed all-comprehensive only when we think it abstractly, i.e., when we think it as a bare form which is supposed to be capable of containing within itself and ordering all other concepts. But when we try to think it concretely, i.e., when we try actually to conceive all other forms in terms of the sort of order and relationship specified by the concept of nature, it cannot be done: the complexities of the concept of the self simply cannot be subsumed under "nature" without giving nature at least as much (self-reflexive) complexity as a self. It is questionable, then, whether the metaphysic implicit in the concept of nature can ever actually be worked out. A naturalistic metaphysics seems plausible because selves are embodied. In some sense we "see" and "experience" them as we do other objects in the space-time order. They obviously stand in some kind of systematic relationship to these other objects, and it seems plausible, therefore, to regard selves as simply part of nature. However, this is to presume that precisely those objective characteristics and relations are exhaustively constitutive for selves, and that is an error.[17]

If the argument just stated (all too briefly) seems excessively abstract and "metaphysical," let me come at the fundamental issues in another way. "Nature," we have seen, is a concept by means of which we intend to indicate the systematic totality of all finite beings and processes (including ourselves). This totality, of course, is never directly experienced by us as an object: it is by means of this *concept,* and this alone, that nature becomes an object to us and for us. But in this way it does become an object to us, i.e., a totality over against us or before us, which we may contemplate. This very fact, however, implies that in some sense we are (must think of ourselves as) over against nature, contemplating it, observing the events and objects that constitute it, seeking means of control over it. Though we think of ourselves as included within nature, unlike all other natural objects we sufficiently transcend nature to make it an object of our thought and to gain some understanding of and control over its processes. In these moves we necessarily think of ourselves as operative *upon* nature as well as *within* nature, as external to it as well as internal. We are that point in nature where nature transcends itself (becoming something other?) and becomes reflexive; thus we are able to enter into deliberate self-conscious operations upon nature. And so we have built up the whole (nonnatural) realm of culture, wherein nature is rearranged not only in accord with our needs (as is true in varying degrees for all forms of life), but in accord with deliberately chosen ends and values which we have ourselves imaginatively created. The concept of nature, we have noted, gets its distinctive quality and feel in large part from the contrast with the artificial, the contrived, the cultural. This being the case, it is not possible (except abstractly and equivocally) to regard this realm of culture, and humans themselves so far as they are cultural beings, as straightforwardly natural. These fall outside or above nature (cf. "supernature") and are superimposed on it.

Unlike other natural beings who are simply under nature's sway, are expressions of its powers and laws, humans have developed modes of existence and reflection which give them considerable powers over nature. And in the course of history they have totally transformed their life from the natural forms which it originally had into the distinctively human form of existence within society and culture. Thus, as Hegel observed, if our nature is said to be (in accordance with the etymology of the word) our original condition, then our nature is characterized by unfreedom, unconsciousness, unculture;[18] for freedom and consciousness and culture all develop only in history, as we move away from our original nature and create for ourselves another, new "historical nature."[19] In (human) history nature becomes something new and different and other from itself.

Thus humans cannot be understood as merely natural beings, i.e., in terms of merely natural powers and processes; if they are to be understood at all, it will be as historico-natural beings. Our recently developed consciousness of and concern with our place in nature, and with the way in which our cultural activity seriously disturbs the ecological balances of nature, will be properly understood only if they are seen as a new stage of historical development and a new level of cultural awareness. Here human reflexive self-consciousness is penetrating deeper into itself as we become increasingly sensitive to hitherto unrecognized repercussions of our activities and thus gain new and deeper levels of freedom from and over the natural world which is our home. It would be a gross and unfortunate misunderstanding if the newly heightened interest in our immersion in nature were taken to mean that human life in culture and society should be disparaged or that we are fundamentally "natural" rather than "historical" beings. It is only because of our historical existence in culture that ecological sensitivities are possible, and it will only be through a further sophistication of our cultural life that the ecological problems of which we have lately become aware may be in some measure met. There is no way "back to nature" for us; there is only the (hoped for) possibility of a movement forward into a more profound and sensitive freedom.

VI

We have not, in these last remarks, in any way lessened the tensions between naturalistic and theistic positions. I am not at this point clear how that is to be done or whether it can be done.[20] I have tried to show that those tensions arise out of our apprehension of the two-sidedness of humanity, our embeddedness in nature and our personal-moral-historical transcendence of nature as free and creative agents. If the natural processes in which human life seems rooted are taken as the clue to the ultimate reality with which we have to do, a naturalistic metaphysics results; if moral and historical experience are paradigmatic, we are led to a concept of God. Both immersion in and transcendence of nature seem to be genuine features of our human existence, and so long as these appear to us as polar opposites, there is little hope that the metaphysical dilemma with which we have been concerned can be resolved.

However, we may be moving toward conceptual developments which will make it possible to gain a more unified view. On the one hand, nature appears to be increasingly understood, in modern science and philosophy, with the aid of analogies and models drawn from our human historical experience;[21] the concepts of process, event, development, evolution have become fundamental, and nature no longer appears as a static and immovable lawful structure but as an exceedingly complex configuration of humming energies. On the other hand, our understanding of psychology and biology is increasingly making clear how all human functions are rooted in and presuppose our bodiliness; Descartes' sharp duality of mind and body is no longer tenable either philosophically or scientifically. If we are moving, then, toward a more profound understanding of the way in which everything historical is deeply rooted in nature and to new conceptions of nature as itself having a history continuous with the evolution and the history of humanity,[22] we may be on the way to developing concepts of historical nature, or the nature of history, which will be inclusive of both what we now call nature and what we now call history.

What implications such a history-nature concept would have for theology and what kind of theological reconstruction it might call for cannot be guessed at this point.[23] But it would seem obvious that neither our traditional theological framework, as we now understand it, nor the naturalistic schemes presently available to us will be able to persist without considerable modification.[24]

9/Metaphysics and Theology

There is an inescapable natural rivalry between metaphysics and theology. Each of these disciplines has an interest in ultimate issues and ultimate claims, but they come at these questions from sharply differing standpoints: from the religious need for a center of orientation for human life in a reality adequate to unlimited human devotion, and from the intellectual need to know "how things really are." In consequence, the concepts and metaphors in terms of which they each grasp that ultimate point of reference in terms of which all else is to be understood differ sharply. On the one hand, in a metaphysical approach such impersonal metaphors as "being" or "nature" or "process" are usually proposed as the most universal or comprehensive terms for grasping that which is ultimately real; on the other hand, in the theological tradition it is claimed that the ultimate reality to which all human life should be oriented can best be grasped in terms of the agential and purposive implications of the concept of "God." Despite the obvious tensions between these diverse metaphors,[1] attempts have often been made to delineate the respective tasks of metaphysics and theology in such a way as to give each an integrity and a domain which could not be decisively determined or dominated

Originally published in *Cross Currents* (1978), 28:325–341.

by the other. But these compromises have never really worked: almost always metaphysics, with its search for rational criteria for assessing all claims about reality and truth, has in fact gained the upper hand.

To take an example: Theologians have often been willing to concede that the proper metaphysical name for that in terms of which all else is to be understood is "being," but that for religious purposes being may be called "God." Clearly such a move gives the metaphysician the last word in defining the actual character even of that which is to be worshiped religiously, and it thus involves subordination of theological claims and concepts to those which are metaphysically derived and defined. In view of this tacit acceptance even by theologians of the priority of metaphysics, it is hardly surprising that metaphysicians have come to consider their work as enjoying considerable independence from the claims and concerns of the theological tradition: as the science of first principles, metaphysics need not subordinate itself to any other discipline or perspective. Moreover, so far as theology attempts to take up such issues, it must look to metaphysics for guidance.

In reaction to this imperialism, some theologians have eschewed the metaphysical task entirely as of no theological significance, holding that theology need concern itself only with God—the creator of all that is—and God's relation to humans, especially in Jesus Christ. When this tack is taken, a confessional theology is developed that may express well the convictions of a particular religious or denominational tradition, but it remains unclear just what is to be made of the truth- or reality-claims being affirmed. Are these merely an expression of opinion—supported, doubtless, by the additional opinion that they are grounded on "God's revelation" in Bible and tradition— with no further certification or justification through experience or rational argument? If so, how can they properly be granted standing as serious claims about or insights into *reality* or *truth?* The metaphysical issues turn out to be

present implicitly in theology, however much they are
avoided explicitly, and failure to acknowledge their importance simply means that the theologian gives up the
possibility of making responsible or legitimate claims to
truth or reality—that is, claims that can properly be given
standing in the common public arena of experience and
debate. Once again the metaphysician—this time by de-
fault—is left in full possession of the field.

One might suppose, then, that if theologians wish their
truth- or reality-claims to be taken seriously, they must
either become metaphysicians in their own right or else
accept the metaphysical position of someone else. But this
move turns out to be more easily suggested than accomplished, for when one turns to contemporary philosophers
for help on ultimate metaphysical issues, one discovers a
powerful inclination to shy away from just those questions
in which we are here interested. Philosophy has become
largely the analysis of concepts and language or the
phenomenological description of the givens of experience;
metaphysical claims about what is *ultimately* real or true
or good seem to most contemporary philosophers to arise
from mistaken attempts to answer pseudo questions.
Doubtless we can engage in a kind of "descriptive metaphysics" that lays out the structures of experience, or in
"conceptual analysis" that makes clear the logic of our
thinking; but claims about "ultimate reality" or about "being-itself," about the "absolute" or the "universal structure of all that is," about ultimate or final norms or standards of Truth, seem inexcusably pretentious and
pompous, far beyond the reach of the finite human mind.
In short, the sort of issues which metaphysics traditionally
addressed, and on which, as we noted above, the theologian has often felt compelled to turn to the metaphysician
for instruction, now seem to the dominant schools of modern philosophy to be beyond their competence. Philosophy today appears no better prepared to assess and certify
theological interpretations of the ultimately real and true

than is theology; worse yet, much contemporary philosophy raises serious, possibly unanswerable, questions about the validity of the whole theological project.

It would appear, then, that the assumption, still common among many theologians,[2] that theology should turn to metaphysics for its final legitimation, should be reexamined. The relationships of theology and metaphysics may be considerably more complex than is thus far evident, and if we are to come to a satisfactory understanding of either of these disciplines, and of their relationship to each other, we had better unravel some of that complexity.

I

Thinking of metaphysics as the science of "first principles" or of "being" may itself be a source of confusion and error. For such an understanding presupposes the possibility that there could be such a "science," that on the basis of careful analysis and interpretation of experience it is possible to come to valid or verifiable conclusions about "how things are," about the "structure of reality," about "being-itself." This notion of metaphysics as the most general or universal science seems based on a model drawn from those sciences which deal with specific regions of experience. Just as it is possible to examine the structure and characteristics of matter (chemistry) and of life (biology), of mind (psychology) and of political struggle and order (political science), so it should also be possible to delineate and explore the structure and qualities which anything whatever must have in order simply to exist, the structure of being. Doubtless this metaphysical science will be much more abstract and general than any of the particular sciences, since it will deal with structures that underlie all these specific sorts of being, and it will be much more difficult to frame concepts precisely and to devise means to test or verify them decisively. (Every conceivable outcome of any experiment, for example, would have to manifest the structure in question, and thus no hypothesized structure could be clearly confirmed—though some might be disconfirmed.) Nevertheless, through creating appropriate investigative techniques and theory-building procedures, similar in their own way to those the particular sciences use in dealing with more restricted domains of experience and knowledge, it may be supposed that a science of metaphysics can be developed. No matter how much such a claim is qualified, and no matter to what degree the much greater difficulty of metaphysics may be acknowledged, when this model is presupposed, metaphysics will appear to be the highest or the most fundamental science, the science that deals with the "structure of reality" presupposed by all other sciences. With such a conception, metaphysics would quite rightly be viewed as the ultimate court of appeal to which major theological concepts must also be submitted.

It was Kant's critical analysis of the nature and function of human reason that most decisively called into question this relatively simple and straightforward way of conceiving the metaphysical task. Kant saw that the central ideas with which metaphysics works—ideas like "God" and "world" and "self"—function differently in our thinking from concepts dealing with objects of direct experience, concepts like "tree" or "man." While the latter are used to organize and classify elements of experience directly, thus helping to make experience itself possible and serving as vehicles through which experience is cognized, the former "metaphysical" notions function at a remove from direct perception or experience: they are used for ordering and organizing our conceptions or knowledge (rather than what is directly experienced) and function, thus, principally as "regulative ideas." The "world," for example, is never an object of direct perception; it is, rather, a concept with which we hold together in a unified totality all our experience and knowledge of objects—everything having its own proper place "within" the world. When the world is treated as itself an object, like the objects of experience, insoluble antinomies arise: Did the world have a beginning in time? or has it existed from all eternity? Is it infinite in extent? or finite? Is it infinitely divisible? or is it made up of ultimate indivisible elements?

The concept of the self—or better, of the "I"—functions in similar ways, and, if misunderstood as the concept of an object given to or in experience, raises similar problems. The "I" also is never directly given or perceived: it is the concept by means of which we hold together in a unified totality all our subjective experience (just as "world" organizes our experience of objects); in fact in a deeper sense the "I" underlies all our experience absolutely, inasmuch as experience must always be *my* experience if I am to experience it at all. But the "I" itself is never directly experienced, and if we treat it as like the concepts of objects which can be experienced, we become victim of a number of serious paralogisms relating to the supposed substantiality of the "I," its endurance through time, and the like. Kant believed that the antinomies and paralogisms to which the concepts of world and of "I" give rise are indissoluble so long as it is supposed that these concepts name objects in any ordinary sense; but they dissolve when we recognize that both these concepts are constructs of the mind, heuristic devices by means of which the mind orders its own content but the objective referents for which we have no way of discovering.

The concept of God, also, can be properly understood only as a construct of the mind. For Kant this concept functioned, on the one hand, as the ultimate unifier of all experience and concepts, both subjective and objective ("God" is the creator or ground of all that is), and, on the other, as the most fundamental postulate of the moral life, that which makes moral experience intelligible through rendering the world in which we live a moral universe. Even less than "world" or "I," then, can "God" be properly understood as an object of experience, or a reality conceivable on the model of an experienceable object. It is the mind's most profound and highest creation, that by means of which it brings unity and significance into all dimensions of its life. To regard God as some kind of describable or knowable object over against us would be at once a degradation of God and a serious category error.

I shall not attempt to summarize or evaluate here the elaborate arguments with which Kant buttressed his analysis. For our purpose, the importance of Kant was his discovery that such central metaphysical concepts as God, self, and world are imaginative constructs, created by the mind for certain intramental functions, and thus of a quite different logical order from the concepts and images which we have of the objects of experience. Developments since Kant in epistemology and the psychology of knowing have largely confirmed his insight here. We now know that all our perception is heavily colored by the interpretive schemes carried in language and culture, that we never perceive objects immediately, uninterpreted by a conceptual framework created by the human imagination. Concepts of selfhood, of God, and of the world, which hold together the whole fabric of a culture's understanding of life and reality, are created only over many generations as men and women seek to make sense of their experience in the terms bequeathed by their ancestors. Such metaphysical notions are thus continually and gradually reshaped and remade into broader, more flexible, and more powerful instruments for bringing order into life. The work of the critical and creative metaphysician on these and related notions is carried on within this context of the cultural and historical development of an understanding of human life and the world, and it makes its own significant impact on the shaping and reshaping of the concepts in terms of which life is most fundamentally and comprehensively grasped and understood.

In the light of these considerations it would appear that the metaphysician's work does not present us so much

with "being-itself" or the "structure of reality" as it does
with the "absolute presuppositions," as R. G. Collingwood
called them,[3] of a given cultural epoch. What the metaphysician does is search out those widest and most comprehensive concepts in the culture (language) of his or her
time, which order and organize all of experience and life
into a meaningful whole within which humans can live
and act. In some periods concepts like "being" and "God"
may perform this function; in others, it may be "evolution," "universe," and "creativity." I do not mean to suggest that there is no overlapping among concepts or periods, or that it is impossible, or inappropriate, for a
metaphysician to use concepts refined in an earlier period
to deal with problems in the present. The continuity of
historical and philosophical development renders any sort
of atomistic interpretation of the independence of different cultural eras simply false. Nevertheless, it is clear that
a style of metaphysical conceptualization that might be
appropriate to Periclean Greece does not quite fit the
breakdown and disintegration of Rome in the time of
Augustine; and the style of the high Middle Ages seems to
most contemporary philosophers highly inappropriate for
understanding the culture and reality of today. Concepts
that in one period seemed best fitted for grasping the
"absolute presuppositions" of human thought and life, in
another time seem archaic and misleading, giving rise to
pseudo problems and failing to illuminate actual human
experience. So other concepts are appropriated and
shaped as the metaphysician attempts to set out the most
fundamental assumptions about life and the world which
underlie and order experience in his or her time.

This historical and cultural relativity of metaphysical
work,[4] which the history of philosophy and of culture reveals, and which a modified version of Kant's interpretation of the indispensable role of regulative ideas renders
intelligible, makes imperative a reexamination of the relations of theology and metaphysics. The claim that theology

must turn to metaphysics for assessment and validation of its truth- and reality-claims presupposes that metaphysics is in a better position to make such an evaluation than is theology: the metaphysician is the expert on criteria of reality and truth, and therefore is in the best possible position to examine the claims of the theologian. But this assumption holds only if in fact there can be a quasi-scientific discipline capable of objectively examining concepts and claims of the widest generality. In the case of the ordinary sciences, analysis and experimentation are carried on within a framework of concepts and theory which determines the objects to be investigated, specifies the methods and objectives of the investigation, and defines what will count as true or valid results. In the case of metaphysics, however, none of these matters are specified; they are themselves the very subjects to be investigated.

We do not, for example, have specific objects of study here, objects which can be compared and contrasted with other objects as we seek to determine their contours and character. Thus, the "world," as we noted above, is never given as an object of experience to be investigated and studied but is rather a regulative idea by means of which we order and hold together the multifarious dimensions of experience in a unified whole. "World" (or "universe") is, in fact, just the idea of the *whole* of reality, and the history of metaphysics and of culture shows clearly that there are many quite different ways of viewing or understanding that whole. It may be viewed as "nature" or "being," as essentially "power" or "energy" or "matter," as "mind" or "will" or "striving," as "mechanism" or "organism"; it may be conceived as the creation and "kingdom" of a sovereign and good God and thus filled with purposive meaning, or as ultimately lifeless and meaningless; it may be apprehended as a realm of impersonal chance and fate or as the proper home for human life and fulfillment and the sufficient ground of a powerful hope for the human future.

In no case, however, is the whole directly available to us to see which of these (or some other) characterizations might be most accurate. Rather, each of these ways of viewing the world, the overall context within which human life falls, represents an imaginative vision. The various conceptions of the whole are constructed by the human mind as it draws upon this or that region or type of experience to provide a paradigm or model in terms of which the meaning of the totality can be understood.[5] The elaboration of a metaphysical position, therefore, is not so much the working out of a scientific theory of the nature of the whole as it is the expression of a *faith* that this or that model or metaphor drawn from experience can properly serve as a paradigm in terms of which the world can be grasped.

Even the concept of the world, taken in its most abstract and formal sense as the whole within which all reality and experience falls, is metaphorical. It is based on a generalization of the familiar experience of numberless objects, each of which is a "whole" made up of "parts." The whole is more than the parts taken simply additively: it is the unified structure of all the parts; it is that which enables us to think this multiplicity as a unity, as one particular thing rather than a mere collection of many things. It may be supposed that this experientially derived concept of whole can be and is used directly to create the notion of world or universe: the world is the whole, the structured unity of all that is. But that would be an oversimple conclusion. Every experiential whole, though a unity of several parts, is itself simply a part of some larger whole that encompasses it. My hand is a whole made up of fingers and thumb, skin and veins and blood, and so forth (each of which is itself a whole composed of parts); but my hand is but a part of the whole that is my body, and my body but a part of the whole self that I am; I in turn am part of many communities that go to make up the larger society; and so on indefinitely. "Whole" and "part" are correlative terms, used in diverse contexts to specify many different sorts of relations, but neither is ever an end term of a series. Every empirical whole can be conceived as but a part of some larger whole; every part, so far as it is seen as a unified structure, is itself a whole made up of parts. This means that the notion of the world—of the whole which contains all that is, the whole which is not a part of some yet larger whole—is really metaphorical. Though it is based on the experiential concept of whole, it uses that concept in a way never directly exemplified in experience. The experiential concept of whole, that is to say, serves as a *model* for constructing the concept of world, but the world is not simply one more example of a whole (in the ordinary sense of the word). "World" is a unique notion, a construction of the mind on the basis of experience, but a construction for which there are no direct experiential correlates.[6]

The general point which I am making here is not peculiar to the concept of "world." It holds equally for other central metaphysical notions such as "being," "nature," "reality," "events," and "experience." The concepts of highest generality with which the metaphysician is principally concerned are in all cases imaginatively constructed on the basis of models or metaphors drawn from ordinary experience but now used in quite extraordinary ways to develop an overall conceptual structure within which all else can be understood.[7] Contemporary culture in all domains is alive with categories and concepts for grasping various dimensions of experience and the world, and with intuitions and visions of what the structure and meaning of the whole might be. There are the interpretations of the cosmos and its development in contemporary astrophysics, the theories about the fundamental building blocks of matter in modern atomic physics, the biological conception of life as a complex evolutionary structure; there are the interpretations of selfhood and society developed by modern psychologists and sociologists, and the vast and diverse illuminations of experience and life provided by poets and prophets, artists and novelists. These various concepts and perspectives determine in many respects our understanding of the different regions of experience, and they influence, often in hidden ways, our conception of the whole. The task of metaphysics is to make the images and concepts that are determinative of our understanding of the whole as explicit as possible, examining and critically assessing them and ultimately unifying and ordering them into a comprehensive, coherent, and convincing conception of reality or the world.

This conception of the world will not be convincing, of course, unless it is grounded on metaphors and models that are so transparently illuminative of contemporary experience as to make them seem—to the contemporary mind which already orders much of its experience in terms of them—almost self-evidently valid and true. Metaphors like "evolution," "creativity," "process," "nature," and "experience" have possessed that sort of illuminating power and validity for many of our contemporaries, and they have been frequently used by recent thinkers, therefore, as the basis for developing comprehensive metaphysical concepts. To be persuasive, such conceptualizations of the whole must provide intelligible interpretations of all the items and dimensions of our actual concrete experience which go to make up that whole. There is, then, a twofold quasi-empirical check on the work of the metaphysician: empirically convincing metaphors must be the basis of the principal metaphysical concepts, and those concepts must order and interpret the actual facts of experience in a convincing way. However, despite these empirical features, the metaphysical task is most fundamentally the constructive and imaginative one of creating an overarching conception of reality or the world within which all the dimensions and elements of experience can be seen, both in their unique individuality and in their interdependence and interconnection with each other.

II

Theology also is preeminently an activity of imaginative construction,[8] construction of a concept of the world and humanity as "under God." Though theologians ordinarily ground their work in scripture and tradition, in every generation they must reformulate and reconceive the claims of faith in the light of contemporary experience, current scientific and philosophical theory, and the insights into the meaning and problems of human life provided by writers and artists. Such reconstructive activity is always in fact a new act of imaginative construction by the theologian, for he or she is engaged in the creation of new and different conceptions of the world, humanity, and God, conceptions which, though rooted in traditional notions, now take account of features and dimensions of experience and life that earlier generations had not seen.

The constructive character of theology, however, is much more radical and far-reaching than this might suggest. The earlier conceptions of human life and of God, found in those traditions and scriptures in which theologians root their work, were themselves also produced by imaginative constructive activity; not only the activity of previous theologians (in the formal sense), but also of apostles and prophets, poets and historians, storytellers and lawmakers. None of these, whether they be well-known biblical authors or the anonymous mythmakers who lie behind their work, have seen God "face to face" and are thus in a position simply to report what they have experienced; and none, certainly, have been in a position to develop their concept of the world—the "heavens and the earth," as the biblical writers called it—on the basis of direct scientific inspection of that overall context within which all life falls. Their portrayals of God, of human life and destiny, and of the world, were as much the product of poetic imagination, constructing a meaningful picture of human existence and its context, as were all those extrabiblical visions and conceptions which the history of culture reveals. Only by virtue of the constructive powers of the human imagination is it possible for men and women to entertain such comprehensive and unifying images and conceptions as "God" and "world"—notions which bind all experience together into a meaningful and coherent whole within which human life has a significant place and task.

Israel's great vision of a world under God, like any metaphysical construction, was based on the use of images and concepts drawn from ordinary experience but now made to serve the extraordinary function of delineating the comprehensive context of all human life. The notion of God—Yahweh—was put together with the help of such common concepts as lord, military leader, judge, shepherd, father, and the like; and God's radical distinctiveness from the finite examples which initially gave content to these notions was developed with the help of another image drawn from ordinary experience: the human creator who constructs or builds artifacts according to his or her own interests and desires.[9] The world and all that is in it, being God's "artifact"—i.e., a reality which would not have come into existence at all without the divine creative activity—is absolutely distinct from God and metaphysically dependent on God in every respect. God, thus, is a ruler and warrior of a qualitatively different sort from any human kind.

The important thing for us to note here is that all the elements used to construct the notion of God were drawn from everyday experience, but they were put together in an imaginative extrapolation which created the image and concept of a new order of reality not directly given to experience: God, the creator of the heavens and the earth and the lord of all history. This imaginative creation of the notion of God could not have been accomplished without the development of a corresponding notion of the world within which humanity lives and over which God is sovereign. The political imagery that was fundamental in developing the idea of God was naturally also employed for understanding the mundane order: the world was grasped as a "kingdom," ordered by laws promulgated by the divine sovereign and ruled by divine kingly power. All creation was subject to the divine lord, but humans particularly were given a body of law from on high which they were to obey if they wished to maintain the favor of God. I shall not elaborate further the point: the biblical writers worked out in great and subtle detail this conception of a "political universe" as the overall context within which human life transpires; and this imaginative creation of many generations of Israelite experience became the normative understanding of life for most of Western history, and the canonical basis for all subsequent Western theological reflection and construction.

Although the central metaphors and models, on which metaphysics and theology rely, differ substantially, there are clearly some very striking similarities between these two disciplines: both seek to present pictures or concepts of the overall or fundamental context within which human life falls, and both create these conceptions through powerful acts of imaginative construction. Both draw from and depend heavily on the creative and constructive work of previous generations, stored up in myth and tradition, but both also always require new acts of creative imagination which take into account dimensions of experience formerly unknown or unappreciated, as well as later developments in scientific and philosophical reflection. These similarities in objectives and procedures, combined with quite pronounced differences in choice of defining models and metaphors, account for the fact that metaphysician and theologian have always felt a close kinship—and often a strong rivalry.

For many centuries theology and metaphysics could each claim distinctive and plausible grounding for their respective positions: theologians believed their concepts were based directly on divine revelation, and thus had an obvious claim to truth; metaphysicians claimed a "scientific" grounding in experience and rational reflection. Although in earlier periods this difference in foundations may have given a distinct advantage to the theologian, the balance has become increasingly tipped in the opposite direction in recent centuries. As doubts about the genuineness of the revelatory foundations of theology grew steadily stronger in the modern period, coincident with the rising authority of human reflection and knowledge in the form of natural science, it seemed increasingly clear that theologians were engaged simply in reworking tradition; and their truth-claims seemed founded largely on the arbitrary acceptance of that tradition—or, in the even narrower form to which the Protestant Reformation especially gave voice, of that portion of tradition called the Bible. Moreover, the personalistic and political metaphors, so prominent in that tradition and to which theologians felt bound, seemed increasingly implausible vehicles for the understanding and interpretation of wide ranges of modern experience. In contrast, metaphysics felt free to employ a wide variety of metaphors and concepts; though its wings were clipped by Hume and Kant, it still could claim to be founded on the only normative grounding actually available to humans: rational critical analysis and reflection. Since the theologians themselves did not understand how fully their own work was rooted in human critical reflection and in human imaginative construction, they did not feel able to move as freely and imaginatively as did the philosophers, when it became increasingly difficult to square traditional conceptions with modern experience. In consequence, it is hardly surprising that theology fell badly in intellectual esteem, and that many theologians came to believe it necessary to turn to metaphysics for validation of their work.

III

It is my contention here that the allegedly "scientific" character of metaphysics, which gave it a claim to cognitive superiority over theology, is a myth (as many contemporary philosophers would also acknowledge), and that the theologians' claim of a direct revelatory foundation for their work is equally a myth. When this is recognized, it becomes clear that metaphysics and theology are in fact very similar activities. Both are concerned with imaginative construction of a concept or image of the overall context (the "world") within which human life transpires, and neither can claim to base that construction on direct inspection of "the nature of things," for the simple reason that such direct inspection is impossible. Various plausible worlds can be constructed, some more accountable to our physical experience, others to the aesthetic or intellectual qualities of life, still others to economic realities or to religious experience. It is not clear which of the various available models or metaphors—all having been taken from within the totality of experience—most adequately represents and portrays the whole. Ordinary methods of "scientific" verification simply cannot be used here, either by metaphysician or theologian. With regard to every object or quality within the world, it is quite proper to ask whether our ideas correspond with some reality "out there," for in such cases we are concerned with the way in which one item in our conceptual scheme relates to and represents one item in what we call (also in our conceptual scheme) experience or the world. But where it is the *world-itself* we are trying to conceive (as in metaphysics or theology), the whole within which everything else falls —including not only all facts but also all our symbols and concepts—there is nothing outside our conception against which we can place it to see whether it "corresponds": just as every thing is within the world, so also everything must be conceived as included within the conception of the world. When we are dealing with metaphysical or theological conceptions, then—with the "world" or the "whole," with "being" or "reality" or "God"—the ordinary truth-criterion of correspondence simply cannot be directly applied. Instead, appeal must be made to the intuitive or self-evident plausibility of the "root metaphors" on the basis of which the principal metaphysical or theological concepts have been constructed.

This appeal can be buttressed, however, by recourse to two other criteria of truth: coherence, and pragmatic usefulness to human life. I shall not say much here about the importance of systematic coherence in metaphysical and theological work; that point would appear to be virtually self-evident. Although, because of the metaphorical and analogical notions that these disciplines necessarily employ, precise definitions and strict deductions are often difficult or impossible to produce, and significant inconsistencies are thus often hard to detect, it remains clear that the principal objective of both metaphysics and theology is to give an ultimate coherence to human life and experience through providing overarching all-inclusive concepts and images which can bring the fragments and pieces of experience into a meaningful unified conception or picture. The imaginative constructive activities in which these disciplines are engaged are the widest and most comprehensive attempts of humans to draw all life and experience into a unified whole. Thus, failure to achieve considerable coherence in metaphysical and theological work is metaphysical and theological failure *per se.*[10]

It is important to examine in somewhat greater detail the relevance to metaphysics and theology of the pragmatic criterion of truth. Let us consider first the way in which the pragmatic criterion applies to metaphysics. What does it mean to ask whether a metaphysical conception "works"? To answer this we must back off a bit and examine more closely the function(s) in human thought which metaphysics performs. What are we trying to *do* when we do metaphysics? If the metaphysician can no longer properly claim to be defining and describing "be-ing-itself" or the "structure of reality," what is he or she doing? I suggested above that metaphysics attempts to articulate and examine the widest and most comprehensive presuppositions of the experience and life of a period, with the objective of clarifying the ultimate conceptual commitments of that period, or of proposing new conceptual formulations that would more adequately interpret experience for that time and place. In this sense the metaphysician is attempting to set out the "world-view" which underlies a segment of human life and history. In doing so, metaphysics helps to bring human experience and life to greater self-consciousness, thus making it possible for men and women to take fuller responsibility for their own life and action. The degree of freedom and responsibility which we enjoy always depends upon our consciousness of the situation in which we are living and acting, upon our awareness of our own capacities and of the alternative possibilities of action that confront us. For most decisions and acts these matters are relatively determinate and re-stricted, issues on which the various arts and sciences and technologies can throw light. Metaphysics, however, goes beyond all these determinate conditions, attempting to expose the structures of meaning and concept which un-derlie the basic patterns of thought and action, of customs and institutions, characterizing an entire cultural epoch. In helping to make possible consciousness of these ulti-mate cultural presuppositions it facilitates gaining some freedom over them, thus enabling the human community to take fuller responsibility for the totality of its historical life. In this respect metaphysics makes its own significant contribution toward fuller human liberation from deter-mination by the powers and forces of that nature from which humanity has gradually emerged.

With this conception of metaphysics as fundamentally

concerned with furthering our liberation and thus our humanization, it becomes possible to state a pragmatic criterion for assessing differing metaphysical positions. How well does the metaphysical interpretation in hand broaden and deepen human consciousness about its most comprehensive presuppositions, thus enhancing human freedom and enabling greater human responsibility for the character and quality of existence? Admittedly the breadth and abstractness of this question is immense, and assessing different metaphysical positions with reference to it will not be easy, but surely the diverse claims of Whitehead and of Heidegger, of James and Marx and Hegel, can be analyzed in terms of their effectiveness in raising human consciousness about its overall situation and thus in furthering human liberation. All knowledge is for action; knowledge of the ultimate presuppositions of our common life is to make possible responsible action with respect to those presuppositions. This is what metaphysics is for.

For theology, also, pragmatic validation is of especial significance.[11] Theistic claims about an ultimate purposive order (and Orderer) cannot in any way be directly tested or verified in this world: God is not an object of experience, accessible to our observation and description. Moreover, the traditional concept of God—rooted in personal and political metaphors—has seemed increasingly implausible to many moderns. In this tradition the most important "proof" to which the theistic position can lay claim is the quality of human life made possible to those individuals and communities who live in terms of that claim. For this reason if it can be shown that, for example, Marxist or materialist conceptions encourage and enable human life of a better and more fulfilling quality, in the long run they will be the ones that prevail, and the theistic view will gradually die out. To the extent that the Christian claim, that true human fulfillment is to be found in the self-sacrificing love epitomized in Jesus' crucifixion, has led to repression of the human (Freud) and to slavishness (Nietzsche), it stands today under heavy criticism for its pretensions. If the Christian understanding of life and the world is not to become increasingly irrelevant in modern culture, or even totally to die out, a much more realistic reconception of its central claims will need to be made. In addition, a thorough reexamination of the principal metaphors and models on which the conception of God has been based clearly seems called for, with a view to radically reconstructing that central theological symbol, so it will once again become a plausible point of reference for understanding all of life and the world.

My discussion of the pragmatic testing of metaphysical and theological conceptions thus far has been in totally abstract terms, as though ideas floated free of institutional structures, of customs and practices, of actual modes of human life, and as if such free-floating ideas could be pragmatically tested. But of course that way of understanding metaphysical and theological ideas is false. If my earlier analysis was correct, these conceptions are always the expression of a particular cultural and historical situation, and they have their significance in the degree to which they in fact enable taking fuller responsibility for that situation. However, with those perspectives which are unable to attract the interest and ultimately the devotion of significant segments of a society, it is not possible to invoke a pragmatic test at all, for there is never an opportunity to observe what modes and qualities of human life they in fact facilitate. Such positions—perhaps some forms of materialism and of determinism are examples—must therefore always remain abstract philosophical speculations, doubtless illuminating and instructive to a few intellectuals but without much power significantly to qualify and transform human existence. Only those metaphysical and theological perspectives and claims that succeed in taking root within actual social and cultural life, creating customs and institutions that perpetuate and extend them and thus transforming whole societies and cultures, are in fact pragmatically testable in the only way open to us with regard to such notions, namely, through the pragmatic effects they have on the character and quality of human life.

It would seem, then, that a testable metaphysics or theology must include much more than abstract speculation. It will have to emerge from the actual institutions and life of people, and it will have to embed itself deeply in social customs and institutional patterns and to express itself in myths and ideologies which can give meaning to the day-to-day life of ordinary folk. In the end, only those metaphysical and theological claims, which successfully articulate and thus help to consolidate and extend what are in effect significant *religious positions* for large masses of people,[12] can hold any hope of actually transforming human existence in some significant ways and are thus pragmatically testable.

In the light of these considerations, the central symbol with which theology has been concerned—God—takes on a significance unequaled in the West by any other metaphysical concept, and there is a human importance to Christian theology which the metaphysical speculation of even some of the greatest philosophers has lacked. Theology has always emerged from the life of a concrete community and has utilized the symbols meaningful to that community. It has attempted to articulate the ultimate presuppositions of that communal life so that the community could more adequately take responsibility for itself, and it has, thus, directly nourished the human cultural and historical process. Doubtless there have been serious corruptions and failures in the Christian community and in its theological self-understanding, but a rather considerable argument can be made that significant human growth and liberation has in many ways been nurtured by the Christian faith and the Christian churches, and thus also by Christian theology. Theology has had an important task and has played an important cultural role in the past, a

260   *The Theological Imagination*

task and role unmatched by any Western metaphysical
tradition.

Whether this faith and this theology have now played
out their role in human history, and the Christian era is
coming to an end, I will not attempt to predict; it is clear
that a powerful new (religious) rival has arisen in Marxism.
Like Christianity, Marxism is no mere abstract metaphysic: it has been able to develop institutional structures
and patterns, and it is capable of presenting itself both in
mythical or ideological forms which appeal to the devotion and loyalties of wide ranges of people, as well as in
sensitive and sophisticated intellectual articulations.
Marxism is a metaphysics that clearly is becoming pragmatically testable, and it sees itself, moreover, as primarily
concerned with the promotion of human liberation. In its
style as a concrete and socially relevant metaphysics, it can
be considered in significant respects more an heir of Christian theology than of the abstract speculation of the academy.[13]

IV

To what point has our consideration of the relations of
theology and metaphysics brought us? We began by considering the contention that theology must look to metaphysics for validation of its truth- and reality-claims. We
soon noted, however, that metaphysics has no easy means
of validation open to it, that beyond a certain appeal to
intuitive persuasiveness, the principal test of metaphysical
contentions is not academic or intellectual but pragmatic:
the character and quality of human life which those claims
articulate and further enhance. Only as a metaphysics
becomes embedded in a social and cultural process can it
really be tested, and only as it actually assists in the growth
of human freedom and responsibility in that process is it
successfully performing its proper task, thus demonstrat-
ing its validity pragmatically. In the light of this considera-

tion we have been enabled to see better the importance
of certain features of the Western theological tradition
and its central symbol, "God." Christian theology has been
in certain respects a pragmatically successful—and thus
significantly "validated"—interpretation of human life
and its overall context precisely because it has been closely
tied to institutional structures and mythical forms of expression which made it widely influential in Western history. Thus it appears—ironically enough—that it is not
only mistaken to suppose theology must rely on metaphysics for "scientific validation"; on the contrary, if a metaphysics is to become truly testable at all, and thus in a
position to make justifiable claims to validity or truth, it
must itself become quasi-theological in its cultural relevance and embeddedness.[14]

For their part, however, theologians should acknowledge much more openly how intuitively implausible the
traditional theological concepts have become, and how
much they are in need of radical reconstruction. Of course
theology would dissolve itself were it to give up its central
symbol, *God;* but much needs to be done in the reconstruction of that symbol so that it becomes more significant
for contemporary life. Metaphysical studies can teach
theologians a good bit about how such reconstructive
work can be carried out, but theology should not defer too
quickly to the judgment of academic metaphysics on questions of truth and validity. In many respects the theological tradition is better equipped to understand the testing
of both metaphysical and theological claims than is academic philosophy. The humiliation of theology before the
philosophers in recent centuries, in large part due to the
fact that theologians have not felt free to reconstruct radically the central theological notions, has prevented clear
realization of this. Hence, instead of careful studies of the
relationship of theological beliefs to actual human praxis
and fulfillment, theologians have all too often engaged in
symbolical speculation at least as abstract as any found in

contemporary metaphysics, and usually much less intuitively persuasive.

The rise and power of Marxism in the modern world should serve to recall both theology and metaphysics to a more adequate understanding of the intimate interconnection of thought and life. It should also serve as a warning to all who, although believing that Christian faith and Christian culture still have much to contribute to human fulfillment, think that the church should dispense with the difficult problems of theological construction and devote itself only to "practical" human service. This is a misleading alternative. The true human fulfillment to which the Christian community is devoted cannot be gained apart from the liberating and humanizing effects of theological and metaphysical self-consciousness and understanding.

10/Christian Theology as Imaginative Construction

The interpretation of theology which I am presenting in this volume is based on an assumption that is so obvious that it has often gone unrecognized by theologians: namely, that theology is human work. Theology is done by humans for human purposes; theological work must be assessed by human standards, and its judges are themselves always ordinary human beings. I mention these truisms because sometimes theologians have proceeded as though they held in their hands superhuman divine truth, the very Word or words of God. Accordingly, they have often held what they received from tradition in such reverence that they felt it inappropriate to criticize or reconstruct in terms of their own best understanding or insights; instead they have reaffirmed in too uncritical a fashion what has been handed on to them from the past as authoritative tradition or truth. But all religious practices, institutions, and beliefs have been humanly created and have changed and developed in a traceable human history, as they have come to serve new needs and have been adapted to new circumstances. This is just as true of theology—of reflection on the language and ideas of faith—as

Originally presented to a Theological Colloquium in Bangalore, India, in 1976 and first published in *A Vision for Man: Essays in Honor of J. R. Chandran,* ed. Samuel Amirtham (Madras: Christian Literature Society, 1978).

of any other aspect of religious life or praxis. Theology also serves human purposes and needs, and should be judged in terms of the adequacy with which it is fulfilling the objectives we humans have set for it. "The sabbath was made for man," Jesus said, "not man for the sabbath" (Mark 2:27). That is, all religious institutions, practices, and ideas—including the idea of God—were made to serve human needs and to further our humanization (what has traditionally been called our "salvation"); humanity was not made for the sake of religious customs and ideas. It is right and proper, therefore, that theologians and others should be continually engaged in examining and reexamining received ideas of God, that we criticize those ideas as sharply as we can in terms of the actual functions they perform in human life, and that we reconstruct those ideas so they will serve more adequately as vehicles of our fuller humanization.

In this concluding chapter I wish to sum up this interpretation of theology as a critical and constructive task, performed by humans for the sake of certain human needs and purposes. I shall do this in the form of an exposition of six theses, beginning with a statement of the nature of theology, moving through an exposition of how theological work is done and setting out the peculiar character of Christian, as distinguished from other sorts of, theology, and concluding with a statement of the implications of this interpretation of Christian theology for the general problem of so-called indigenization into "non-Christian" customs, institutions, and patterns of thought and action. I hope these remarks will show in summary form in just what respect and to what extent Christian theology is bound to criteria and norms which cannot be compromised, and to what extent theology is free to adapt itself to the forms and images and concepts of the context in which it is working and which it is attempting to serve. We begin with a general thesis on the nature of theology.

THESIS I. The proper business of theology *(theos-logos)* is the analysis, criticism, and reconstruction of the image/concept of God.

Elucidation: This thesis, which may sound tautological, has a number of implications which should be made explicit, for it rules out certain traditional ways of understanding the theological enterprise.

In the first place, this thesis means that theology is not to be understood as primarily or chiefly exposition or interpretation of the several creeds of the church or of the ideas of the Bible. Doubtless both the Bible and the creeds are relevant and important for understanding the image/concept of God and for judging what are proper, and what improper, uses or formulations of that symbol, but it is their utility for getting at the image/concept of God that gives the Bible and the creeds their importance for theology, not the other way around. That is, it is because we are trying to understand who God is that we are interested in the Bible and the creeds; it is not because we are obliged to accept what is taught in creeds and Bible that we are interested in God. God is the object of our interest and concern here, and the Bible and the creeds are secondary to and derivative from that primary theological focus. This implies, of course, that the creeds and the Bible are subject to a standard other than themselves in terms of which they themselves must continually be judged, namely, the concept of God. This is the primary subject matter of theology and that to which everything else must be subordinated. It is not good enough, then, to show that a theological conception is biblical, or that it conforms to a creedal statement. On the contrary, biblical and creedal conceptions can properly be introduced into theological work only if they themselves conform to requirements laid down by the conception of God.

It should be clear that our first thesis has similar implications for other sorts of claims that are often made about theology. It is often held, for instance, that Christian theology is primarily the exposition of Christian doctrines or dogmas, as though these doctrines and dogmas were givens which the theologian must simply accept, and which he or she is then called upon to explain or interpret. But according to our thesis this is once again the wrong way around. The only given (and this is a very peculiar "given") with which the theologian works is God: all doctrines and dogmas are attempts to express and interpret what we mean by "God" and they have their significance in the degree to which they are successful in doing that. Doctrines and dogmas, then, are not simply to be accepted; they are to be examined, criticized, and often rejected, in the light of the image/concept of God that finally commends itself to us. It is God who is the ultimate authority and point of reference for the theologian; no doctrine or dogma can be given that high place without falling into idolatry.

It is sometimes said that theology is primarily anthropology, an interpretation of the nature of the human, and that therefore the first task in theology is to develop a conception of the human. But this once again is putting the cart before the horse. Though we certainly cannot develop an interpretation of God without simultaneously working out an understanding of our human condition, and though different conceptions of our human condition, and different views of our human nature, will have diverse implications for what or who we understand God to be, the primary business of theology is to work out an understanding not of humanity but rather of that supreme focus for human service and devotion, God. And our understanding of what humanity really is will have to be secondary to and derivative from what we conclude God to be.

It is God, then, who is the unique and peculiar focus of attention and interest in theology. No other intellectual discipline has this as its special and peculiar object in the way theology does. The disciplines of biblical scholarship, church history, history of doctrine, philosophical anthropology, and the like all have importance for the theologian, but they are all subordinated to the primary task of getting clear what we mean by "God." Doubtless we will not be able to do this without considering God's relation to the world and to humanity—and thus doctrines of creation, of sin and salvation, of providence, of the church, and the like will all have their contribution to make to the theological task. But these are all only instruments of, or vehicles for, the central theological task: interpreting and reconstructing the image/concept of God.

If the central business of theology, then, is the analysis, criticism, and reconstruction of the symbol of God, it is important for us to get as clear in our minds as possible just what sort of symbol this is, how it is constructed and how properly defined. That is the subject of my second thesis.

THESIS II. The image/concept of God, a human construct like all other symbols, is, and always has been, built up through an extrapolation or development of certain finite metaphors or models, in such a way that it can serve as the ultimate point of reference for grasping and understanding all of experience, life, and the world.

Elucidation: There are two points being made in this second thesis. The first is that by *God* we mean to be indicating what can be called our "ultimate point of reference," that in terms of which everything else is to be understood, that beyond which we cannot move in imagination, thought, or devotion. Traditional characterizations of God often make just this point. To refer to God as the "Creator of all things visible and invisible," for example, is to say that everything that exists has its source in God's activity and can be rightly understood only in relation to God's purposes for it. To think of God as "Lord" of history and of nature is to understand that everything that happens has its ultimate explanation in God's intentions and actions, that God's sovereign will rules the entire movement of nature and history, and that the real meaning of that movement, therefore, cannot be grasped without reference to what God is doing. To speak of God as "the Alpha and the Omega" is explicitly to state that God defines or circumscribes everything else, and there is no way to get beyond God to something more ultimate or more significant. By "God," then, we mean the ultimate point of reference for all understanding of anything; by "God" we mean the ultimate object of devotion for all human life.

It is precisely this ultimacy that distinguishes God from all idols, and it is only because of this ultimacy that God can be considered an appropriate object of worship, a reality to which self and community can properly give themselves in unlimited devotion. To give oneself in worship and devotion to anything less than "the ultimate point of reference"—anything less than God—is to fall into bondage to some other finite reality, eventually destroying the self and making true human fulfillment (salvation) impossible. All idolatry is enslaving and destructive: by "God" we mean that reality which rescues us from all these enslavements into which we continually fall, that reality which brings human life to its full realization. But it is only in virtue of being the "ultimate point of reference" that God can in this way be the savior from all idols. We may conveniently refer to this feature of the concept of God as "The Principle of God's Absoluteness."

If God has this kind of ultimacy—if God is in this way beyond everything finite, not to be identified with any of the realities of our experience in the world—then God is absolutely unique, one who cannot be grasped or understood through any of our ordinary concepts or images. This is the second point being made in our second thesis. At best, all of the concepts and images—always drawn from our experience in the world—which we use to grasp God and to understand God will be only analogies or metaphors, symbols or models; they will never be applicable literally. The concept of God is built up in our minds by playing off one metaphor against another, by criticizing and qualifying this image through juxtaposing it with that concept, by carefully selecting finite models which will enable us to gain some sense of that which is behind and beyond everything finite but which cannot be identified directly with anything finite. Our concept of God, thus—if it is the "ultimate point of reference" we are attempting to conceive—will never be finished or fixed in some definitive form or definition; rather it will always be that which escapes our every definition but to which we aspire as we formulate our definitions. By "God" we mean that, as Anselm so well put it, "than which nothing greater can be conceived," that is, that which is beyond our every finite conception.

In order that these two points which are implicit in Thesis II should be completely clear and explicit, I shall summarize them in two sub-theses.

SUB-THESIS A. The "ultimate point of reference," as that to which every item of experience and every object within the world, as well as the world itself, is to be related, transcends all experience and the world and may not be confused or identified with any item of experience or object within the world (Principle of God's Absoluteness).

SUB-THESIS B. All concepts and images which are used to give content or concreteness to the image/concept of God are drawn from particular human experiences within the world; they must be regarded, therefore, as only models or metaphors or analogies on the basis of which the symbol of God is built up.

These two sub-theses taken together give us Thesis II. They state that whatever else we mean by "God," we mean at least that which transcends the world and all that is in it, that which shows everything finite to be but an idol if it is treated as an object of worship or devotion; whatever else we mean by "God," we mean at least that which

can be known only through treating our concepts—all of
them drawn from our experience of realities within the
world—as models or metaphors or analogies, never as literally defining the divine.

It will be obvious from Thesis II that the way in which
God is conceived is always heavily dependent on the models and metaphors we use. A God conceived in terms of
the metaphor of creativity or constructive power, for example, will be very different from a God conceived in
terms of violent destructiveness; a God conceived by
means of images of loving-kindness and merciful forgiveness will be very different from one conceived as impersonal process or abstract unity. There are many different
notions of God abroad, and that which distinguishes them
from each other are the concrete models and images they
employ in putting together their several conceptions.
That which distinguishes the specifically *Christian* conception of God from others is the configuration of metaphors and images in terms of which it is constructed. The
next question to which we must address ourselves, therefore, has to do with the models and metaphors that define
and characterize the Christian conception of God. That is
the subject of Thesis III.

THESIS III. The Christian image/concept of God draws
heavily on human metaphors and models—for example,
father, lord, judge, son, word, love, mercy, forgiveness—
thus suggesting that the "ultimate point of reference" may
properly be understood in human, or at least humane,
terms and that God relates Godself to humankind in ways
which promote and enhance human development and
fulfillment (Principle of God's Humaneness); to the extent
that the man Jesus Christ is regarded as the final or definitive revelation of God, God's humaneness becomes further specified as essentially suffering love.

Elucidation: The Christian conception of God was of
course built upon foundations drawn from the Old Testa-

ment where anthropomorphic metaphors like lord, king, mighty warrior, and judge were heavily used and in fact provided the defining images. God was conceived as a mighty personal being, creator of the world and lord of history. The characteristically Christian metaphors qualify this conception in the direction of de-emphasizing God's arbitrary imperial power and highlighting his personal and humane character: God is depicted preeminently as loving, gracious, forgiving, faithful, a "father." In radical forms of Christianity, where Jesus is taken as the definitive revelation of God—that is, as the definitive image or model in terms of which God is finally to be understood— the notion of God is radically transformed from its Old Testament origins in the image of a "mighty warrior" who "lords it over" all others into a conception (also drawn from the Old Testament) of one who is essentially a "suffering servant" who in love and forgiveness sacrifices self completely that humans might have fulfillment and life (Mark 10:42–45). When Jesus is the key model in terms of which God is understood, God is grasped as essentially suffering and forgiving love. At the very heart of the Christian conception of God, therefore, are images which depict God as essentially *humane*.

We can say, then, that alongside the Principle of God's Absoluteness, which characterizes all (monotheistic) notions of God, Christian faith puts a "Principle of God's Humaneness" as equally central and defining. In some ways, these two principles defining the divine correspond to what in traditional Christian theology was developed as the first and second persons of the trinity—God the transcendent creator, and God the incarnate savior. To these two, traditional theology added the Holy Spirit as third person of the trinity, proceeding from both the Father and the Son. The Spirit was the continuous presence of God— of the Father and the Son, of Absoluteness and Humaneness—in all times and places and especially in the community of the faithful. In terms of our formulation, the doctrine of the third person thus means that the one who is properly characterized as both truly absolute and truly humane must also be understood as always and everywhere present, and thus, in particular, as present here and now.

The central features of the Christian concept of God have now been sketched. There are three principal criteria or norms in terms of which every proposed idea of God is to be assessed and criticized and reconstructed: absoluteness, humaneness, and presence, derived from the three principles that define the essentials of the Christian conception of God. We are now in a position, therefore, to state more directly the task of specifically Christian theology. That is the burden of Thesis IV.

THESIS IV. The task of Christian theology is to assess and criticize received ideas of God in terms of their adequacy in expressing God's *absoluteness* and God's *humaneness,* and to reconstruct the image/concept of God so that it will express these motifs as adequately and meaningfully as possible in the contemporary situation, i.e., so that God's *presence* in contemporary life becomes intelligible.

Elucidation: We can now see more clearly the fuller significance of something that we noted under Thesis I, that theology is not properly understood either as primarily biblical exegesis or as the exposition of traditional dogma or doctrine. Christian theology is essentially *construction*—construction, as carefully as possible, of a Christian view of God. Doubtless the Bible has a great deal to contribute to this constructive work; indeed, it would not have been possible to formulate our three criteria for theological construction—absoluteness, humaneness, and presence—without recourse to biblical materials. It is in these materials that we have the fullest record of the origins and growth of the notion of God as it developed in Israel's history, and here also are to be found the only extant records of the life and ministry of Jesus of Nazareth, the one taken by Christians to be the definitive revelation of God's true nature. So the understanding of what is indispensable to the conception of God obviously is biblically based. And yet no theologian ever has understood himself or herself simply to be reproducing biblical ideas; every theologian has been engaged in the work of translating these ideas into terms that would be effective and meaningful in his or her own time and place and culture. That is, theologians have always been engaged in the task of analyzing, criticizing, and reconstructing received ideas of God into terms which seemed more appropriate and adequate and true for their own time and place. This critical and reconstructive work was already going on in the Bible itself—as one can easily see if one observes the development of the ideas of God from Moses through the Yahwist and Amos to Second Isaiah, and then finally to Jesus, Paul, and John—and it continued in the work of the second-century Apologists, in Origen, Athanasius, Augustine, Anselm, Aquinas, Luther, and Calvin and all the way down to Karl Barth and Paul Tillich in the last generation.

Theology thus cannot be regarded as primarily biblical exegesis, however important biblical study is to the constructive work of the theologian. Nor can theology be regarded as essentially the reproduction and exposition of traditional doctrines and dogmas. The long history of Christian experience and reflection is doubtless a great help to the theologian's understanding of God, but it never directly provides the theologian with that construction: that is what the theologian himself or herself must do. In fact, the central thing that can be learned from this long history—as the recital of names just given ought to indicate—is that in each generation the image/concept of God has to be reconstructed anew, bringing in new elements not thought of before, eliminating motifs that now seem inadequate, misleading, or even downright false, correcting what now appear to be the misconceptions or misinterpretations of previous generations. However important biblical and historical materials are to the reflection of the theologian, they never can function as final authorities. In every generation it is the theologian herself or himself who makes the final decision about what contours the notion of God will have on the pages being written.

Theology is now, and always has been, human construction of a concept of God. That is both the glory and the frailty of theology: glory, in that it is the conception of God, the highest idea known to the human mind, which is being contemplated and constructed; frailty, in that every such conception is, after all, only one more human conception, subject to all the limitations of finitude, relativity, prejudice, and sin which infect every piece of human work, thus necessarily to be criticized and corrected by others.

Once we recognize that our theology is fundamentally our own construction of a notion of God believed appropriate for our time, we will see that we cannot divest ourselves from taking full responsibility for our theological work. *We* are the ones who must persuade ourselves what the principles of absoluteness and humaneness can and must mean for our time and our world and our experience, and we are the ones who must decide how their conjunction in a reality appropriate to focus the worship and devotion of modern men and women can be understood. We are the ones, in short, who must construct the conception of God which will be meaningful and significant for our day. There is simply no one else to do it. To be called to the vocation of Christian theologian is to be called to just this task of construction. How is constructive work, appropriate to our contemporary life and culture, to be done? That question brings us to Thesis V.

THESIS V. Criticism and reconstruction of the image/ concept of God will involve continuous reference to contemporary forms of experience and life—personal, social, moral, aesthetic, scientific—all of which must be related to, and thus relativized and humanized by, the concept of God, if God is indeed to function as "ultimate point of reference" in contemporary life.

Elucidation: The task of theology is not only to speak of God's absoluteness and God's humaneness (the first and second persons of the trinity), but also to show that the One who is truly absolute and truly humane is *present* (the third person of the trinity), i.e., that God can be and in fact is the "ultimate point of reference" for *our* lives, our world, our experience, and our devotion. This means that the theologian must show, at least in principle, that all of contemporary life and experience can be brought into relation with what God is believed to be, that no nook or cranny of life or of the world—as we moderns experience and understand life and the world—remains disconnected from or out of relation to God. To the extent that segments or portions of our life or our experience remain unrelated to God, God is not in fact the "ultimate point of reference" for all our world; and thus God is not indeed *God,* and we are not God's worshipers: we are polytheists and idolaters. Just as important, therefore, as formulating an adequate idea of God—or rather, an essential part of the formulation of an adequate idea of God—is showing the way in which God is related to every segment and every dimension of our experience and world. The theologian, thus, must develop an understanding of the world, of human culture and human life, which takes into full account what is known and believed about each of these matters in modern wisdom and science; no domain of culture or of learning may be overlooked if God is to be not only "the God of the fathers" but also the proper and true ultimate point of reference for our time and our world.

As we bring the various segments of contemporary life and experience into connection with God, however, they will necessarily be simultaneously brought under the criticism and judgment of God's absoluteness and God's humaneness. Our awareness of God's absoluteness will show every point of view, every custom, every institution, every style of life, which we find in our world, to be finite and limited and relative, and we will be enabled to recognize how often we and others have falsely absolutized one or another of these into idols before whom we have fallen down in worship. God is the great relativizer of all false absolutes, the One who unmasks all the idols, and as we begin to understand who God is in our time and place, we will be enabled better to see also what the idols are in our society and culture, the idols that have held our neighbors and us in bondage, and have otherwise corrupted and threatened to destroy our common life.

God is also conceived as truly humane. So as we bring the customs and institutions and practices of our life into connection with the concept of God, we will be enabled better to see where they have been inhuman, depersonalizing, destructive of our humanity. To be aware of God, the truly humane one, is to be aware of a tremendous demand upon us to humanize the inhuman structures of our world, to free those who are in bondage to degrading and depersonalizing institutions and practices.

Thus, the theological task of bringing all of life and the world into relation with God will simultaneously facilitate and require our criticizing the idolatries and the inhumanities that are degrading and destroying contemporary human beings. Theology, if it truly speaks of God, always becomes simultaneously social criticism and ethics.

This conception of Christian theology, as the construction of a concept of God which shows the meaning and significance of God for our own time and place, puts us into a position to ask about the way in which, and the degree to which, Christian theology should be "indigenized" in the culture in which it is being practiced. This brings us to my sixth and last thesis.

THESIS VI. A continuing and full indigenization of all theological metaphors, models, and concepts is both appropriate and necessary, no matter how far this departs from biblical or traditional conceptions; but simultaneously all those indigenous forces, ideas, and institutions reaching for an idolatrous absolutization, as well as those responsible for continuing injustice and dehumanization, must be relativized and resisted in the light of that loving One who alone is absolute.

Elucidation: Once we recognize clearly what theology is, namely, new construction of the concept of God in terms of the experience and needs and demands of each new situation in which believers find themselves, we can see that so-called indigenization is no new or unique problem at all. The problem of theology has always been the problem of reconceiving and reinterpreting the concept of God in terms which are indigenous to a new situation but which had not previously been used theologically. The whole history of theology is nothing else than the story of the appropriation of such new terms and concepts, thus transforming and developing the concept of God and at the same time showing God's relevance to ever wider reaches of experience. Doubtless as one moves from cultures which have long spoken of the Christian God and which have developed whole vocabularies to express the modes and dimensions of God's relationship to all the various features of the world known to them, to cultures which have been formed religiously according to other patterns and vocabularies, the difficulties of the theological task become more obvious and the demands placed on human imagination and creativity become more urgent. But in principle nothing is changed; it is only that we can now see more clearly and obviously just what theology really always is—a task of creative construction, both glorious and very fragile. Indigenization of all theological metaphors and concepts is always essential to good theological work.

278 The Theological Imagination

But it is equally essential, of course, as the idea of that One who is truly absolute and truly humane is constructed in terms supplied by a new cultural context, that God's absoluteness and humaneness become significant norms in terms of which the false idols, and the inhuman and unjust institutions, of that culture are effectively exposed, criticized, and reformed. If indigenization were to mean that the idea of God became so completely adapted to the concepts and norms and practices of a new culture that it no longer could serve as a radical standard of criticism for that culture, and thus failed to exert tension toward significant transformation of that culture in the direction of fuller humanization, full indigenization of the idea of God would be its destruction. For the conception of One who is at once truly absolute and truly humane is never completely "at home" in the relativities and imperfections and inhumanities of any culture; so far as the idea of God is vital and significant in the life of a people, it provides a basis for criticism and a motivation for reform, or even revolution. Thus, successful indigenization of the idea of God can never mean its full adaptation to the norms and values of a culture; it must mean, rather, the formulation of the idea in concepts and metaphors which make its critical bearing on that culture truly relevant and effective for those living there.

As the truly absolute and humane One becomes the ultimate point of reference in terms of which all human life and experience is understood, all the institutions and practices and beliefs of the culture necessarily become exposed to a theological judgment on their idolatry and their inhumanity. In this way God no longer remains merely the God of the tradition but becomes the *living God* for persons living in that culture.

Thus, Christian theology is completely free—indeed, theology is under the imperative—to become fully indigenous in every respect in each culture in which Christian believers live and work, so long as the Principle of God's Absoluteness and the Principle of God's Humaneness are maintained. The central task of theologians in every culture is to work out, to construct, an image/concept of God appropriate to contemporary life.

Notes

Chapter 1/CONSTRUCTING THE CONCEPT OF GOD

1. Even in perception of ordinary objects the mind always employs "subsidiary" clues, feelings, and impulses in order to achieve "focal" awareness of the object or meaning with which it is concerned; such constructive activity is indispensable to the grasping of any meanings by the mind (see Michael Polanyi and Harry Prosch, *Meaning* [University of Chicago Press, 1975], esp. Chs. 2 and 4). With a reality or meaning—such as "God"—which is not and cannot be directly perceived, the mind's construction of the image or concept out of subsidiary concepts and images, which it uses but to which its attention is not at the moment directed, is (as I will argue below) completely constitutive.

2. For detailed discussion of the significance of the narrative form of the Bible, and the way in which this form itself contributed importantly to the notion of God and the kind of meaning that notion has had in much of Western history, together with an interpretation of the historical breakdown of that notion in modern times, see Hans Frei, *The Eclipse of Biblical Narrative* (Yale University Press, 1974).

3. In summarizing biblical and other traditional material, I use the male linguistic forms found there in refer-

ence to God. When representing my own position, I shall avoid sexist expressions.

4. For a fuller statement of the view that all theology is, and always has been, essentially imaginative construction, see my *Essay on Theological Method* (Scholars Press, 1975; rev. ed., 1979. All references are to the revised edition).

5. The provisional or preliminary conception of "God" with which one begins an attempt at theological reconstruction may have very far-reaching consequences. In this chapter I am following an "existential" approach to the analysis of God-talk rather than a "cosmological" approach (see my *Essay on Theological Method,* p. 69, n. 8, and pp. 70–71, n. 18). That is, I am attempting to get at the meaning of the concept of God by exploring its use in concrete personal and communal life instead of emphasizing (initially) its claims to universality and ultimacy. Beginning in this way with the "subjective" rather than the "objective" pole of the concept facilitates interpreting God's transcendence or absoluteness in a more immanental or this-worldly way—and thus, perhaps, in a way more plausible to modern consciousness—than I was able to achieve in the *Essay on Theological Method.* But it does so at the cost of sacrificing something of God's absoluteness and universality, characteristics which in that *Essay* were taken to be the marks which distinguish God from everything else in the world and even from the world itself (see esp. pp. 49–68).

6. H. Richard Niebuhr's analysis of God as a "center of value" is the most suggestive I know in developing these themes. See his *Radical Monotheism and Western Culture* (Harper & Brothers, 1960), esp. Chs. 1, 2, and Supplementary Essays 2, 3.

7. If we were adequately to define and characterize that center, devotion to and service of which will bring about human fulfillment and meaning, we would need answers to two major questions: *(a)* What is human "fulfillment,"

and how is that to be determined? Obviously there are many and various views on this issue, and procedures for deciding among them would have to be worked out. Chapter 6, below, presents some suggestions on how this issue might be addressed. *(b)* Which among the many possible "objects of devotion" most fully contributes to or facilitates such fulfillment? This second would seem to be an empirical issue which cannot be given a precise answer apart from appropriate psychological, sociological, and other studies. In a fully articulated contemporary constructive theology it would be necessary to devote considerable attention to each of these questions; but here I shall have to pass by most of the issues which they raise.

8. See Dietrich Ritschl, *Memory and Hope* (Macmillan Co., 1967).

9. It might be noted in passing that I am setting myself firmly here against Schleiermacher's view that the notion of God is grounded fundamentally and directly in a "feeling of absolute dependence." (Cf. *The Christian Faith* [Edinburgh: T. & T. Clark, 1928], § 4.)

10. In any functional approach to the understanding of religion (such as the present one), it is especially important that this motif of God's otherness be emphasized. For it is a short step from uncovering the "function" which human practices, ideas, or institutions perform to supposing they can be understood exhaustively as simply the means or instruments for meeting certain human needs, achieving certain human objectives, fulfilling certain human wishes (cf. Marx, Nietzsche, Freud); and thus the trap of anthropocentrism remains unbroken. The "function," however, which the motif of God's radical transcendence and independence performs is precisely to spring that trap, to provide a center for human endeavor and affection which is not simply a direct projection of human wishes and needs, to give us a center outside of and beyond ourselves. Orientation on such a center, which gives a kind of critical leverage in terms of which all that we are and do can be

"independently" appraised and thus creatively transformed, may, of course, also be understood to be a human
"need"—especially in view of the difficulties and even
chaos into which our proclivities toward egocentrism and
anthropocentrism inevitably draw us. But it is a need of
quite a different order from ordinary human wishes and
desires, for it is the "need" to break loose from enslavement to our wishes and desires, to break out of the tight
little circle that is centered on us (and our "needs"),
becoming open and significantly related to that which is
beyond us. In this respect, the idea of God's transcendence
has the highly dialectical function of reordering human
life and insight so they will not be simply "functions of
human needs" but will be open to all that lies beyond the
human. It can give a vantage point from which our consciousness can be broken loose from the ideologies and
rationalizations which always entrap us into pursuit of our
own interests and into defense of our own values, ideals,
and ideas—even when we are trying to be "scientific" and
open to "how things are"—thus helping to provide us with
a true disinterestedness in our search for truth and with a
critical leverage against even that which we now hold
most dear. (". . . whoever would save his life will lose it; and
whoever loses his life for my sake and the gospel's will save
it," Mark 8:35.) It is highly desirable that contemporary
reconstruction of the concept of God retain in some significant and effective form the motif of God's radical otherness or transcendence; without this, "God" would be
little more than a projected fulfillment of our own wishes.
(For a contemporary sociological discussion of the importance of the motif of transcendence or otherness, if God-
talk is to be truly effective in undergirding human identity
and in performing other essential religious functions in
modern society, see Hans Mol, *Identity and the Sacred*
[Free Press, 1976], esp. Ch. 6.)

    11. For fuller discussion, see Chapter 5, below.
    12. For a presentation of a conception of God which

attempts to utilize Jesus as a "model" and which highlights points like these, see my *Systematic Theology: A Historicist Perspective* (Charles Scribner's Sons, 1968, 1978), Pt. I, esp. Chs. 11–14. As the new preface to that work indicates, although I now regard its methodological foundations as quite unsatisfactory, the material development there of the concept of God (though it remains largely in the mythic mode) and of the human, still seems to me to be substantially correct.

13. H. R. Niebuhr's term. For his illuminating and powerful discussion of radical monotheism, in contrast with henotheism and polytheism, see his *Radical Monotheism and Western Culture.*

14. In my *Essay on Theological Method,* in which I followed the "cosmological" approach to the analysis of the concept of God (see note 5, above), a defining significance was given to the dualistic metaphor of creator/creation. The more or less traditional interpretation of God's transcendence or otherness which this metaphor fosters helped to conceal, in that work, the tension in the concept of God between the mythic and the metaphysical dimensions.

15. Cf., among others, H. R. Niebuhr, *Radical Monotheism and Western Culture,* pp. 31–44, 122–126.

Chapter 2/ATTACHMENT TO GOD

1. The fullest discussion of this phenomenon, together with the exposition of an original and highly suggestive theory explaining it in relation to its evolutionary biological antecedents, appears in the work of John Bowlby, *Attachment and Loss,* 2 vols. (Basic Books, 1969 and 1973).

2. This is of course no recent discovery. Every primitive tribe of which we know values the group above the individual, and philosophers from Socrates on have attempted to understand and expound this priority of the group. With Hegel, Marx, and more recent theorists like George

Herbert Mead, the fundamentally social nature of self-hood becomes a central theme. However, in modern times, particularly since the Enlightenment, this theme has been muted, and the solitary individual, rather than the person-in-community, has often been taken to be the paradigmatic human reality; much modern psychology and philosophy has proceeded on that assumption. The work of such psychologists as Bowlby, as well as much contemporary sociology and anthropology, makes clear that the essentially social character of human life can no longer be regarded as a matter for dispute.

3. Bowlby, *Attachment and Loss,* Vol. II, p. 359.

4. Ibid., Vol. I, p. 201.

5. Paul Tillich, *The Courage to Be* (Yale University Press, 1952).

6. This is why it is impossible for us directly to *observe* ourselves; my "self" is too complex and symbolic a reality to be directly "seen." We can "observe" only objects which are in some sense distinct from and over against us, as B is distinct from A; but we can never observe the "I" who is doing the observing in the moment it is observing —though of course we can observe (e.g., in a mirror) our bodies or parts of our bodies. The fact that our bodies can become object to ourselves, to the observing "I," that the "I" can and does thus distinguish itself from its own body, is of course the basis for the age-old (but erroneous) supposition that persons are composed of two distinct substances, soul (the "I") and body (an observable object).

7. See G. Ernest Wright, *The Old Testament and Theology* (Harper & Row, 1969), esp. Chs. 4 and 5.

8. I have attempted to sketch out what is involved in such a conception of theology in *An Essay on Theological Method.* The present volume represents a further explication of that conception.

Chapter 3 / THE IDEA OF RELATIVITY
AND THE IDEA OF GOD

1. Karl Barth, *The Epistle to the Romans* (London: Oxford University Press, 1933), p. 170.

2. Anselm, *Proslogium,* Ch. 2.

3. This unique logical standing by itself, of course, would not be sufficient to give God such far-reaching religious significance. For that it is necessary to hold God to be loving, just, faithful, etc., as well as "transcendent" or "absolute."

4. In what follows I do not mean to suggest that the employment of the concept of God in criticism is its only, or even its most important, use. Obviously it has many other religious uses. It is in its use as an instrument of criticism, however, that its special significance for understanding the problem of relativism comes most clearly into view.

5. I have attempted elsewhere to articulate more fully this dialectical moment in the idea of God through a distinction between the "real" and the "available" God (see the essay on "God as Symbol" in my *God the Problem* [Harvard University Press, 1972]). A powerful contemporary example of the self-corrective character of the idea of God is the criticism, especially by "women's liberation" theologians, of the use, in Western thought about God, of almost exclusively male imagery and language, rendering all such thought ideological, idolatrous, and oppressive in certain crucial respects (see, e.g., Mary Daly, *Beyond God the Father* [Beacon Press, 1973]).

6. The Christian believer Kierkegaard saw, even more clearly than did Marx, how deeply these dangers were rooted in the idea of God itself, and he attempted to articulate this in his notion of "the teleological suspension of the ethical." See especially his analysis of God's command to Abraham to sacrifice Isaac, in *Fear and Trembling* (Princeton University Press, 1945).

7. It is this revolutionary critical power of the idea of God that underlies much current so-called liberation theology and that helps to sustain many current reformatory and revolutionary social and political movements.

8. I would not claim that the concept of God is the only possible concept that can function as a critical principle calling into question every human posture and work. In Buddhism, for example, the concept of "emptiness" plays a similar critical role (for an analysis and exposition of this concept, see F. J. Streng, *Emptiness: A Study in Religious Meaning* [Abingdon Press, 1967]), and it is conceivable that other concepts with such possibilities have been, or could be, developed. I do want to emphasize, however, that the insights and understanding underlying and expressed through both "God" and "emptiness" emerged in contexts of religious reflection on the nature and meaning of human existence, and it seems doubtful that narrowly epistemological or methodological inquiries, however technically precise and logically sophisticated, could produce concepts of equal critical power and scope. In the West, at any rate, the most radical and comprehensive instrument of criticism and self-correction which has thus far appeared is the concept of God. It is to be regretted that the recent secularization of the West—however desirable that might be in itself—has led to ignorance or suppression of this point, and thus has denied us the use of one of our most valuable cultural assets. In the current crisis of Western culture, we can ill afford to do without this most powerful instrument of critical insight and understanding.

9. I should observe here that I cannot claim originality in giving this sort of theological interpretation to relativism. This was a central theme in the thought of H. Richard Niebuhr (see esp. *The Meaning of Revelation* [Macmillan Co., 1941] and *Radical Monotheism and Western Culture*), and he was building on the earlier work of Ernst Troeltsch and Karl Barth, as he himself acknowledged.

10. I want to emphasize that in holding that theology is

"essentially" critical, I do not mean to be limiting theology to criticism. The concept of God has other moments than "transcendence" or "aseity" (which are the basis of its critical power), and these have scarcely been touched on here. (See other chapters in this volume, e.g., Chapter 5, for my approach to these issues.) A full treatment of the concept of God cannot be developed without making far-reaching constructive claims. Such a constructive position, however, worked out without taking account of the full critical—and self-critical—consciousness which we can now see the concept of God itself demands, could only be regarded as naive and unsuitable for today's world.

Chapter 4/THE CHRISTIAN CATEGORIAL SCHEME

1. Since Yahweh is always referred to with male pronouns in our texts, I shall also refer to him in these terms here whenever I am dealing with the Hebraic conception. Later, when I proceed to construction of a contemporary conception of monotheism, I will refrain from such sexist language.

2. The text used here is taken from *Christology of the Later Fathers,* ed. Edward Rochie Hardy, Vol. III of The Library of Christian Classics (Westminster Press, 1954), p. 338.

3. Text cited from ibid., p. 373.

4. For some address of this issue, see Chapter 5, below.

5. I might just observe in passing that the position I am articulating here is not to be confused with the claim of Karl Barth that all our thinking about God and the human is to be *derived* from Christ, as if the idea of Christ contained within itself the whole of Christian theology. On the contrary, I am holding here that the Christian worldview is structured by *four* fundamental categories, each with its own intrinsic meaning and thus a certain independence from the others, yet dialectically interconnected and interdependent with each of the others. It is always an

open and difficult question *how far* the concept of God is to be defined with reference to Christ, how far independently on the basis of other considerations; *how far* the human is to be defined by Christ, how much in terms of general human experience or Freudian insights or Marxist perspectives or Buddhist understandings. Our attempt to clarify the Christian categorial scheme does not foreclose any of these questions; it simply specifies the issues to which serious attention must be given and the points of reference in terms of which Christian theology works.

Chapter 5/TOWARD A CONTEMPORARY INTERPRETATION OF JESUS

1. See John Knox, *On the Meaning of Christ* (Charles Scribner's Sons, 1947).
2. For discussion see, for example, Willi Marxsen, *The Beginnings of Christology* (Fortress Press, 1979); Norman Perrin, *A Modern Pilgrimage in New Testament Christology* (Fortress Press, 1974); Ferdinand Hahn, *The Titles of Jesus in Christology* (World Publishing Co., 1969); James M. Robinson and Helmut Koester, *Trajectories Through Early Christianity* (Fortress Press, 1971).
3. See Chapters 1 and 4, above, and Chapter 9, below. See also my *Essay on Theological Method.*
4. Perhaps some note should be taken here of the double meaning which "world" has had in Christian reflection, sometimes indicating the overall context of human life (God's good creation of "heaven and earth"), sometimes indicating the corrupted situation or condition into which humanity has fallen and from which it must be saved. In the latter—more gnostic—uses the world is never taken to be the "appropriate" context for human life, giving us sustenance and support, but represents all that from which believers must turn away; it is the corrupted and evil domain of the devil. Clearly, my use of "world" to

designate a fundamental moment of the theistic categorial scheme is not to be confused with this special theological use. I use the term to refer to the (metaphysically) true or actual context of human life (however that context might be conceived materially), that context without which human existence could not be (or become) what it truly and properly is (or should become).

5. See in this connection Stephen Crites, "The Narrative Quality of Experience," *Journal of the American Academy of Religion* (1971), 39:291–311.

6. In the present volume some of these issues are briefly touched on in Chapters 1, 6, 7, and 9.

7. For a thorough analysis of Barth's christology which decisively demonstrates the way in which the traditional Christian myth informs Barth's thinking at every point, see Charles Waldrop, "Karl Barth's Alexandrian Christology" (Unpublished Ph.D. thesis, 1975, now in Harvard Divinity School Library).

8. I do not mean by this statement to suggest that we are in a position to develop a full-blown picture of "the historical Jesus." Research has revealed that our information about Jesus is much too fragmentary for that. But it is possible for historians to work back through the layers of tradition, distinguishing those parables and sayings which, with high probability, can be regarded as coming from Jesus himself from those more likely to have other origins, and similar distinctions can be made with regard to the reported events of Jesus' life. And thus one can reconstruct what Van Harvey has called a "perspectival image of Jesus" (see his *The Historian and the Believer* [Macmillan Co., 1966; reprint ed., Westminster Press, 1981], pp. 265ff.). For some recent discussion of some of the historical issues involved here, see the titles cited in note 2, above.

9. Cf. Rudolf Bultmann's famous characterization of myth: "Mythology is the use of imagery to express the otherworldly in terms of this world and the divine in terms

of human life, the other side in terms of this side" (*Kerygma and Myth,* ed. H. W. Bartsch [London: S.P.C.K., 1953], p. 10, n. 2).

10. Cf. Helmut Koester: ". . . we are confronted . . . with the question, whether and in which way that which has happened historically, i.e., in the earthly Jesus of Nazareth, is present . . . as the criterion—not necessarily as the content—of Christian proclamation and prophecy. . . . The only point of departure from which the earthly Jesus becomes the criterion of faith [in the canonical gospels] is his suffering and death. All other traditions of Jesus' words and deeds are legitimate, not because they preserve the exact memory of Jesus' life, but because they serve as parts of a theological introduction to the proclamation of Jesus' passion and death. In this way, the church in the canonical gospel tradition remains subject to an earthly, human, 'real,' and historical revelation which is the criterion of the tradition" (Robinson and Koester, *Trajectories Through Early Christianity,* pp. 117, 162–163).

11. See Hans Frei, "Theological Reflections on the Gospel Accounts of Jesus' Death and Resurrection," *The Christian Scholar* (1966), 49:263–306; and *The Identity of Jesus Christ* (Fortress Press, 1975). I am using Frei's excellent phrase rather differently than he intended. He uses it primarily to indicate the way a literary or novelistic account brings out the identity of a character, and he argues on these grounds that Jesus' resurrection is decisive for understanding who he is as the Gospels depict the matter; I am using Frei's phrase to indicate the significance of that *historical* moment in a person's career where we see most distinctly who he or she is—in the case of Jesus, that moment is, in my opinion, the crucifixion, not the (mythic) resurrection.

12. See Chapter 1, sec. V, above.

13. It will be noted that in citing this early characterization of Christ, I have deliberately omitted the mythic frame within which it appears in the New Testament.

14. For further discussion of the significance of this vision of the human for our pluralistic world, see Chapter 7, below.

Chapter 7/CHRISTIAN THEOLOGY
AND THE MODERNIZATION
OF THE RELIGIONS

1. It should be observed here that I no longer subscribe to such an undialectical view of the relations of the symbols "God" and "Christ." See Chapter 4, above, especially pp. 114-120, for a more carefully nuanced interpretation.

Chapter 8/THEOLOGY AND THE CONCEPT OF NATURE

1. An early expression of the now common emphasis will be found in Joseph Sittler, "A Theology for Earth," *The Christian Scholar* (1954), 37:367-74. See also, among many others: Conrad Bonifazi, *A Theology of Things* (J. B. Lippincott Co., 1967); Philip J. Hefner, "Towards a New Doctrine of Man: The Relationship of Man and Nature," in Bernard E. Meland (ed.), *The Future of Empirical Theology* (University of Chicago Press, 1969); Frederick Elder, *Crisis in Eden: A Religious Study of Man and Environment* (Abingdon Press, 1970); H. Paul Santmire, *Brother Earth: Nature, God and Ecology in Time of Crisis* (Thomas Nelson & Sons, 1970); *Christians and the Good Earth* (Alexandria, Va.: Faith-Man-Nature Group, 1967); Michael Hamilton (ed.), *This Little Planet* (Charles Scribner's Sons, 1970); Ian Barbour (ed.), *Earth Might Be Fair: Reflections on Ethics, Religion, and Ecology* (Prentice-Hall, 1972); John B. Cobb, Jr., *Is It Too Late? A Theology of Ecology* (Bruce Publishing Co., 1972). A useful annotated bibliography of relevant theological and other writings will be found in Kenneth P. Alpers, "Starting Points for an Ecological Theology: A Bibliographical Survey," in M. E. Marty and D. G. Peerman (eds.), *New Theol-*

ogy, No. 8 (Macmillan Co., 1971), pp. 292–312.

2. *A New English Dictionary on Historical Principles,* ed. J. A. H. Murray (Oxford: Clarendon Press, 1901–1933), Vol. 6, Pt. 3, pp. 41–42. See also *The Century Dictionary and Cyclopedia,* ed. W. D. Whitney (Century Co., 1889–1900), Vol. 5, p. 3943.

3. For as long as the term "nature" has been used with cosmic scope and reference, it has been more closely identified with the material universe than with the spiritual. In consequence "naturalism," which in its more recent formulations has attempted to do full justice to the "spiritual" side of human "nature"—thus directly employing the ambiguity in the concept with which we are here concerned —was often in earlier versions basically materialism. For discussion of these points, see A. C. Danto, "Naturalism," *Encyclopedia of Philosophy,* ed. Paul Edwards (Macmillan Co. and Free Press, 1967), Vol. 5, pp. 448–450; also Y. H. Krikorian, *Naturalism and the Human Spirit* (Columbia University Press, 1944).

4. Here the modern concept of nature differs substantially from classical views, particularly Greek. In the classical period, nature, the context of human life, was understood as a teleological order within which human life—and also human purposes—were meaningfully situated (see C. J. Glacken, *Traces on the Rhodian Shore: Nature and Culture in Western Thought from Ancient Times to the End of the Eighteenth Century* [University of California Press, 1967], Chs. 1–3). Nature, even the earth itself, was viewed as a living organism of which humanity was a functioning part. However, as humans have come to be understood (in the West) as essentially personal and purposive beings, able to envision and create whole worlds within which to live, nature progressively lost its intrinsic teleology and became impersonal and dead. Perhaps the historical intervention of the Christian doctrine of creation was partly responsible here, for in the Christian perspective nature became viewed not as ordered by its own immanent vital

principles, but as an artifact from the hand of God, given such order and direction as God extrinsically imposed. In this scheme purposiveness is lodged in the creator, not in nature itself. And therefore it is in relation to the creator that human purposiveness finds a meaningful metaphysical ground, not in relation to the world of nature taken in and by itself. It is this naked and impersonal nature, now, that is the "natural order" studied by science and taken for granted in most of our experience and life. The development here is similar to that which occurred with the Cartesian dualism of mind and matter (and is not unrelated). Once mind (purpose) was wholly abstracted from matter, it was no longer possible to think of matter (nature) as a teleological order or organism; it was simply "dead." Such a material (natural) order can never provide an adequate context for human existence, as the nature of the ancients did, for there is no intelligible grounding here for the purpose, meaning, and value which have such importance in human life. In this situation humans must resign themselves to existence in an impersonal and ultimately inhuman world (nature) or seek to live in relation to some extranatural ground of meaning and purposiveness (God). It was Kant who perceived this development and its significance most clearly, constructing his metaphysics and ethics accordingly. "Against the eighteenth-century position that man is a part of nature and ought to be subservient to her laws, Kant reacted by inverting the order and making nature what she is because of how she appears to us. Then he transcended even this Copernican venture by daring to weigh nature in the scales of reason and to declare that she is wanting and does not contain the destiny of man. The practical—what man ought to be and how he ought to transform his existence—in this conception takes precedence over what nature is and what she demands of man as part of her order. Nature produced man but brought him to the stage where he can finally assert his independence of her" (L. W. Beck, *A Commen-*

tary on Kant's Critique of Practical Reason [University of Chicago Press, 1960], p. 125).

5. This is already foreshadowed in Scotus Erigena's four-fold concept of nature-God: (1) nature uncreated and creating, or God in Godself; (2) nature created and creating, or God as cause of all things; (3) nature created but not creating, or the world as continuous process; (4) nature neither creating nor created, or God as the consummation of the whole process.

6. As Paul Tillich has noted, the well-known modern formula *"deus sive natura . . .* indicates that the name 'God' does not add anything to what is already involved in the name 'nature' " (*Systematic Theology* [University of Chicago Press, 1951], Vol. I, p. 262).

7. There are, of course, a variety of natural powers and processes which can serve as metaphysical paradigms, e.g., the vitality, growth, and evolution characteristic of life as understood in the biological sciences in contrast with the endless motion, mathematical order, and entropy characteristic of the matter studied in physics. Usually it is not simply the bare notion of "natural process" which provides the basis for the metaphysical concept of nature (i.e., nature viewed as the ultimate context of human life); rather it is one of these more concrete and particular kinds of natural order. In general one can say that if the subject matter of biology is given this paradigmatic function, nature appears filled with vitality and activity and even teleological development, and human existence may seem meaningful and with hopeful prospects; when the subject matter of physics provides the paradigm for understanding nature, however, we are confronted with images of mechanism and lifelessness and an ultimate future of icy death. (For elaboration, see Stephen Toulmin, "Contemporary Scientific Mythology," in S. Toulmin, R. W. Hepburn, and A. MacIntyre, *Metaphysical Beliefs* [London: SCM Press, 1970], pp. 60–65.)

8. See, e.g., Michael Foster, "The Christian Doctrine of Creation and the Rise of Modern Natural Science," *Mind* (1934), 43:446–468; and "Christian Theology and Modern Science of Nature," *Mind* (1935), 44:439–466 and (1936), 45:1–27; R. G. Collingwood, *An Essay on Metaphysics* (Oxford: Clarendon Press, 1940), Pt. IIIA; and Francis Oakley, "Christian Theology and the Newtonian Science: The Rise of the Concept of the Laws of Nature," *Church History* (1961), 30:433–457.

9. See esp. Lynn White, Jr., "The Historical Roots of Our Ecologic Crisis," *Science* (1967), 155:1203–1207.

10. For fuller discussion of the Christian "categorial scheme," see Chapter 4, above.

11. It is worth remembering in this connection that the Hebrew vocabulary did not even have a term corresponding to our word "nature." The fundamental unity and order of the context within which humans lived was provided directly by God. (See H. W. Robinson, *Inspiration and Revelation in the Old Testament* [Oxford: Clarendon Press, 1946], Ch. I.)

12. The turn away from such highly anthropocentric ways of interpreting the details of nature began during the high Middle Ages. Lynn White regards St. Francis as quite important in this respect. "St. Francis first taught Europe that nature is interesting and important in and of itself. No longer were flames merely the symbol of the soul's aspiration: they were Brother Fire. The ant was not simply a homily to sluggards, the worm not solely a sermon on humility: now both were autonomous entities. St. Francis was the greatest revolutionary in history: he forced man to abdicate his monarchy over the creation, and instituted a democracy of all God's creatures. Man was no longer the focus of the visible universe. In this sense Copernicus is a corollary of St. Francis . . . it was no accident that his order attracted men who flung themselves into furthering the new natural science and who became its leading expo-

nents in the thirteenth century" ("Natural Science and the Naturalistic Art in the Middle Ages," *American Historical Review* [1947], 52:433–434).

13. Boyce Gibson is correct in suggesting that precisely this notion of God is the ground of the strong sense of the meaningfulness of human life and activity characteristic of Hebrew culture. "Nowhere does fate play a smaller part than among the Hebrews; and the reason is that they resisted more firmly than any other civilization the assimilation of God to nature. Even the arbitrariness of their God had its compensations" (*Theism and Empiricism* [London: SCM Press, 1970], p. 189).

14. Albrecht Ritschl put this in an especially sharp way: ". . . nature is called into being to serve as a means to God's essential purpose in creating the world of spirits . . . the creation of nature by God is . . . a relative necessity, the necessity, namely, of serving as a means to God's previously chosen end of calling into being a multitude of spirits akin to Himself. . . . For the apparatus by which the individual life and all commerce in things spiritual is carried on, presupposes for its permanent existence the whole immeasurable system of the world, mechanical, chemical, organic. . . . The whole universe, therefore, considered thus as the precondition of the moral kingdom of created spirits, is throughout God's creation for this end" (*The Christian Doctrine of Justification and Reconciliation* [Edinburgh: T. & T. Clark, 1900], pp. 279–280). This general point of view was just as characteristic of neo-orthodoxy as of liberalism. See, e.g., the extensive examination of Karl Barth's theology with respect to the understanding of nature by Paul Santmire, "Creation and Nature: A Study of the Doctrine of Nature with Special Attention to Karl Barth's Doctrine of Creation" (Unpublished Ph.D. dissertation, 1966, now in Harvard Divinity School Library).

15. I have myself frequently taken this route, most obviously perhaps in my *Systematic Theology: A Historicist*

Perspective, esp. in Pts. II and III (cf. also the Introduction), and in *God the Problem,* Ch. 6.

16. "... everything depends on grasping and expressing the ultimate truth not as Substance but as Subject as well" (G. W. F. Hegel, *Phenomenology of Mind* [London: George Allen & Unwin, 1931], p. 80).

17. Of course, there always have been, and doubtless there always will be, materialist or physicalist interpretations of selfhood, and much is to be learned from studying these. These perspectives are always based, however, on a preferred status given to the objective or observable sides of selves, i.e., to third-person language. One does not need to move all the way to idealism to be persuaded that there is a dimension of selfhood ("subjectivity") which cannot be handled in purely objective or descriptive categories; first-person language seems *in principle* not to be reducible to second-person or third-person language. It would seem to be impossible in principle, therefore, to grasp these dimensions of selfhood (the "I") in terms of the concept of "nature" with its essentially descriptivist or objectivist categories. Something—precisely that which essentially characterizes the "I" as *I*— will always be left out.

18. See, e.g., G. W. F. Hegel, *Philosophy of History* (Dover Publications, 1956), pp. 40–41.

19. Cf. Karl Marx: "It is that nature which he develops in history which is the real nature of man" (quoted in *Philosophisches Wörterbuch,* ed. G. Klaus and M. Buhr [Berlin: Europäische Buch, 1970], p. 769).

20. For some suggestions on this matter, worked out since this article was written, see Chapter 1, secs. V and VI, above.

21. See R. G. Collingwood, *The Idea of Nature* (Oxford: Clarendon Press, 1945).

22. Cf. C. F. von Weizsäcker, *The History of Nature* (University of Chicago Press, 1949).

23. See note 20, above.

24. Some may regard Whitehead's philosophy, with its stress on nature as process, as already showing the way to this new notion of nature-history; others may see such possibilities in Hegel. Although both of these men have contributed much toward an understanding of reality as processive and historical, I do not think either succeeds in resolving the issues with which we are here concerned. Hegel is certainly sensitive to the problems of conceiving the self and reality in such a way as to make place for the distinctive self-reflexive character of selfhood; however, though he attempts to carry through his dialectical metaphysics into the interpretation of nature, he does not succeed in developing a very persuasive conception, probably in part because he was working prior to both modern evolutionary biology and also the new physics, and thus did not have available to him means to interpret natural phenomena in historical or processive terms. On the other hand, though Whitehead certainly exploits such modern scientific developments in working out his philosophy of organism and process, and thus produces a concept of nature in many ways open to reconciliation with the problems raised by history and selfhood, even using concepts and images drawn from self-experience (e.g., "subjective aim," "feeling," "decision") to articulate his understanding of the ultimate metaphysical realities, he does not seem to have clearly grasped the distinctive self-reflexive character of the self and the peculiar problems which this raises for metaphysical conceptualization, and he devotes very little attention to the consequently peculiar character of the historical order in contrast with evolutionary and other natural processes. Instead, his conception seems rooted largely in his analysis of the notions of process, event, and organism, as these grow out of the contentions and claims of the (largely objectivist) natural sciences. Whereas Hegel thus seems too far on the history side of the history-nature polarity with which we have been concerned, Whitehead remains too far on the nature side;

neither is sufficiently aware of the problems raised by both sides of this polarity to be able to transcend it and produce a truly unifying conceptual scheme. Some might wish to claim that Teilhard de Chardin has produced such a conceptual apparatus. Certainly he has provided us with a unified *vision* of nature-history, and that is undoubtedly an important achievement. But it is not clear that his fundamental notions have been thought through with sufficient rigor to enable us actually to *conceive* nature and history in one unified and comprehensive metaphysical scheme. More significant in this regard, perhaps, is Paul Tillich. Volume III (1963) of his *Systematic Theology,* the importance and originality of which has not been widely noted, attempts to work through these issues by developing the concept of *life* as an all-embracing metaphysical category. Tillich's work here certainly calls for careful consideration. However, I suspect that the development of concepts adequate for grasping history-nature awaits some future genius. Or perhaps it is never to be accomplished. Perhaps the contrasts of self and world, of mind and body, of history and nature, of subject and object, of humanity and the rest of creation are finally irreducible (cf. Kant), and we will have to be satisfied with various compromises and partial perspectives.

Chapter 9/METAPHYSICS AND THEOLOGY

1. I have attempted to analyze the distinctions and tensions between concepts of "nature" and of "God" in Chapter 8, above.

2. Outstanding representatives of such a view in the contemporary scene are the Whiteheadian theologians, on the one hand, and the Heideggerians, on the other; some followers of the later Husserl may also be in this camp. The most recent to argue this general claim is David Tracy, in *Blessed Rage for Order* (Seabury Press, 1975), esp. Ch. 7.

3. Collingwood, *An Essay on Metaphysics.*

4. For a much fuller discussion of these issues, see my *Relativism, Knowledge and Faith* (University of Chicago Press, 1960).

5. For an elaboration of the way in which different metaphysical positions are developed on the basis of such paradigms or models or "root metaphors," see Stephen Pepper, *World Hypotheses* (University of California Press, 1942).

6. As the argument here suggests, I find E. Husserl's talk of "world" as directly intuitable or experienceable (see, e.g., *The Crisis of European Sciences and Transcendental Phenomenology* [Northwestern University Press, 1970], Pt. IIIA) to involve a serious oversimplification of the origin and basis of that concept.

7. This claim is of course the reverse face of Wittgenstein's point that metaphysicians put ordinary language and concepts to odd and extraordinary uses which often result in logical tangles, category mistakes, and the raising of pseudo problems. These dangers and difficulties must certainly be admitted, and they should be guarded against; but their possibility, and even likelihood, in no wise renders the metaphysical task either useless or avoidable.

8. See above, esp. Chapters 1, 2, and 4, and Chapter 10, below. For a fuller argument of this claim, see my *Essay on Theological Method,* esp. Chs. 2 and 3. At a number of points in this chapter, I have paraphrased or quoted sentences from that work without specific acknowledgment.

9. See, e.g., allusions to the potter who works in clay, found in the earliest creation story, Gen. 2, as well as in such passages as Isa. 29:16 and 45:9 and Rom. 9:20f., where the absolute superiority of God over God's creations is emphasized through use of the imagery of potter and pot.

10. I do not think the claims of Kierkegaard and others, that theology deals with ultimately unintelligible paradoxes, in any way nullify this point. Despite his ridicule of Hegel's system-building, Kierkegaard's own work repre-

sented a highly consistent attempt to set out a doctrine of the meaning of human finitude in the light of the "absolute qualitative distinction" of the finite and the infinite. The "paradoxes" in which S.K. delighted became in their own way quite intelligible (to himself and his sympathizers) within the overall metaphysical picture of humanity before God which he sketched.

11. This has always been to some extent understood in the theological tradition: ". . . faith by itself, if it has no works, is dead" (James 2:17); "You will know them [true prophets and false prophets] by their fruits. . . . A sound tree cannot bear evil fruit, nor can a bad tree bear good fruit" (Matt. 7:16, 18).

12. Cf. the definition of religion by the anthropologist Clifford Geertz: "A *religion* is (1) a system of symbols which acts to (2) establish powerful, pervasive and long-lasting moods and motivations in men by (3) formulating conceptions of a general order of existence and (4) clothing these conceptions with such an aura of factuality that (5) the moods and motivations seem uniquely realistic" ("Religion as a Cultural System," in *The Interpretation of Cultures* [Basic Books, 1973], p. 90).

13. For a recent discussion of the interpretation of Marxist metaphysical and Christian theological claims, together with an attempt to develop a radical "post-theistic" Christian metaphysical position, see Thomas Dean, *Post-Theistic Thinking: The Marxist-Christian Dialogue in Radical Perspective* (Temple University Press, 1975).

14. Perhaps in this connection note should be taken of one or two important Western metaphysical positions. Platonism, for example, has had immense cultural and historical significance, including considerable influence on Christian theology. But Platonism has never had an institutional base comparable to the Christian church, and it has never had influence over the masses of ordinary people comparable to the Christian faith. Modern naturalism (the "scientific world-view") in some respects underlying

and in some respects the expression of modern science, may also be considered a powerful Western metaphysical position: it certainly has created institutions, myths, and communities which have decisively transformed and in many ways contributed to the liberation of human life. It remains to be seen, however, whether naturalism can integrate and order and meaningfully interpret all the diverse features and dimensions of human experience, and can provide symbols of sufficient power and universal appeal to focus and discipline the devotion of the masses of ordinary humans.

Index of Names

Index of Subjects

Anthropology, theological, 163–166, 266

Anxiety, 59–67

Bible, authority of, 23f., 145f., 265, 272–274

Categorial scheme, 102
  Christian, 101–103, 113–122
  monotheistic, 109–113, 128–130

Christ. *See* God: as defined by Christ; Jesus

Christology, 114–120, 123f., 135–142
  Chalcedonian, 44f., 116–118, 134f.

Conceptual framework. *See* Framework of interpretation

Cosmic history, 37f., 40f., 49, 55

Evil, 157–162, 166–168

Evolutionary historical process. *See* Cosmic history

Faith, 31, 49–51, 111, 191, 247

Finitude, 82, 84–92

Framework of interpretation, 27–31, 159–161, 244–249.

See also Categorial scheme; World-views

God, Ch. 1, 14f., 67–78, 80–88, 103–109, 266–279
  absoluteness of, 17, 33–39, 42f., 80–84, 187f., 267–279
  as critical principle, 84–88, 274–278, 288f.
  as defined by Christ, 45, 116f., 123f., 144, 147–154
  as focus of devotion, 32–46, 50f., 112, 147–154, 186f.
  as humanizing, 39–41, 43–46, 120, 186–190, 274–279
  as imaginative construction, 21–34, 72–75, 267–270
  as relativizing, Ch. 3, 35–39, 74f., 274–279
  as trinity, 271f.
  as ultimate point of reference, 29, 80–88, 103–110, 266–270, 274–276
  aseity of, 27, 81f.
  criteria of, 154–156, 187–192, 272–274
  existence of, 36–38, 46–51, 56, 82, 147–154
  Hebraic origins of, 25–27, 106–109

Salvation, 157–162, 166–170, 199, 203f. *See also* Human, the: fulfillment of; Humanization
Self, 60–67, 74f., 243, 286, 298f.
Self-awareness, 63–67, 233–235, 286
Sexism (in theology), 15f., 43f., 281f., 289
Sin, 35–37, 90f. *See also* Idolatry
Symbol(s). *See* Categorial scheme; Framework of interpretation; God: image/concept of

Theism, 15
Theological imagination, 12
Theology
  as criticism, 93–95, 125–128, 272–279. *See also* God: as critical principle
  as imaginative construction, Ch. 10, 11–13, 30–33, 125–134, 250–259
  authoritarian, 138, 178–180, 192, 201f. *See also* Revelation
  Christian, 44–46, 114–122, 145, 177f.
  criteria of, 154–156, 168–170, 182–184, 187–206

task of, 76, 102, 120f., 170, 179f., 264–267
traditional, 93f., 99, 163f., 177–180, 182–184, 253, 265f.
truth in. *See* Truth: theological
Trinity, 124, 271f.
Truth
  metaphysical, 33f., 48–51, 249, 254–261
  theological, 47–51, 121f., 239f., 254–261
  relativity of, 88–92

Ultimate point of reference. *See* God: as ultimate point of reference

World, concept of, 110f., 118–120, 216–218, 242f., 246–249, 290f.
World-views, 26–31, 33f., 101f. *See also* Framework of interpretation
  Christian. *See* Categorial scheme: Christian; Theology: Christian
  Hebraic, 26f., 37f.
  monotheistic, 37f., 48–51. *See also* Categorial scheme: monotheistic; Monotheism